Banking Modern America

The passage of the National Currency Act of 1863 gave the United States its first uniform paper money, its first nationally chartered and supervised commercial banks, and its first modern regulatory agency: the Office of the Comptroller of the Currency. The law marked a milestone in the development of the U.S. financial system and the modern administrative state. Yet its importance has been largely overlooked.

Banking Modern America aims to address that gap. With its unique multidisciplinary approach that brings together scholars from disciplines including history, economics, the law, and finance, this book lends a new dimension to studying the origins and development of a system that touched many aspects of modern America. Chapters examine key episodes in the history of Federal banking, looking at the Civil War origins of the national banking system and the practical challenges of setting up a new system of money and banking. The essays in this volume explore the tensions that arose between bankers and Federal regulators, between governmental jurisdictions, and even between regulators themselves.

This book will be essential reading for academics of banking and finance, regulation, numismatics and history, as well as professional economists, historians and policy makers interested in the history of the US financial system.

Jesse Stiller is the Special Advisor for Executive Communications and Historian at the Office of the Comptroller of the Currency (OCC), a bureau of the U.S. Department of the Treasury, USA.

Financial History
Series Editors: Farley Grubb and Anne L. Murphy

For a full list of titles in this series, please visit www.routledge.com/series/FINHIS

18 **Camille Gutt and Postwar International Finance**
    Jean F. Crombois

19 **Taxation and Debt in the Early Modern City**
    Edited by José Ignacio Andrés Ucendo and Michael Limberger

20 **Money in the Pre-Industrial World**
    Bullion, debasements and coin substitutes
    Edited by John H. Munro

21 **Reforming the World Monetary System**
    Fritz Machlup and the Bellagio Group
    Carol M. Connell

22 **Debt and Slavery in the Mediterranean and Atlantic Worlds**
    Edited by Gwyn Campbell and Alessandro Stanziani

23 **Bonded Labour and Debt in the Indian Ocean World**
    Edited by Gwyn Campbell and Alessandro Stanziani

24 **The Globalization of Merchant Banking before 1850**
    The case of Huth & Co.
    Manuel Llorca-Jaña

25 **Monetary Statecraft in Brazil 1808–2014**
    Kurt Mettenheim

26 **Banking Modern America**
    Studies in regulatory history
    Edited by Jesse Stiller

Banking Modern America
Studies in regulatory history

Edited by Jesse Stiller

LONDON AND NEW YORK

First published 2017
by Routledge
2 Park Square, Milton Park, Abingdon, Oxon OX14 4RN

and by Routledge
711 Third Avenue, New York, NY 10017

Routledge is an imprint of the Taylor & Francis Group, an informa business

© 2017 selection and editorial matter, Jesse Stiller; individual chapters, the contributors

The right of Jesse Stiller to be identified as the author of the editorial material, and of the authors for their individual chapters, has been asserted in accordance with sections 77 and 78 of the Copyright, Designs and Patents Act 1988.

All rights reserved. No part of this book may be reprinted or reproduced or utilised in any form or by any electronic, mechanical, or other means, now known or hereafter invented, including photocopying and recording, or in any information storage or retrieval system, without permission in writing from the publishers.

Trademark notice: Product or corporate names may be trademarks or registered trademarks, and are used only for identification and explanation without intent to infringe.

British Library Cataloguing in Publication Data
A catalogue record for this book is available from the British Library

Library of Congress Cataloging in Publication Data
Names: Stiller, Jesse, editor.
Title: Banking modern America: studies in regulatory history / edited by Jesse Stiller.
Description: New York: Routledge, 2017. | Includes bibliographical references and index.
Identifiers: LCCN 2016020585| ISBN 9781138213807 (hardback) | ISBN 9781315447568 (ebook)
Subjects: LCSH: National banks (United States) – History. | Banks and banking – State supervision – United States – History. | United States. Office of the Comptroller of the Currency – History.
Classification: LCC HG2555.B36 2017 | DDC 332.1/2230973–dc23
LC record available at https://lccn.loc.gov/2016020585

ISBN: 978-1-138-21380-7 (hbk)
ISBN: 978-1-315-44756-8 (ebk)

Typeset in Bembo
by Saxon Graphics Ltd, Derby

Printed and bound by CPI Group (UK) Ltd, Croydon, CR0 4YY

Contents

List of illustrations		vii
Notes on contributors		ix
1	**Introduction** JESSE STILLER	1
2	**Origins of the National Bank Act and national currency** PETER HUNTOON	6
3	**National Bank Notes and the practical limits of nationalization** FRANKLIN NOLL	20
4	**Charter No. 1: first among national banks** MARIANNE BABAL	32
5	**E.T. Wilson and the banks: a case study in government regulation and service** PAULA PETRIK	50
6	**Stabilizing the national banking system, 1864–1913: the role of bank examination** EUGENE N. WHITE	67
7	**Founding the Fourth Branch: the Office of the Comptroller of the Currency** JESSE STILLER	88
8	**National bank preemption and the Financial Crisis of 2008** RAYMOND NATTER	109

9 **The measure of a regulator: the Office of Thrift Supervision, 1989–2011** 129
PAULA DEJMEK WOODS

Index 146

Illustrations

Figures

2.1 This note, from the very first sheet of national bank notes, was given to Salmon P. Chase. It was signed by the bankers and issued on December 21, 1863 at their bank. Notice that Chase wrote "First national bank note issued" on the back along with his initials. Bank sheet number 1 can be observed at the base of the left vignette. The 9 in the upper right corner is the Treasury sheet number, which was arbitrarily started at 9   7

2.2 Pre-national bank note-era note issued by a state chartered bank. Some of these, including this one, were as good as gold. Others proved to be worthless   9

2.3 This is a Civil War-era legal tender note, a piece of circulating national debt carrying a promise to pay a dollar of unspecified value at some unspecified future date. These notes were derisively called greenbacks and were discounted against gold until 1879. Notice that Secretary of the Treasury Salmon P. Chase had his portrait printed on the note   10

2.4 Ohio Republican Senator John Sherman was responsible for strengthening and pushing the National Currency Act through the Senate   11

2.5 The largest contributor to the verbiage and flow of the National Currency Act was the Ohio General Banking Law passed in 1845. Whig state senator Alfred Kelley was responsible for moving that bill through the Ohio legislature   13

2.6 Hugh McCulloch, the first Comptroller of the Currency, was memorialized by having his portrait placed on $20 Series of 1902 national bank notes   13

2.7 Graph showing the value of legal tender notes as priced in gold between 1863 and 1879. National bank notes were discounted equally because they were redeemable in legal tender notes   15

2.8	The U.S. Treasury honored the pivotal role that Secretary of the Treasury Salmon P. Chase played in keeping the U.S. Treasury afloat during the Civil War by placing his portrait on $10,000 bills beginning with this Federal Reserve Note in 1918	16
2.9	The look of the nation's currency was standardized and reduced to two-thirds of its former size between 1928 and 1929. This resulted in the creation of the Series of 1929 national bank notes. Shown is the very last $10 Series of 1929 note from the last shipment of notes sent to a bank, an event that occurred on July 10, 1935	17
6.1	National bank insolvencies and voluntary liquidations 1864–1913	73
6.2	National bank insolvencies and payout ratios 1865–1913	73
9.1	Number of *de novo* OTS regulated thrifts 1996–99	138

Tables

6.1	The examination workforce	74
6.2	Monthly National Bank Examination Reports, August 1896	77
9.1	OTS staffing ratios	134

Contributors

Jesse Stiller is Advisor for Executive Communications at the Office of the Comptroller of the Currency, US Department of the Treasury, USA.

Peter Huntoon is a private scholar in Boulder City, CO, USA.

Franklin Noll is President at Noll Historical Consulting, Greenbelt, MD, USA.

Marianne Babal is a historian at Wells Fargo and Co, San Francisco, CA, USA.

Paula Petrik is a Professor of History at George Mason University, Fairfax, VA, USA.

Eugene N. White is Professor of Economics at Rutgers University, New Brunswick, NJ, USA.

Raymond Natter is a partner at Barnett, Sivon & Natter, PC, Washington, DC, USA.

Paula Dejmek Woods is a financial analyst at the Office of the Comptroller of the Currency, US Department of the Treasury, USA.

1 Introduction

Jesse Stiller

The 150th anniversary of the U.S. Civil War triggered a predictable outpouring of literature on the fight and those who fought. It occasioned considerably less scrutiny of the other ways in which the war years left an imprint on American life. Yet the changes that took place between 1861 and 1865 in such fields as public education, transportation, civil rights, science and technology, farming and land use, commerce and industry, and the structure of government had a lasting effect on the nation's future development, even if they were less compelling to contemporaries—and to most writers since—than the war itself.

Banking is another area that underwent substantial change during the war. On February 25, 1863, President Lincoln signed into law the National Currency Act, laying the groundwork for a uniform paper money and a system of locally owned, nationally chartered, and nationally supervised banks. The bill had survived a difficult trip through Congress, passing the Senate by a mere two-vote margin. Even this slim victory was achieved only because the Senate leadership promoted the measure as a source of quick funding to support the war effort. As Peter Huntoon points out in the opening chapter in this collection, the Currency Act, which required national banks to purchase government securities as collateral for their note obligations, did provide a shot of revenue to the Treasury and, over the long haul, reduced the cost of financing the war effort.

But, for Lincoln, Treasury Secretary Salmon P. Chase, and Senate Republicans who led the fight for its passage, the National Currency Act, like other key Civil War-era legislation, was as much about the post-war future. For these leaders, a uniform national currency and a banking system that enjoyed public confidence were indispensable to a thriving, integrated national economy. From closer commercial interactions, they saw, would come a resurgence of nationalist sentiment, especially in the areas recently in rebellion against the government, and with it, the promise of a more permanent Union.[1]

Although the pre-Civil War experience provided Congress with lessons to draw upon in shaping national banking policy, some of those lessons were ambiguous. Banking had long been among the more polarizing issues in American political life, resulting in wide variations in state banking practices and standards. It also led to abrupt shifts in national policy, as evidenced by the rise and fall of the two proto-central Banks of the United States (BUS). During their successive 20-year tenures, these two institutions played an important role in, among other things, monitoring and, where necessary, constraining the notes issued by state-chartered banks. Although this form of oversight helped stabilize the money supply and discourage fraud and speculation, it antagonized the state-chartered banks, those who benefited from easier access to credit, and those who viewed the BUS as a symbol of an overweening centralism that threatened state institutions and states' rights.

In fact, the authors of the National Currency Act felt considerable pressure to abolish state banking outright, to ensure that the high banking standards established for banks formed under the Act were not undercut by non-national banks operating under different and possibly more permissive rules. For various reasons, the authors of the Currency Act chose to pursue that goal indirectly, by taxing state banknotes. But further than that lawmakers would not go—a matter of regret then and later for those entrusted with responsibility for the system's success. Most members of Congress in 1863 concluded that it was unfair, if not illegal, to impinge on private property in the hands of bankers who, despite their state charters, were at least nominally loyal to the Union—especially since the government was still dependent on financing provided by those same bankers. Moreover, there was a recognition that banking, except for a few large institutions in New York and a handful of other large cities, was still essentially a local business, relying on local capital and local customers. There was widespread feeling that it should remain that way.

The arrangement codified in the National Currency Act laid the foundation for what would become one of the distinguishing characteristics of banking in the United States, namely thousands (tens of thousands at its high water mark) of independent unit banks instead of the approach based on nationwide branching that was increasingly in favor in other advanced countries. Unit banking gratified the national preference for banks that were limited in size and power, but it came at the expense of the system's stability; unit banks tended to be weaker banks and therefore more susceptible to failure. Not until 1927 were national banks accorded limited branching powers, but the bias against branching remained strong.

One feature of the pre-Civil War banking system that Congress more fully embraced was free banking, so called because it was open to any group that met the conditions spelled out in the jurisdiction's banking law. This approach, which was ultimately adopted by nearly two-thirds of the states, was a decided improvement over the previous practice of requiring organizers to obtain special permission from the state legislature before they could operate. One of Congress's major goals was as much as possible to depoliticize banking, a goal not likely to be achieved if Congress was responsible for approving or denying individual banking charters.

Congress also intended to depoliticize bank supervision. The free banking acts in the various states usually made provision for a more systematic approach to government inspection of the freely formed institutions, whose numbers grew steadily. Several states in the 1820s saw the emergence of the professional bank examiner, appointed to their positions on the basis of banking expertise. In these early days, examinations tended to be cursory, primarily because examiners were impossibly overstretched. Michigan's 1837 law provided for three "commissioners" to inspect each free bank up to four times a year. Within a year there were 40 free banks in operation, with dozens more in organization, dispersed over the vast and rugged expanse of a frontier state.[2] Of necessity, these examiners spent more time in transit between banks than in them, and their authority was easily evaded by bankers determined to do so.

These state-based innovations found their way into the National Currency Act, which was later revised and renamed the National Banking Act. It provided for the creation of an "independent bureau" of the Treasury Department, the Office of the Comptroller of the Currency, to superintend the new national currency and the new banks that would issue it. Compared to the sometimes dubious issues of state banks, national currency was twice-secured, by reserves national banks were required to hold and by U.S. government securities deposited with the Comptroller, to be liquidated in the event the bank was unable to meet its obligations. The Comptroller was further authorized to appoint the needed number of examiners "to make a thorough examination of all the affairs of the bank." How thorough was still an open question; in 1887, one OCC examiner had responsibility for 90 national banks scattered over seven states.

Despite the ample precedent for many of the provisions of the National Currency (Bank) Act, the measure thrust the federal government into a new role, with mixed results. Within little more than a decade, the national bank-issued currency, which represented a major improvement over the profusion of local currencies it was meant to replace, fell out of favor with bankers and investors. For all intents and purposes, the currency lapsed into practical disuse after 1935. Today this currency survives as prized collectables that illustrate their historical importance, but as a component of the money supply it is no longer of any importance.

The national banking system itself remained hobbled by steps Congress had chosen not to take in the formative years, including the termination of state banking. Many state bankers were attracted into the national system, but not all were, and, in time, the number of state banks (although not their asset size) exceeded the number of banks with the word "national" in their titles. Although the "dual banking system," another unique characteristic of U.S. banking, refers specifically to the state/national dichotomy, non-bank financial institutions, such as trust companies, credit unions, life insurance companies, and mortgage companies, were also able to take advantage of commercial opportunities that national banks either spurned or were prohibited by law from pursuing. Thus, where Congress envisioned an orderly financial marketplace in which national banks would be the dominant, if not the sole player, the reality proved to be far more diverse and chaotic.

Yet there can be no denying that, flawed as the Civil War banking legislation was, it accomplished many of the goals of its founders. Banks, which were generally held in low public esteem before the Civil War, were restored to a measure of respectability. They became catalysts for the country's capital accumulation and, therefore, for the rapid development of the post-Civil War period. National banks in particular became associated with higher standards of safety and soundness. In this sense, Lincoln's dreams were realized.

So while the Civil War banking legislation was a mixed success as a business model, its legacy endures. The federal banking system, so named because it now incorporates both national banks and federal savings associations previously supervised by the federal Office of Thrift Supervision, still holds a large majority of the nation's banking assets. Just as important were the ways in which the National Bank Act broke new ground in redefining the relationship between the federal government and the states, between the public and private sectors of the economy, and between the executive and legislative branches of the government. The chapters in this book address some of these larger questions, while also focusing on the practical challenges inherent in the creation and administration of a novel system of banking based on local ownership and federal oversight.

The immediate inspiration for this collection is the 150th anniversary of both the national banking system and the government agency that, from the beginning, has been the regulator and supervisor of a substantial segment of the U.S financial services industry. What we believe distinguishes this collection is that it brings together specialists from various disciplines to examine these issues from their own unique professional perspectives. Here we have historians drawn from the ranks of government, academia, business, and consultancy; an economist, a legal scholar, an expert in national currency itself, and a bank examiner from the Office of the Comptroller of the Currency (OCC), who looks at a critical recent episode in the history of financial regulation.

A note on usage is in order. The official name of the act of February 23, 1863 creating the national banking system was the National Currency Act, sometimes abbreviated in this book as NCA. As noted above, a revised version of that legislation was signed into law on June 4, 1864. Unofficially, it was referred to as the National Bank Act, or NBA, a title change that was made official in legislation adopted on June 20, 1874. Depending on context, both titles are used throughout the essays in this book.

This book owes much to several individuals who supported its preparation and publication, although they are not responsible for the opinions expressed in this book. Among OCC officials, the list includes the 30th Comptroller of the Currency, Thomas J. Curry; Chief of Staff Paul Nash; Deputy Comptroller for Public Affairs Robert M. Garsson; and Director for Public Affairs Operations Bryan Hubbard. History Associates, Inc. of Rockville, Maryland provided invaluable editorial support. After 42 years of marriage, my wife, Deborah Stiller, deserves the greatest thanks of all.

Notes

1 Heather Cox Richardson, *The Greatest Nation of the Earth: Republican Economic Policies during the Civil War* (Cambridge, MA: Harvard Historical Studies, 1997), pp. 66–102.
2 T.H. Henchman, *Banks and Banking in Michigan, With Historical Sketches, General Statutes of Banking …* (Detroit, 1887), pp. 29–33.

2 Origins of the National Bank Act and national currency

Peter Huntoon

Introduction

The two factors most responsible for adoption of the National Currency Act in February 1863—the near insolvency of the Civil War Treasury and the longstanding need for a uniform, reliable national money supply—have been duly recognized by historians. Less attention has been paid to how effectively the new system answered those needs and the reasons for its successes and failures.

In this chapter, currency historian Peter Huntoon challenges several widely held views: that the Currency Act owed its language to New York State's free banking law of 1838; that the system's advent had little or no constructive impact on the Treasury's cash flow; and that enactment represented a clear triumph of hard money over soft. Instead, he traces the currency legislation to the Midwestern states, home to many of the legislation's sponsors and advocates. He argues that the national banking system and its currency lent more support to the Union cause than has been commonly believed. He points out that the national banking system in fact represented a political compromise that incorporated soft money with Federal oversight of banking. Huntoon offers a fresh perspective on the origin of the system.

There is real significance in the fact that the National Currency Act of 1863[1] amended by Congress the following year did not officially become known as the National Bank Act until 1874. Only then did the two impulses behind the legislation achieve parity: to create a standardized paper money that would circulate without resistance across the land and a system of nationally chartered and supervised banks to issue it. Until then, the currency piece clearly held center stage.

National currency was a child of the darkest days of the Civil War, fathered by an all but bankrupt U.S. Treasury desperate to fund a war with no end in sight and its costs spiraling out of control. It fell to Treasury Secretary Salmon P. Chase[2] to find a solution. As Doris Kearns Goodwin and others have detailed, Chase was a man of immense ambition who considered himself far better qualified to be president than Abraham Lincoln, but who was edged out by Lincoln at the Republican Convention of 1860.[3] Lincoln cagily bought a degree of peace by appointing him to his cabinet as Secretary of the Treasury.

Figure 2.1 This note, from the very first sheet of national bank notes, was given to Salmon P. Chase. It was signed by the bankers and issued on December 21, 1863, at their bank. Notice that Chase wrote "First national bank note issued" on the back along with his initials. Bank sheet number 1 can be observed at the base of the left vignette. The 9 in the upper right corner is the Treasury sheet number, which was arbitrarily started at 9.
Source: Mark Hotz.

Chase recognized that national currency could be another weapon in his arsenal to finance the war. It also offered a means to mitigate to a degree the serious inflation brought about by his previous remedy, the issuance of fiat legal tender notes.

A fundamental provision in the national currency legislation was a failsafe mechanism to ensure that the currency national banks issued always would be fully redeemable, even if the issuing bank failed. Bankers would purchase bonds from the U.S. Treasury and deposit those bonds with the Treasurer as security for national currency that the Treasury would issue to them.

This quid pro quo was a boon to the Treasury. It not only obligated bankers to buy Federal debt that the Treasury needed to sell, it also caused them to purchase those bonds with legal tender notes, a form of currency issued by the Treasury that was nothing more than circulating mini-notes of indebtedness that paid no interest to the holder. Thus the national currency system created a market for both Federal bonds and legal tender notes, two forms of Federal debt that had been meeting resistance in the marketplace.

The concept of bond-secured currency was not new.[4] Free banking laws were passed in eighteen of the thirty-two states during the two decades preceding the Civil War, wherein the term "free banking" meant a banking system with free entry and bond-secured note issues.[5] The difference between those issues and national currency was that national currency was to be secured solely by U.S. Treasury bonds, whereas some states permitted banks to hold various kinds and qualities of bonded debt.

Legal tender notes issued by the U.S. Treasury and national currency issued under Federal supervision represented a major departure from pre-Civil War currency. Before the war, Federal currency was limited to gold coinage supplemented by minor silver and copper coins, but in relatively modest amounts. In 1860, the total volume of specie—gold coin—in the country was a bit over $250 million for a nation of some 27 million free people.[6]

Paper currency issues prior to the Civil War were the preserve of private bankers, corporations operating under state corporate laws, banks chartered under state banking laws and state banks authorized by state legislatures.[7] Banks and the currency issued by them were regulated by heterogeneous state laws, producing a chaotic system of currency that tended to be a drag on commerce and a nuisance to the public.

Congress chartered two Banks of the United States in part to serve as a constraint on the issuance of unsound currency, the first of which operated from 1791 to 1811 and the second from 1817 to 1836. These institutions served as banks of redemption for the paper money then in circulation by cycling the notes back to the issuing banks, thereby constantly testing the integrity of the issuers. President Andrew Jackson, who opposed all paper currency in favor of gold specie, vetoed extension of the charter for the Second Bank of the United States in 1831, so its Federal charter expired in 1836.

Approximately 1,600 entities issued some $200 million in notes of 7,000 different designs and denominations during the free banking era that followed. All were theoretically redeemable at the counter of the issuing entity for specie.[8]

Many of these currencies were as good as gold and circulated with little resistance. Others were of doubtful value, and were discounted or repudiated in commerce, the discount being a function of the reputation of the issuer and the distance that would have to be traveled to the counter of the issuing bank to redeem a note. The value of currencies issued by failed banks was predicated on proceeds allocated to their redemption realized from the liquidation of the banks as well as the duration of the wait for the release of those funds.

A primary function of pre-Civil War banks was the currency exchange business—the acceptance of currency purchased at a discount and redemption of it with the issuer. The bankers profited greatly from these transactions.

Bank note reporters were periodicals that quoted the discount for such currency.[9] The reporters were multi-page documents much like stock quote sheets that were subscribed to by bankers, merchants and others who handled

Figure 2.2 Pre-national bank note-era note issued by a state chartered bank. Some of these, including this one, were as good as gold. Others proved to be worthless.
Source: National Numismatic Collection, Smithsonian Institution.

currency. The availability of this information significantly discouraged over issuances[10] and resulted in less loss to the public than was often claimed.[11]

There was serious question concerning the constitutionality of Congressionally authorized issuances of Federal paper money because that power was not specifically enumerated in Section 8 of the Constitution. Easy money factions, often in the guise of laissez-faire economists and states' rights activists claiming ideological descent from Thomas Jefferson, held that through this silence such authority was withheld by the framers. Sound money advocates and champions of Federal oversight beginning with Alexander Hamilton claimed that it was an implied power.

The currency issue became a surrogate battleground in the ongoing contest over a strong or weak Federal government. The Southern delegations generally opposed strong Federal controls of any stripe, preferring to hide behind the banner of states' rights in order to shield slavery. A strong central bank or even national banking that ceded authority to the Federal government was politically distasteful to them. Once the Southern states broke away, the balance of power in Congress tilted toward a more liberal reading of the Constitution, one that empowered the Federal government to engage in and regulate the issuance of currency.

Civil War demand notes and greenbacks

When the war broke out, the primary source of revenue for the Treasury was customs taxes, which were payable in gold. The Treasury had a limited amount of gold on hand, enough to fund the small Federal government at the time, but certainly not enough to fund a protracted war. Furthermore, the war would cause the customs revenue stream to diminish.

Chase had to quickly devise means to finance the war, which was running up costs averaging $2 million per day.[12] All recognized that the Treasury was

Figure 2.3 This is a Civil War-era legal tender note, a piece of circulating national debt carrying a promise to pay a dollar of unspecified value at some unspecified future date. These notes were derisively called greenbacks and were discounted against gold until 1879. Notice that Secretary of the Treasury Salmon P. Chase had his portrait printed on the note.
Source: Heritage Auction Archives.

virtually without resources and there would be a substantial lag between the time new taxes could be authorized and the money would arrive.

As an interim measure Congress passed an act in 1861 authorizing the issue of Federal demand notes amounting to $50 million.[13] Another $10 million was authorized in 1862.[14] These notes were circulating Federal debt with the promise of convertibility into specie, yet gold was not set aside in the Treasury for their redemption. Their value lay in the fact that Treasurer Francis E. Spinner proclaimed that the notes were receivable for all public dues including customs taxes, which were required to be paid in gold.[15] Consequently they universally were regarded as coin notes. However, their issuance certainly did not rest on hard money principles.

As the situation worsened for the Treasury, it and an increasingly compliant Congress did what is common for treasuries and legislative bodies to do in such dire straits. Congress authorized Chase's Treasury to do two things: first, to float bond issues in the United States and abroad to infuse its coffers and, second, to issue mini-bonds in the form of paper money that was circulating national debt bearing a promise to pay dollars of unspecified value at some unspecified future date.

The Act of February 25, 1862, authorized the first $150 million of United States notes, followed by another $150 million in July, 1862, and yet another $150 million in March 1863.[16] These notes were declared to be legal tender by law, which is why they became known as legal tender notes, but they were universally and often derisively labeled greenbacks by the public. They were supplemented by various interest bearing legal tender emissions. This type of debt aggregated $684 million by August 1865.[17] The legal tender notes were distinguished from demand notes in that they were explicitly precluded from use for payment of customs taxes.

Figure 2.4 Ohio Republican Senator John Sherman was responsible for strengthening and pushing the National Currency Act through the Senate.
Source: Wikipedia.

Thus the Treasury attempted to market massive amounts of bonds and pass off legal tender currency to any creditor willing to take it. These instruments encountered stiff resistance, so both the bonds and currency were discounted in the marketplace.

Passage of the National Currency Act

Chase required allies in Congress to push his national currency concept forward.[18] The torch was picked up by Republican New York Representative Eldridge. G. Spaulding, who cobbled together a draft bill over the Christmas recess of 1861 that incorporated Chase's concepts. Spaulding's bill languished, primarily because he concluded that the printing and issuance of more legal tender notes was a quicker expedient to create the currency needed by the Treasury.

Representative Samuel Hooper, Republican from Massachusetts, revived Spaulding's initiative in July 1862, but dropped it in January 1863 after two failed attempts to move it through the House Ways and Means Committee.

In desperation, Chase turned to Ohio Republican Senator John Sherman, who had replaced him as Senator upon his appointment as the Secretary of the Treasury in 1861. Sherman strengthened the bill and pushed it through the Senate, where it narrowly passed. It was immediately introduced into the

House where it survived the Ways and Means Committee and a subsequent floor vote, and was signed into law by President Lincoln on February 25, 1863.

Spaulding and Hooper had operated at a disadvantage. They were easterners painted as pawns of the eastern banking establishment. Sherman had more credibility precisely because he was not an easterner.

The fundamental principles underlying the National Currency Act were laid out by Alexander Hamilton in preparing the charter for the First Bank of the United States. However, much of the language in the act was borrowed from state banking law, with that of New York generally viewed as the inspiration behind the National Currency Act.

When Richard Erb[19] placed the New York Free Banking Act of 1838, the Ohio General Banking Act of 1845, and the National Currency Act of 1863 side-by-side, he made a revealing discovery. Twenty-two sections of the National Currency Act were copied verbatim from the Ohio law. Another seven sections that appeared only in the Ohio law were not copied but the content in them was covered in like manner. Furthermore the flow of the Federal sections paralleled that of Ohio law.

As it transpired, only six sections were copied from the New York law, probably at the hand of New York Representative Spaulding in 1861 and 1862. The provisions borrowed from New York were mostly concerned with administrative details such as reporting of conditions of banks, organization certificates, engraving and printing of currency, and custody of plates. Seventeen sections in the National Currency Act do not appear nor are their contents addressed in the New York Free Banking law of 1838.

Clearly much of the language in the National Currency Act was modeled on Ohio law. That said, the earlier New York legislation had to have influenced the Ohio legislators. It would be naive to believe that the Ohio legislators did not have a copy of the New York bill at their fingertips when they framed their own law less than a decade later.

However, once the mantle for handling the National Currency Act was passed to Ohio's Sherman, the Ohioan, possibly in league with Chase himself, preferentially lifted language from the Ohio act. After all, the last to handle the bill controlled the language. As a result the fingerprints of Ohioans are all over the final draft of the National Currency Act.

Wolka[20] probed the origins of the Ohio act in order to identify who deserves ultimate credit for the structure and much of the language in the National Currency Act. The laurels fell to Alfred Kelley, a Whig State Senator from Cleveland, who shepherded it through the Ohio legislature early in 1845.

Ohio banking law prior to 1845 was weak, so paper money abuses there required serious remedy. The Whigs swept both houses of the Ohio legislature in the election of 1844, with banking and currency reform a major campaign issue. Once in power, the 1845 act was introduced on January 7, and passed along strict party lines on February 24.

National Bank Act and national currency 13

Figure 2.5 The largest contributor to the verbiage and flow of the National Currency Act was the Ohio General Banking Law passed in 1845. Whig state senator Alfred Kelley was responsible for moving that bill through the Ohio legislature.
Source: Wendell Wolka.

Figure 2.6 Hugh McCulloch, the first Comptroller of the Currency, was memorialized by having his portrait placed on $20 Series of 1902 national bank notes.

The first Comptroller of the Currency under the National Currency Act was Hugh McCulloch, another Midwesterner. McCulloch, 1808–95, was the president of the sound, large and very influential State Bank of Indiana. He descended on Washington to lobby against enactment of the pending national banking legislation because it posed a threat to the profitability of his note-issuing bank.[21] The ever wily Chase prevailed upon McCulloch to become the first Comptroller of the Currency, thus transforming this formidable foe to the concept into a gifted advocate who had the stature and acumen to guide it to success during its formative years.

Bond-secured national bank notes

The concept of bond-secured paper currency was straightforward. Bankers would accumulate money and use that money to purchase interest-bearing U.S. Treasury bonds. They would deposit those bonds with the Treasurer of the United States to be held in trust as security to back national currency that the Treasury would issue to them. From 1863 to 1900, the Treasury, through the Office of the Comptroller of the Currency, would send the bankers 90 percent of the face value of the bonds in the form of national currency. After 1900 the amount was raised to 100 percent. The bankers would then have money in hand that they could loan.

The redeemability guarantee was that, if the bank failed, the Treasurer would sell the bonds, deposit the proceeds in a redemption fund, and have cash to redeem the outstanding notes issued from the bank. Thus the note holder was protected.

From the Treasury's standpoint, a key advantage to the scheme was that it helped create a market for greenbacks, which bankers needed to accumulate in order to purchase their bonds. Greenbacks met the lawful money criteria for the purchase of their bonds and were the cheapest money available relative to gold.

Furthermore, the bankers were required to hold greenbacks to meet reserve requirements to enable them to redeem their notes and to cover deposits. This removed large volumes of greenbacks from circulation.

The incentive for bankers to engage in the issuance of national currency was that they earned interest twice on the same investment. That is, they earned interest on their bonds and also on the national currency that they received and could loan.

Both the bonds and the national currency that the bankers received were redeemable in greenback dollars, so national currency circulated at par with greenbacks and was discounted the same as greenbacks against gold. At first the discount was a measure of insecurity that the United States might not survive the war. Later, as the war dragged on but winning became increasingly assured, the discount reflected inflation caused by the fact that the government had pressed such huge volumes of greenbacks into circulation.

Figure 2.7 shows the value of greenbacks and national currency against gold.[22] The low occurred in 1865, when it took almost two and a half greenback dollars to purchase a dollar in gold.

National Bank Act and national currency 15

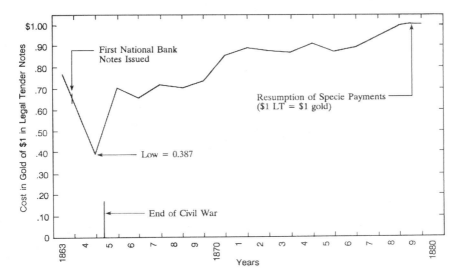

Figure 2.7 Graph showing the value of legal tender notes as priced in gold between 1863 and 1879. National bank notes were discounted equally because they were redeemable in legal tender notes.

The long view

The National Currency Act was in part sold on its short-term potential to boost Treasury revenue. But did it?

That question can be answered in broad strokes using some gross statistics from the Civil War-era.[23] Total Federal expenses during the war were $3,415 million. Total Federal revenues were $771 million. Therefore the total additional debt accrued by the Government during the war years was $2,644 million, most of it attributable to war spending.

At the beginning of October 1865, six months after the war had ended, national banks owned $276 million in bonds to secure their currency.[24] The implication is that the bankers soaked up only about 10 percent of the war debt. Furthermore, they only started buying this debt at the end of 1863, halfway through the war. It is therefore easy to dismiss the National Currency Act as coming too late with too little impact. Such an assessment understates the gravitas of the act.

Omitted from these figures is the volume of Federal debt locked away in the form of legal tender notes within national banks at the beginning of October 1865 to cover deposits and notes in circulation that totaled at least $137 million.[25] Those reserves represented another 5 percent of the national debt.

But more importantly and probably historically underappreciated was the psychological impact of national bankers on both the currency and bond markets after passage of the National Bank Act in 1863. Although the price of legal tender currency in gold continued to erode during the following two years, the ultimate magnitude of the rout was probably lessened through their actions.

Wars cannot be won by nations with bankrupt treasuries. Chase's Treasury operations were as crucial in saving the Union as the actions of its most decorated generals. What Chase accomplished through deft debt management can be attributed to the sheer strength of his character and the confidence in the Treasury that his bearing instilled. The Treasury Department never forgot Chase, and memorialized him by placing his portrait on $10,000 Federal Reserve notes beginning in 1918 and next on $10,000 gold notes in 1928. However, Chase beat them to it. He already had put his portrait on the $1 legal tender notes of 1862.

It was not lost on Chase that the exigencies of the times required the issuance of highly inflationary greenback and national currency of dubious constitutionality. Ironically, as Chief Justice of the Supreme Court, the position to which Lincoln appointed him in June 1864, Chase joined the Court's majority in 1870 in declaring his Civil War legal tender issues unconstitutional. Once the composition of the Court changed and overturned that decision in 1871 and 1873, he wrote eloquent dissents in support of the 1870 finding.[26]

Perhaps there is no irony here. Chase's reversal more likely stands as a measure of a man of high integrity objectively carrying out his duties to the nation, but cognizant of the differing roles that he shouldered, first as Secretary of the Treasury and later as Chief Justice. Chase's Treasury actions reflected the pragmatism of the Union leadership as they navigated the shoals of the Civil War. Chase chose courses of action that kept the Union financially afloat even though they ran against his principles.

There can also be little doubt that by 1863 economists understood that the highly inflationary legal tender debt needed to be reined in. The national bank scheme applied some brakes by creating demand for the legal tender notes while simultaneously causing large volumes of them to be taken out of circulation to be held as reserves in national banks.

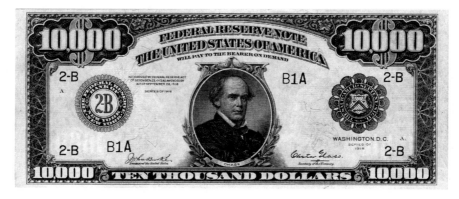

Figure 2.8 The U.S. Treasury honored the pivotal role that Secretary of the Treasury Salmon P. Chase played in keeping the U.S. Treasury afloat during the Civil War by placing his portrait on $10,000 bills beginning with this Federal Reserve Note in 1918.

Source: National Numismatic Collection, Smithsonian Institution.

One often overlooked but significant provision in the National Currency Act of February 25, 1863, speaks to the cautious approach employed to defuse political opposition to its enactment. This involved the all-important limit on corporate succession of national banks built into Section 11 that gave banks a life of 20 years or less from the date of passage of the act, the duration to be chosen by the bankers. Congressmen less than enamored with the concept but voting for it under cover of patriotic support for the war effort could return to their constituents and claim that the thing would go away after the current crisis had passed.[27]

The National Currency Act could hardly be called a win for any particular economic doctrine. The currency that it created was soft, being secured by and redeemable in legal tender currency, which was anathema to hard money advocates. Yet the act provided for Federal oversight of national banks in the form of regularly published reports of condition and intrusive examinations, which was anathema to laissez-faire banking sensibilities. It was a pragmatic compromise that represented the complexion of Congressional interests remaining in Washington after the Southern delegations left. It can be judged a positive step in the nation's continuing effort to create a workable monetary system.

The national bank currency that was created proved to be seriously flawed. Paramount was that it was an inelastic currency, the volume of which was predicated on the relatively fixed collective capitalization of the banks rather than being linked to the fluctuating demands of commerce. As such it exacerbated periodic money panics. National currency was inordinately cumbersome and costly to administer for both the government and the bankers. Furthermore, national banks were brittle; that is, they were stand-alone so-called unit banks that failed even under moderate stress, with severe consequences to depositors.[28]

Figure 2.9 The look of the nation's currency was standardized and reduced to two-thirds of its former size between 1928 and 1929. This resulted in the creation of the Series of 1929 national bank notes. Shown is the very last $10 Series of 1929 note from the last shipment of notes sent to a bank, an event that occurred on July 10, 1935.
Source: Photo courtesy of Jess Lipka.

Because the shortcomings of national currency were never overcome, it was inevitable that Congress would move on to a sounder alternative, which it did with the more elastic Federal Reserve currency beginning in 1914. National currency left the monetary stage in 1935 when the last of the bonds used to secure it were called by the Treasury.

However, thanks to the safeguards provided by the framers of the National Bank Act, no one ever lost money through the inability to redeem a national bank note.

Notes

1 National Currency Act of February 25, 1863, 12 Stat. 665 (1863), an act to provide a national currency, secured by a pledge of United States stocks, and to provide for the circulation and redemption thereof. This act was revisited by the National Bank Act of June 3, 1864, 13 Stat. 99 (1864), an act to provide a national currency, secured by a pledge of United States bonds, and to provide for the circulation and redemption thereof.
2 Salmon P. Chase (January 13, 1808–May 7, 1873) was a liberal Democrat from Ohio who was elected senator under the Free Soil banner and served from 1849 to 1855 and subsequently served as governor of Ohio from 1855 to 1860.
3 Doris Kearns Goodwin, *Team of Rivals: The Political Genius of Abraham Lincoln* (New York: Simon & Schuster, 2005).
4 Fritz Redlick, *The Molding of American Banking, Men and Ideas (1781–1910)* (Eastland, CT: Martino Fine Books, 1951).
5 Hugh Rockoff, "The Free Banking Era, a Reexamination." *Journal of Money, Credit and Banking.* 6:2 (1974).
6 A. Barton Hepburn, *A History of Currency in the United States*, rev. edn (New York: MacMillan Company, 1924), 177.
7 Howard Bodenhorn, *State Banking in Early America: A New Economic History* (New York: Oxford University Press, 2002).
8 Hepburn, *A History of Currency in the United States*, 180.
9 William H. Dillistin, "Bank Note Reporters and Counterfeit Detectors." *American Numismatic Society Notes and Monographs,* 114 (1949).
10 Gary Groton, "Reputation Formation in Early Bank Note Markets." *Journal of Political Economy*, 104:2 (1996).
11 Arthur J. Rolnick and Warren E. Weber. "Banking Instability and Regulation in the U. S. Free Banking Era." *Federal Reserve Bank of Minneapolis Quarterly Review.* 9:3 (1985).
12 John Jay Knox, *United States Notes: A History of the Various Issues of Paper Money by the Government of the United States* (New York: Charles Scribner's Sons, 1884), 85.
13 National Loan Act of July 17, 1861, 12 Stat. 259 (1861), an act to authorize a national loan, and for other purposes; Act of August 5, 1861, 12 Stat. 316 (1861), an act supplementary to an act entitled "An act to authorize a national loan, and for other purposes."
14 Act of February 12, 1862, 12 Stat. 338 (1862), an act authorizing an additional issue of United States Notes.
15 Knox, *United States Notes*, 89–90.
16 Legal Tender Act of February 25, 1862, 12 Stat. 136 (1862) an act to authorize the issue of United States Notes, and for the redemption or funding thereof, and for funding the floating debt of the United States; Act of July 11, 1862, 12 Stat. 532 (1862), an act to authorize an additional issue of United States Notes, and for other

purposes; Act of March 3, 1863, An act to provide ways and means for the support of the Government.
17 Knox, *United States Notes*, 85.
18 Ross M. Robertson, *The Comptroller and Bank Supervision: A Historical Appraisal*, with a new chapter and foreword by Jesse H. Stiller (Washington, DC: Office of the Comptroller of the Currency, 1995), 40–41.
19 Richard T. Erb, "The National Banking System: Who Deserved the Credit" (unpublished manuscript, undated). Erb served successively as Acting Deputy Comptroller and Licensing Manager in the Comptroller of the Currency's Office circa 2000.
20 Wendell Wolka, "The True Roots of the National Banking System" (PowerPoint presentation, Central States Numismatic Society National Bank Note Symposium, Higgins Museum, Okoboji, Iowa, August 3, 2006).
21 Hugh McCulloch, *Men and Measures of Half a Century* (New York: Charles Scribner's sons, 1888), 163–6.
22 John Jay Knox, *Annual Report of the Comptroller of the Currency to the Second Session of the Forty-fifth Congress of the United States*, December 3, 1877 (Washington, DC: U.S. Government Printing Office, 1877), XIII; John Jay Knox, *Annual Report of the Comptroller of the Currency to the Third Session of the Forty-fifth Congress of the United States*, December 2, 1878 (Washington, DC: U.S. Government Printing Office, 1878), XXVI.
23 Hepburn, *A History of Currency in the United States*, 203.
24 Freeman Clarke, *Report of the Comptroller of the Currency to the First Session of the Thirty-ninth Congress of the United States*, December 4, 1865 (Washington, DC: U.S. Government Printing Office, 1865), 15.
25 Freeman Clarke, "Report of the Comptroller of the Currency to the First Session of the Thirty-Ninth Congress of the United States, December 4, 1865": Washington, DC: U.S. Government Printing Office. The National Currency Acts of February 25, 1863, and June 3, 1864, required country national banks to hold reserves of 15% of their deposits and outstanding circulation and banks in specified reserve cities to hold reserves of 25% of their deposits and outstanding circulation. The amount of $137 million is calculated from the data on page 144.
26 Knox, *United States Notes*, 156–6.
27 The National Bank Act was periodically amended to allow for extensions of corporate life to banks (Acts of July 12, 1882, April 12, 1902 and July 1, 1922) and ultimately to grant perpetual corporate life (Act of February 25, 1927).
28 Robert Craig West, *Banking Reform and the Federal Reserve 1863–1923* (Ithaca, NY: Cornell University Press, 1974), 24.

3 National Bank Notes and the practical limits of nationalization

Franklin Noll

Introduction

It was one thing to create the national banking system on paper. It was quite another to bring it to fruition in the midst of the Civil War. Offices and furnishings had to be secured, staff hired, and operating procedures developed. Reviewing hundreds of applications for national bank charters was a major administrative hurdle in the best of circumstances, but in this case it had to be done with a staff of four: Comptroller Hugh McCulloch, Deputy Comptroller Samuel T. Howard, and two clerks. That McCulloch was able to accomplish most of this in the roughly 10 weeks that elapsed from the date of the National Currency Act's passage to May 9, 1863, when the office's doors swung open for the first time, was a small organizational miracle.

One issue was not so easily resolved—designing, engraving, and printing the new national currency that the national banks were to place into circulation. Congress and the Comptroller had high hopes that this currency would become the nation's only paper money, driving out the thousands of varieties of notes issued over the years by state banks. Furthermore, Treasury Secretary Salmon P. Chase and Spencer M. Clark, the engineer who headed the office that later became the Bureau of Engraving and Printing (BEP), had the idea that a national currency should be produced by a new government agency rather than by the private sector firms that had long had the business to themselves of printing paper money and other financial instruments.

As Franklin Noll shows in this chapter, Chase and Clark's plan underestimated the challenges of their undertaking. Ultimately, the failure to deliver the national currency in a timely manner undermined support for the entire system and led to doubts fed by the banknote printing industry, which faced the loss of lucrative government contracts under Clark's plan. The industry's resistance helped regain the contracts, but not for long. In 1877 the BEP became the sole producer of all U.S. currency.

Noll reminds us that while good policies are important, implementation is crucial—that history is as often shaped in the frictions that play out behind the scenes as those that occupy center stage.

Dr. Noll, who received his Ph.D. from the University of Maryland, is the president of Noll Historical Consulting, LLC, which administers the history and museum programs for the BEP.

In 1863 an act was passed establishing a national currency that was to be circulated via a new national banking system. This act, along with other wartime initiatives, such as war bonds, a federal income tax, and the transcontinental railroad, marked an unprecedented expansion of federal authority into the United States economy. Further, the new Office of the Comptroller of the Currency would administer and oversee the bond-backed currency, issued by banks chartered by the government and declared a legal tender of fixed value by the government. Secretary of the Treasury Salmon Chase had already established a government printing operation in the U.S. Department of the Treasury to print the new currency, making the national bank note a national as well as a nationalized currency. The printing operation was a precursor to the Bureau of Engraving and Printing.

Yet in 1863, Hugh McCulloch, the first Comptroller of the Currency, decided to have the national currency printed by private companies rather than by the government printing agency set up for that purpose. Was the decision the result of McCulloch, the former Indiana banker, being biased against the idea of the government printing its own currency? Did he believe that there should be limits to currency nationalization? Was it his way of maintaining private participation in an otherwise federal venture? Is this episode illustrative of lingering misgivings over the expansion of federal authority inherent in the establishment of a national currency and a national banking system?

The evidence shows rather that McCulloch's decision was a practical rather than an ideological one. He was driven to use private banknote companies in New York by a sense of urgency to issue his office's new currency. Ultimately, frustrated by delays in the Treasury Department's note production and determined to get the new system up and running, McCulloch fell back on established ways of producing banknotes.

The urgent need for a national currency

Upon taking office in May 1863, McCulloch's goal was to get the national currency into circulation as quickly as possible. At the start of the war, the major forms of currency were state banknotes and gold. Issued by private, state-chartered banks, state banknotes made up a privatized currency system that was less than ideal, with thousands of different types of banknotes in circulation, many of which were worthless. Meanwhile, the stress of the Treasury Department's borrowings of gold coin to finance the war forced eastern banks off the gold standard on December 28, 1861. The Treasury followed suit on December 30, and a monetary crisis ensued. Gold and silver disappeared from circulation, leaving only a sea of state banknotes of questionable value and that by law could not be accepted or used by the Treasury Department. As a temporary fix, United States Notes, also known as legal tenders or "greenbacks," were created by Congress in February 1862. National currency, backed by government securities, was believed to be the solution.

Once authorized, it was imperative to get the notes rapidly into circulation to revive the economy and to establish the credibility of the new banking and currency systems—and the credibility of the Comptroller himself. Because of the war, currency had to be the law's first priority. McCulloch made this clear in his first annual report to Congress, asserting that "The national currency system contemplates the organization of national banks," not vice versa.[1]

By April 1863, McCulloch was hard at work evaluating charter applications from bank organizers. Bonds intended to secure the currency were arriving daily, but McCulloch had no notes to issue, as he was compelled to inform applicants.[2] For bank organizers, every day without notes to issue in the form of a loan was a day's loss of interest income.[3] No doubt, the lack of available notes gave some pause when considering forming a new national bank.[4] Samuel T. Howard, Deputy Comptroller, wrote to McCulloch in June 1863, "We have been receiving telegram after telegram from parties anxious to commence," but they were put off by the lack of notes for issuance.[5]

The longer it took to get notes into circulation, the more time opponents had to organize, and the success of the new national banking system was not guaranteed. Many of the nation's banks were hostile to the new institution. And it was not long before the New York Clearing House Association drew up plans to block the entrance of national banks into the New York banking arena, and members refused to convert to a federal charter.[6]

The failure to get the national currency into circulation also hindered the war effort.[7] In 1863 the war was being paid for by the sale of war bonds to the general public and the issuance of greenbacks. However, the bond sales were hindered by the lack of a medium that the people could use to purchase them, as the Treasury Department could only accept gold and greenbacks in payment. As the new National Bank Notes were legal tender, they would be another means of payment acceptable to the Treasury.[8] Absent these notes, bond sales lagged expectations, meaning less cash flowing in to the needy Treasury.

Production plans

Chase's plan was that national currency would be printed in Washington, DC, by the Treasury's new banknote operation. It was located in the southwest corner of the Treasury building's basement and run by Spencer M. Clark, acting engineer in charge of the Bureau of Construction of the Treasury Department. Clark's operation, established in mid-1862, was in charge of processing the greenbacks arriving from the New York banknote companies. Within a few months of its founding, Chase pronounced Clark's enterprise a "perfect success," offering a "prodigious advantage to the Government."[9]

As 1862 progressed, Chase and Clark explored a Treasury-based alternative to ordering notes from the banknote industry, which was controlled by a few companies in New York: the American Bank Note Company, National Bank Note Company, and Continental Bank Note Company. With a few companies dominating production, competition suffered. Clark reported, when he became involved in printing at the Treasury Department, that he "was amazed to find the enormous prices that had been paid for the work."[10] The companies had a hard time meeting their production deadlines, leading to continual conflicts with and complaints from Chase.[11]

Sometime in late December 1862, Chase met with Clark on the possibility of printing coupon bonds inside the Treasury building.[12] In January 1863, the *Boston Daily Advertiser* reported that the banknote companies were "criminally behind" in providing greenbacks and that the Treasury Department was making plans to do the printing itself.[13]

Given this state of affairs, it was not surprising that Chase became interested in severing ties with the companies and doing the printing in-house.[14] As McCulloch explained the matter to his friend George Hatch, president of the American Bank Note Company, "In a matter of so great importance and permanent importance as that of providing for a National Bank Note Circulation, the Secretary considered it to be his duty (with which opinion my own entirely accords) to place the Government, in view of future contingencies, on a position of perfect independence of Bank Note Companies."[15] In other words, a truly national currency should be produced by the government. The plan drawn up by Chase and Clark was to have all the New York banknote companies prepare components of the printing plates for shipment to the Treasury Department, which would then create the final plates and do all the printing.[16]

Clark had grand design ideas for the national currency. He wanted state-of-the-art notes bearing complex designs and anti-counterfeiting features, printed with cutting-edge presses and special paper. The note Clark envisioned consisted of one with an ornate obverse and reverse, both of which would have vignettes of a national or historic character. In addition, the obverse would have the words "National Currency" printed in gold. The reverse would have its central vignette flanked by two ovals in which would be seals printed in gold. One seal would be of the state in which the national bank resided and the other would be a national seal.[17]

This gold-colored printing was important for the security of the note. Known as bronzing, the reflective nature of the bronzing prevented photographic reproduction of National Bank Notes. In the black-and-white photography of the day, these gold letters and images would appear black, preventing accurate copies.[18] Bronzing was a new feature on currency, but it could be accomplished using established machines and methods. The technical challenge in Clark's design lay in the placement of the bronze lettering and the bronze shields on the notes. Failure to get the text or the shields in exactly the right location on each note would result in the National Bank Notes not looking alike, raising concerns among the public as to whether the notes were counterfeit. Widespread anxiety on this point could result in the failure of the national currency.

The only way to produce the notes Clark wanted was through an experimental type of printing known as hydrostatic printing. At the time, and indeed through the 1950s, currency was printed using engraved plates via a "wet" method. Before each printing of a back, front, or tint, the paper being used was soaked until damp to make it more pliable. After printing, the paper would be allowed to dry so that the ink would set. The pliability from wetting was needed because the presses of the time could not exert enough pressure to force stiffer, dry paper into the grooves of the plate. The problem with wet printing was that each soaking-drying cycle caused the paper to shrink and expand in arbitrary ways, meaning that the already-printed images on the paper moved unpredictably.

In order to avoid this problem and get accurate registration for multiple printings, a dry printing method had to be used. This meant using dry paper that, in turn, required a press capable of producing tremendous forces during the printing process. The only instrument capable of doing this was a hydrostatic press, which used hydraulics to generate the force necessary to complete the printing. However, these presses were rather crude and still experimental at the time of the Civil War.[19] For Clark to use dry printing in producing National Bank Notes, he would have to perfect—if not reinvent—hydrostatic printing for long, high-quality production runs.

Clark worked on development of the press with Stuart Gwynn, an inventor working at the Treasury Department since late 1862, to provide a new, distinctive banknote paper that contained colored fibers embedded in the paper.[20] As a further layer of anti-counterfeiting protection, Clark wanted this newly developed, distinctive paper to be produced only in the Treasury building. The main concern was whether Gwynn could produce the paper in large enough quantities, as only small batches had been produced during development.[21]

The struggle for a national currency

During the spring of 1863, Clark was largely left in charge of getting the National Bank Notes under production, as McCulloch was busy attending to his new role in Washington. Despite all the initial planning, however, progress was slow. Final designs for the National Bank Notes did not begin arriving from the banknote companies until June.[22] It was now four months since the start of the design process and five months since the passage of the authorizing act, and no engraved pieces had yet been produced. Why was it taking so long given the critical need to produce notes as quickly as possible?

One reason was the contentious relationship between the Treasury Department and the banknote companies. In later testimony, Clark argued that the banknote companies intentionally delayed the delivery of contracted work to the Treasury in an attempt to discredit Clark and thus win back the government's work. This was on top of government unhappiness with the companies' performance in producing bonds and greenbacks.[23] In April 1863, an exasperated Chase assigned Clark to produce the bonds internally, giving him only six weeks to do the job.[24]

It was not surprising that National Bank Notes were so long in coming. With heavy preoccupations of his own, McCulloch was not deeply involved in the printing problems until May, when he evidently received the depressing news on the state of the notes. "I do not think that Circulating Notes can be prepared and ready for delivery in much less than three months," he wrote to one banker.[25] This became the official response to those badgering the office for a time when the currency would be ready. Throughout early summer, every inquirer was given the stock answer that the notes would not be ready for three months.

As McCulloch settled into his new office, he began to pay more attention to the currency that was at the heart of it. "If the Engravers fulfill their contract, and no unexpected hindrance occurs," he wrote more confidently in July, "circulation will be ready for distribution . . . as early as the first part of October next."[26] He repeated this conviction many times to correspondents and appeared happy to leave production concerns to Clark.

However, problems persisted. On July 7, Clark met with McCulloch and informed him of the realities that confronted them. The first set of plates was not scheduled for delivery until mid-September. Also, there were not enough transfer presses to produce all the needed plates. The only solution was to have private firms build and ship transfer presses to the Treasury Department.[27] The next day, McCulloch addressed a letter to Chase urging him to give Clark the authority to go ahead with acquiring more presses. Otherwise, the "preparation of notes for the Associations which are being organized, will be greatly delayed to their injury and the prejudice of the system."[28] Evidently, Chase gave his approval to the plan, as McCulloch paid no further attention to currency production and continued relaying to inquirers that the notes would be ready in early October.[29] During the rest of the month and into August, Clark focused on his other duties while he waited for the work of the New York banknote companies to arrive. However, the newly chartered national banks were losing patience, complaining to Chase that, while they had purchased the bonds required by law, the government was reneging on its part of the bargain by not delivering notes.[30]

When September came and went without appreciable progress, McCulloch raised concerns over the cutting-edge, practically experimental nature of the Treasury's print operations and wondered out loud whether it would be better for the established banknote companies to produce the national currency despite the additional cost.[31] Adding to McCulloch's anxiety were the first calls for organized opposition to the national banking system coming from within the New York Clearing House Association on September 23.[32] The association later released a report that was a "vicious" attack on the national banking system and "intended to frighten the public."[33]

After early October, the date promised by McCulloch for release of the currency notes, the number of new national banks continued to grow apace, no doubt in expectation that business could start at once with enough national currency to go around.[34] Yet there were no notes. There were not even any plates. The banknote companies were not living up to their contracts, delivering only proposed models that Clark and McCulloch found unsatisfactory in execution but accepted anyway for the sake of speed. "The failure to meet contractual guidelines is unwarranted," McCulloch wrote, "but as the immediate issue [of notes] is now of the utmost importance, I shall not direct their alteration, fearing delay."[35]

His impatience growing, McCulloch began to intervene personally in negotiations with the banknote companies. He was still committed to the idea of the Treasury Department producing the notes and saw the sticking point in the timely production of the necessary plates. He therefore began discussions with the banknote companies to create the final plates, effectively cutting Clark out of the process.[36] An October agreement between Clark and McCulloch laid out the plan: the New York companies would produce the plates and Clark's office would print the notes, with the caveat that the companies could also be called upon to print notes if necessary.[37] Clark was irate that "the companies' non-compliance with the Secretary's order should inure, as they expected it would, to their pecuniary gain and Government loss," but there were no other options.[38]

By November, with time ticking away, McCulloch and Clark were in daily communication about their progress.[39] On November 16 Clark reported that the hydrostatic presses were still not ready for full production.[40] McCulloch now felt he had no choice but to exercise the option of contracting some of the printing outside the Treasury Department.

Thus, on November 18, the Continental Bank Note Company was directed to start printing $5 notes for First National Bank of Washington, DC, using standard banknote paper—not Gwynn's distinctive paper, of which none had been prepared. To keep as much of Clark's plan as possible, McCulloch had Clark supply the paper to Continental with the bronzed type already printed on it as an anti-counterfeiting measure.[41] Clark sent the paper reluctantly, predicting that McCulloch would be dissatisfied with the results: "The Bank Note Companies have told you, that they can print these notes with an accurate register, according to my plan. I have told you they cannot and . . . I sincerely believe you will be disappointed."[42] Because the companies used wet printing, the paper would shrink and expand irregularly, causing the bronze title to appear in different locations on finished notes. Clark's prediction proved correct, but by then McCulloch was willing to sacrifice quality for timeliness. And he felt that Clark, by focusing too much on unproven processes, had fallen short.[43]

Clark was "pained" to learn that his plans for the government to be the exclusive source of national currency were being cast aside. It was also a disappointment to Chase, but he had delegated the organization of the Comptroller's Office to McCulloch, and he felt bound by that decision.[44]

In his Annual Report to Congress of November 28, McCulloch admitted that "the work of preparing the national circulation has been attended with unlooked for delays." But the production of notes was under way, and he promised Congress that within two months all the current national banks would receive the notes due them.[45]

This eventuality could not come soon enough. On the same day as McCulloch's report to Congress, the New York Clearing House published a committee report written by John E. Williams denouncing the national banking system. And a few days later the Clearing House voted their approval of the Williams report and called for a boycott of the national banking system.[46]

At last, on December 18, 1863, $5 notes for First National Bank of Washington, DC, were received by the Treasury Department from the Continental Bank Note Company and numbered.[47] The first $20,000 worth of these notes was dispatched from the Treasury to the bank on December 21. Five months had passed since the bank had deposited its security for those notes.[48]

Conclusion

McCulloch's goal in 1863 was to get the national currency into circulation as quickly as possible. Secretary Chase and Spencer Clark had agreed to use an embryonic in-house capability to produce that currency. But as one deadline after another slipped away, McCulloch turned the task of producing the national currency over to private companies, which would be involved in National Bank Note production—to their immense profit—for the next 15 years.[49]

There were basically three reasons for this outcome:

- The New York banknote companies had engaged in delay and subterfuge. Under contract to produce elements of the printing plates to the Treasury Department, they repeatedly failed to live up to the terms of their contracts, belatedly delivering shoddy goods. Clark concluded that this was a ploy to force McCulloch to hire the banknote companies to do the entire job, and there is considerable justification for Clark's conclusion.
- If Clark fell short, there was reason for it. He was overburdened with the responsibility for creating a new production facility and with a big backlog of orders for government bonds and notes. It did not help that he sought to adopt new and unproven technologies, such as hydrostatic presses and advanced papers. Clark simply did not have the time or resources to accomplish all this work, and he allowed the production of National Bank Notes to fall by the wayside.[50]
- Hugh McCulloch basically took a hands-off approach to note production until it was too late to save the plan for in-house production. If McCulloch had used his many connections in the industry to his advantage, the plan might have been more successful.

Thus, McCulloch's decision to have notes printed privately was not an ideological decision but a practical one. He had no bias against the idea of the government printing its own currency. Instead, he had simply run out of time.

If there was any conflict between the federal expansion of power in the economy and McCulloch's actions, it was between a desire for a national and nationalized currency and the difficulty of making it a reality.

Notes

1. U.S. Department of the Treasury, *Report of the Secretary of the Treasury on the State of the Finances* (Washington, DC: Government Printing Office, 1863), 55; Fritz Redlich, *The Molding of American Banking: Men and Ideas, Part II: 1840–1910* (New York: Hafner Publishing Co., 1951), 102, 104–5; Bray Hammond, *Sovereignty and an Empty Purse: Banks and Politics in the Civil War* (Princeton, NJ: Princeton University Press, 1970), 143.
2. Chase was receiving queries in early March 1863. Entry 11: letters from private individuals, banks, and trust companies, and Government officials, 1863–1909, box 1, Record Group 101: Records of the Office of the Comptroller of the Currency (hereafter RG 101), National Archives and Records Administration, College Park (hereafter NARA-CP).
3. Redlich, *The Molding of American Banking*, 110.
4. Hugh McCulloch to J. C. Finlay, June 11, 1863, entry 2-A: letters sent by the Comptroller of the Currency, April 8, 1863–July 16, 1863, RG 101, NARA-CP.
5. Samuel T. Howard to Hugh McCulloch, June 23, 1863, entry 2-A: letters sent by the Comptroller of the Currency, April 8, 1863–July 16, 1863, RG 101, NARA-CP.
6. David M. Gische, "The New York City Banks and the Development of the National Banking System, 1860–70," *American Journal of Legal History* 23, no. 1 (January 1979): 40–47; John A. James and David F. Weiman, "The National Banking Acts and the Transformation of New York City Banking During the Civil War Era," *Journal of Economic History* 71, no. 2 (June 2011): 339–43; Redlich, *The Molding of American Banking*, 106–13; Hammond, *Sovereignty and an Empty Purse*, 145.
7. Schuyler Colfax to Hugh McCulloch, April 16, 1863, Hugh McCulloch Papers, 1855–1905, vol. 1, Library of Congress.
8. Hammond, *Sovereignty and an Empty Purse*, 315, 110, 304.
9. See diary entry for September 13, 1862, in David Donald, ed., *Inside Lincoln's Cabinet: The Civil War Diaries of Salmon P. Chase* (New York: Longmans, Green and Co., 1954), 139.
10. "Report to the Secretary of the Treasury from the First Division of the National Currency Bureau," H.R. Rep. No. 50–38, at 8 (1865) (hereafter "Report to the Secretary of the Treasury").
11. Tracy Edson to Salmon Chase, April 16, 1862, entry 542: correspondence with bank note companies, folder: 1861–62, box 2: American Bank Note, RG 53: Records of the Bureau of the Public Debt (hereafter RG 53), NARA-CP. See also Tracy Edson to Salmon Chase, August 12, 1862, idem.
12. Spencer Clark to Salmon Chase, December 27, 1862, entry 679-C: documentary history of the U.S. Treasury Department, 1775–1963, folder: 1847–66, box 3: Records of the Office of the Chief Clerk, Records of the Treasury Library, RG 56: Records of the Department of the Treasury, NARA-CP.
13. Hammond, *Sovereignty and an Empty Purse*, 340.
14. *Report of the Select Committee to Investigate Charges against the Treasury Department*, H.R. Rep. No. 38–140, at 124 (1864) (hereafter *Report of the Select Committee*).
15. Hugh McCulloch to George W. Hatch, June 27, 1863, entry 2-A: letters sent by the Comptroller of the Currency, April 8, 1863–July 16, 1863, RG 101, NARA-CP.

16 "Report to the Secretary of the Treasury," 20, 32.
17 Barbara Bither, "Bronzing Planned for the Nationals," *Bank Note Reporter* 60, no. 1 (January 2011): 22–4.
18 Barbara Bither, "Green Ink, Blue Threads, and Gold Circles: The BEP Fight Against Civil War Counterfeiting," *BEP Communicator*, September 2008, 8–10.
19 "Report to the Secretary of the Treasury," 25, 28–9, 33.
20 *History of the Bureau of Engraving and Printing, 1862–1962* (Washington, DC: Government Printing Office, 1962), 19; "Report to the Secretary of the Treasury," 17–19.
21 Barbara Bither, "The Federal Government's Quest for Distinctive Paper," *ANS Magazine* 11, no. 2 (2012): 19–27.
22 Spencer Clark to W. D. Wilson, July 10, 1863, entry 1: official and miscellaneous letters received, 1864–1912, box 1, Salmon Chase to George Hatch, 13 July 1863; Spencer Clark to Salmon Chase, July 15, 1863; Spencer Clark to Salmon Chase, July 17, 1863, *idem*.; Spencer Clark to George Hatch, July 23, 1863; Spencer Clark to W.D. Wilson, July 25, 1863; Spencer Clark to George Hatch, July 25, 1863, entry 5: press copies of official and miscellaneous letters sent, 1862–1912, vol. 2; all in RG 318: Records of the Bureau of Engraving and Printing (hereafter RG 318), NARA-CP; Hugh McCulloch to George Harrington, May 28, 1864, *Report of the Select Committee*, 310.
23 *Report of the Select Committee*, 116–19.
24 "Report to the Secretary of the Treasury," 20.
25 Hugh McCulloch to Henry W. Cushman, May 18, 1863, entry 2-A: letters sent by the Comptroller of the Currency, April 8, 1863–July 16, 1863, RG 101, NARA-CP.
26 Hugh McCulloch to Abraham Becker, July 6, 1863, entry 2-A: letters sent by the Comptroller of the Currency, April 8, 1863–July 16, 1863, RG 101, NARA-CP.
27 Spencer Clark to Hugh McCulloch, July 7, 1863, entry 5: press copies of official and miscellaneous letters sent, 1862–1912, vol. 2, RG 318, NARA-CP.
28 Hugh McCulloch to Salmon Chase, July 8, 1863, entry 2-A: letters sent by the Comptroller of the Currency, April 8, 1863–July 16, 1863, RG 101, NARA-CP.
29 Hugh McCulloch to Simon Gebhart, July 16, 1863, entry 2-A: letters sent by the Comptroller of the Currency, April 8, 1863–July 16, 1863, RG 101, NARA-CP.
30 John Niven, ed., *The Salmon P. Chase Papers, Vol. 4: Correspondence, April 1863–1864* (Kent, OH: Kent State University Press, 1997), 98.
31 *Report of the Select Committee*, 116–17.
32 Gische, "The New York City Banks," 43.
33 Redlich, *The Molding of American Banking*, 107.
34 U.S. Treasury, *Report of the Secretary of the Treasury on the State of the Finances*, 49.
35 Comptroller of the Currency to George Hatch, October 12, 1863, entry 5: press copies of official and miscellaneous letters sent, 1862–1912, vol. 2, RG 318, NARA-CP.
36 Hugh McCulloch to George Hatch, October 23, 1863, *Report of the Select Committee*, 298–9; Hugh McCulloch to George Hatch, October 28, 1863, and Hugh McCulloch to F[itch] Shepard, October 28, 1863, entry 5: press copies of official and miscellaneous letters sent, 1862–1912, vol. 2, RG 318, NARA, College Park.
37 Spencer Clark to Salmon Chase, October 28, 1863, entry 5: press copies of official and miscellaneous letters sent, 1862–1912, vol. 2, RG 318, NARA-CP.
38 Spencer Clark to Hugh McCulloch, October 30, 1863, entry 5: press copies of official and miscellaneous letters sent, 1862–1912, vol. 2, RG 318, NARA-CP; Salmon Chase to Alexander Wilson, 9 November 1863, *Report of the Select Committee*, 290.
39 *Report of the Select Committee*, 117.

40 Spencer Clark to Salmon Chase, November 16, 1863, entry 602: correspondence relating to the Bureau of Engraving and Printing, 1862–93, 1907–13, box 1, RG 53, NARA-CP.
41 Salmon Chase to W. D. Wilson, November 18, 1863, and Spencer Clark to Hugh McCulloch, November 25, 1863, entry 5: press copies of official and miscellaneous letters sent, 1862–1912, vol. 2, RG 318, NARA-CP; *Report of the Select Committee*, 108.
42 Spencer Clark to Hugh McCulloch, 23 November 1863, entry 5: press copies of official and miscellaneous letters sent, 1862–1912, vol. 2, RG 318, NARA-CP.
43 Ibid.
44 *Report of the Select Committee*, 124; Hugh McCulloch, *Men and Measures of Half a Century* (New York: Charles Scribner's Sons, 1888), 166, 232–3.
45 U.S. Treasury, *Report of the Secretary of the Treasury on the State of the Finances*, 58.
46 Gische, "The New York City Banks," 44, 47.
47 S. R. Wilkins to Spencer Clark, December 18, 1863, entry 1: official and miscellaneous letters received, 1864–1912, box 1, RG 318, NARA-CP.
48 Entry 14: National Currency and Bond ledgers, 1864–1935, vol. 1, 96–97, RG 101, NARA-CP.
49 Franklin Noll, "The United States Monopolization of Bank Note Production: Politics, Government, and the Greenback, 1862–78," *American Nineteenth Century History* 13, no. 1 (2012): 15–43.
50 *Report of the Select Committee*, 126.

Bibliography

Abraham Lincoln Papers.
Bither, Barbara, "Bronzing Planned for the Nationals." *Bank Note Reporter* 60, no. 1 (January 2011): 1, 22–4.
Bither, Barbara, "The Federal Government's Quest for Distinctive Paper." *ANS Magazine* 11, no. 2 (2012): 19–27.
Bither, Barbara, "Green Ink, Blue Threads, and Gold Circles: The BEP Fight Against Civil War Counterfeiting." *BEP Communicator*, September 2008, 8–10.
Donald, David, ed. *Inside Lincoln's Cabinet: The Civil War Diaries of Salmon P. Chase*. New York: Longmans, Green and Co., 1954.
Gische, David M. "The New York City Banks and the Development of the National Banking System, 1860–70." *American Journal of Legal History* 23, no. 1 (January 1979): 21–67.
Hammond, Bray. *Sovereignty and an Empty Purse: Banks and Politics in the Civil War*. Princeton, NJ: Princeton University Press, 1970.
History of the Bureau of Engraving and Printing, 1862–1962. Washington, DC: Government Printing Office, 1962.
James, John A. and David F. Weiman. "The National Banking Acts and the Transformation of New York City Banking During the Civil War Era." *Journal of Economic History* 71, no. 2 (June 2011): 338–62.
McCulloch, Hugh. *Men and Measures of Half a Century*. New York: Charles Scribner's Sons, 1888.
McCulloch, Hugh, Papers. Library of Congress.
Macdonald, James. *A Free Nation Deep in Debt: The Financial Roots of Democracy*. New York: Farrar, Straus and Giroux, 2003.
Niven, John, ed. *The Salmon P. Chase Papers, Vol. 4: Correspondence, April 1863–1864*. Kent, OH: Kent State University Press, 1997.

Noll, Franklin. "The United States Monopolization of Bank Note Production: Politics, Government, and the Greenback, 1862–78." *American Nineteenth Century History* 13, no. 1 (2012): 15–43.
Noyes, Alexander Dana. *Thirty Years of American Finance*. New York: G.P. Putnam's Sons, 1898.
Records of the Bureau of Engraving and Printing.
Records of the Bureau of the Public Debt.
Records of the Department of the Treasury.
Records of the Office of the Chief Clerk.
Records of the Office of the Comptroller of the Currency.
Records of the Treasury Library
Redlich, Fritz. *The Molding of American Banking: Men and Ideas, Part II: 1840–1910*. New York: Hafner Publishing Co., 1951.
"Report to the Secretary of the Treasury from the First Division of the National Currency Bureau." H.R. Rep. No. 50–38 (1865).
Report of the Select Committee to Investigate Charges against the Treasury Department. H.R. Rep. No. 38–140 (1st sess. 1864).
Richardson, Heather Cox. *The Greatest Nation of the Earth: Republican Economic Policies during the Civil War*. Cambridge, MA: Harvard University Press, 1997.
Robertson, Ross M. *The Comptroller and Bank Supervision: A Historical Appraisal*. Washington, DC: Office of the Comptroller of the Currency, 1995.
Scalia, Michael. "'I commenced work … ' Origins of the Bureau of Engraving and Printing." Unpublished manuscript, September 2004.
U.S. Department of the Treasury. *Report of the Secretary of the Treasury on the State of the Finances*. Washington, DC: Government Printing Office, 1863.

4 Charter No. 1

First among national banks

Marianne Babal

Introduction

The organizers of the national banking system were right to be concerned about whether the new national charter would be attractive enough to potential bank organizers. Certainly, it would be an embarrassment to the Lincoln administration—and a setback to the grand scheme the system embodied—if bankers were unmoved by the call to join the system to save the Union. Given the grumbling and outright opposition to the legislation in certain quarters, there was a distinct possibility that the administration's appeal to patriotism might not be enough to override concerns about the burdens and uncertainties of an untested regime—especially in states such as California, which harbored deep suspicion of chartered banking of any kind. Would the law's benefits—including the right to circulate a personalized, yet uniform currency and to operate under the license and authority of the national government—outweigh the costs and nuisances it clearly entailed? Would restrictions on bank activities, the heavy capital and reserve requirements, the congeries of new forms and reporting responsibilities, and the lengthy delays in getting the new national currency designed, printed, and distributed to the bankers keep others away? Only time would tell.

Fortunately, as Marianne Babal explains in this chapter, the inducements proved more compelling than the drawbacks. In the case of the First National Bank of Philadelphia, the subject of Babal's work, the prestige of a high charter number turned out to have real value in the financial marketplace, which the bank's founders and its successors turned to commercial advantage in the nineteenth century and beyond. Wells Fargo Bank, the corporate heir to the First National of Philadelphia, touts its status as National Bank Charter No. 1 to this day. The Philadelphia bank also had the advantage of the leadership of brothers Jay and Henry Cooke, who had been indispensable allies of Treasury Secretary Chase in the passage of the National Currency Act. They joined the effort in part because they hoped to take advantage of the business opportunities the new system created. In turn, the Cookes' high-level connections helped them attract investors and obtain favorable treatment from the government. The coveted "first of the first" appellation was one of the products of these connections.

Marianne Babal is a corporate historian and vice president at Wells Fargo and Company at its headquarters in San Francisco. In that capacity she develops exhibits and publications on Wells Fargo's storied history. She is also an active participant in *professional organizations dedicated to the practice of public history. She holds a graduate degree from the University of California at Santa Barbara.*

On June 20, 1863, First National Bank of Philadelphia received National Bank Charter No. 1 from the Office of the Comptroller of the Currency. It was the first among thousands of national bank charters issued by the OCC over its 150-year history.

In his first annual report to Congress, in December 1861, Secretary of the Treasury Salmon P. Chase decried the nation's lack of a uniform currency and its reliance on a hodgepodge of notes issued by state-chartered banks. "The value of the existing bank note circulation depends on the laws of thirty-four States and the character of some sixteen hundred private corporations," he declared, noting sardonically that this currency was "usually furnished in greatest proportions by institutions of least actual capital."[1]

The public's lack of confidence in such a varied currency was particularly acute in western states and territories, where merchants conducted business far from the banking centers of New York, Philadelphia, and Boston. The severe Panic of 1857 compounded distrust and uncertainty and crippled business and investment just as increasingly strident sectional animosity consumed the nation's attention. In April 1861 those animosities erupted into the Civil War, which many on both sides believed would be short-lived. These illusions were soon shattered, and a harsh new reality set in: the war would be much longer, bloodier, and vastly more expensive than anyone had imagined. Secretary Chase reported to Congress that for the fiscal year ending July 1, 1862, the federal government's outstanding obligations, including interest payments and already mounting war expenses, would total $318.5 million, a staggering sum that exceeded the total value of coins then circulating throughout the nation's economy.[2]

In his December 1861 report, Chase advocated for the establishment of a national banking system made up of associations empowered by the federal government to issue circulating banknotes. Redemption of this currency would be secured by deposit of United States bonds with the federal treasury.[3] Elements of this bond-backed currency system followed models established previously by some state banks, including the State Bank of Ohio, which Chase was familiar with as that state's former governor, and existing state free-banking laws, particularly that of New York. The Secretary's proposal for a new national banking system would have a dual desired effect: providing a uniform national currency and expanding the federal government's wartime borrowing capacity by creating demand for sale of government bonds.[4] In addition to Chase's advocacy and the immediate pressure for war financing, one additional factor contributed to the advancement of the national banking proposal. Secession had removed anti-central bank Southern Democrats from Congress, giving the Republican Party leadership enough votes to pass its favored currency and banking legislation.[5]

Opposition to Chase's proposed national banking system included state banking interests, who understandably opposed a system of federally sanctioned banks that would potentially overwhelm or absorb existing state-chartered banking institutions. Also suspicious of the proposal were those who feared a reprise of government-sanctioned concentrated economic power such as that exerted by the defunct Bank of the United States a generation before. "It is complained against Secretary Chase's banking project that it gives to the administration great and dangerous power; that it will build up something more obnoxious than was the United States Bank," the *Philadelphia Ledger* noted before dismissing such talk as "all clap-trap for there exists no sort of comparison of the proposed plan of banking on pledge of government securities with the uncontrolled action and unlimited issues and discounts of the old United States Bank."[6]

The national currency concept proffered by Chase attracted much debate but no immediate legislative action, forcing the Secretary to borrow $150 million from banks in New York, Philadelphia, and Boston, which in turn depleted bankers' gold reserves.[7] Meanwhile, wartime hoarders and speculators gathered precious metal, coins disappeared from circulation, and banks suspended specie payment on banknotes.[8]

Congress chose to temporarily meet the exigency by approving $50 million in demand notes and, soon after, several issues of legal tender notes, which became popularly known as "greenbacks."[9] These notes were designated legal tender for all debts, public and private, with two notable exceptions: the U.S. Department of the Treasury continued to pay interest on outstanding public debt in specie, and federal customs duties required payment in hard currency of gold or silver only.[10]

By 1864 some $415 million in greenbacks had been printed and put into circulation. These notes and the sale of bonds had provided the federal government with a financial stopgap at a time when the war, by the summer of 1861, was draining the federal treasury at a rate of $1 million per day.[11] The war had ballooned the national debt from $65 million at the end of fiscal year 1860 to over $1.1 billion in the fiscal year ending 1863.[12]

The Treasury Department's earlier attempt to float a bond issue for $150 million in the autumn of 1861 was made difficult by Secretary Chase's requirement that banks purchase the bonds in increasingly scarce specie.[13] A new bond offering in late 1861 was offered more broadly. These three-year notes, dubbed "seven-thirties," because they paid 7$3/10$ percent interest, drew buyers who flocked to offices of subscription agents such as Jay Cooke & Co. in Philadelphia, which had extensively advertised the investment opportunity in newspapers. Cooke's success in marketing these notes resulted in Chase appointing Cooke as a special agent in selling larger later bond offerings.[14]

The Secretary had a long-standing relationship with Jay Cooke and the Cooke family, extending back to Chase's time as governor of Ohio. One of three sons of a prominent Sandusky attorney, young Jay left home at the age of 17 for Philadelphia, where he took a clerk position in the investment bank founded by Enoch W. Clark and Edward Dodge. The able and ambitious Cooke at age 21 became a partner in the business and managed E.W. Clark & Company's Philadelphia banking house upon the death of founder Clark in

1856. The following year, Cooke left the firm to pursue other ventures in canal and railroad construction before establishing his own investment banking firm, Jay Cooke & Company, in 1861. While Jay Cooke made his name in Philadelphia's financial circles, brother Henry became editor of the Buckeye State's leading Republican newspaper, the *Ohio State Journal,* before following his brother into banking. Throughout their careers, the Cookes nurtured relationships with important political figures such as Chase and Ohio senator John Sherman and lobbied heavily for Chase's appointment as Secretary of the Treasury in the Lincoln cabinet.[15]

The first Legal Tender Act of February 1862 had given the Secretary of the Treasury authority for sale of $500 million in 6 percent bonds, redeemable in 5 years and payable in 20.[16] Jay Cooke & Company, in anticipation of such an opportunity, had recently opened a banking house in the nation's capital and, together with its existing banking house in Philadelphia and numerous sub-agents, expected to sell a million dollars of the five-twenty bonds per day.[17] In order to achieve the desired results, Cooke's sales and publicity networks stoked patriotic fervor among citizen investors and saturated northern states with advertisements, editorials, and broadsides reminding those investors of their "solemn duty" to support the gallant army and naval forces fighting to preserve the Union.[18]

Establishment of a network of new national banks, each required to secure circulating currency with government bonds, would greatly expand the market for sale of bonds. Reporting to Congress in December 1862, Secretary Chase repeated his desire for a uniform currency and national banking system.[19] The Secretary needed to attract torchbearers to his cause in the Senate and House chambers. Samuel Hooper of Massachusetts introduced the proposal in the House of Representatives on January 19, 1863.[20] One potential ally in the U.S. Senate was John Sherman, an Ohioan like Chase and banker brothers Henry and Jay Cooke. On January 23, 1863, Henry Cooke reported to elder brother Jay on his efforts to enlist Senator Sherman's support for a currency and national bank bill, which the younger Cooke asserted was done at the request of Secretary Chase:

> I had an interview with S. last evening and again to-day. Sherman has not positively promised to champion the bill, but from his talk to-day I think he will do it. I am sure he will do so if Governor C. [Chase] will consent to two slight modifications, viz.: restricting the charter (which at present is perpetual) to twenty years, and, to prevent inflation, limiting the amount of circulation to be issued and apportioning it among the states.[21]

Sherman introduced the bill for a national currency and gave an impassioned speech in the Senate in favor of its passage on January 26.[22] Advocates such as the Cooke brothers put considerable effort into garnering support for the uniform currency act in Congress. The Cooke brothers authored and placed numerous articles and advertisements. Newspapers that had carried advertisements for the five-twenty bonds devoted column inches to the inadequacies of existing state banking systems and the anticipated benefits of a national currency system. The Act's proponents employed letters of support and handbills in their lobbying efforts, reproduced many copies of the bank bill, and even clipped favorable press reports on the topic from home districts of members of Congress, who found the clippings neatly piled upon their desks in legislative chambers in the Capitol.[23]

The National Currency Act legislation, officially entitled "A Bill to provide a national currency, secured by a pledge of United States stocks, and to provide for the circulation and redemption thereof," passed the Senate on February 13, 1863, by a close vote of 23 to 21, followed soon after with approval in the House of Representatives by a vote of 78 to 64.[24] President Lincoln signed the act into law on February 25, 1863. After the act passed, Secretary Chase wrote to Jay Cooke expressing appreciation for his support. "Your services in behalf of the Uniform Currency bill are fully appreciated by me: except that appreciation of the consciousness of usefulness to your country must be your sole reward."[25]

The Philadelphia financier had every intention of participating in the new system. Cooke's years of experience with bankers E.W. Clark & Company and his own firm gave him access to a wide circle of investors and significant sums of capital. Under provisions of the national currency legislation, an association of five or more persons could obtain a national bank charter from the Comptroller of the Currency, a newly created federal office within the Treasury Department. Persons forming associations could submit a request for a charter by submitting a notarized certificate stating the name of their association, place of business, amount of capital stock—a minimum of $50,000, but $100,000 in large cities—number of shares, names of stockholders, and quantity of shares subscribed to, and commencement and termination dates of the association.[26]

At the time of commencement of business for any national banking association, at least 30 percent of the capital stock had to be paid in and government bonds equal to at least one-third of such capital had to be deposited with the federal government. After authentication by the Comptroller's office, a certificate was issued authorizing associations to commence business circulating notes; discounting bills, notes, and other debt; receiving deposits; buying and selling gold and silver, coins, and bills of exchange; and loaning money on real and personal security.[27] Associations established in compliance with the Act were entitled to receive and circulate banknotes from the Comptroller of the Currency in amounts up to 90 percent of the value of bonds deposited with the Treasury.[28]

Bankers and business leaders in a number of cities quickly began to organize with the intention of forming national banking associations under the law, even as government employees struggled to quickly activate the new system. In Philadelphia, Jay Cooke mobilized a group of associates and leaders in Philadelphia's commercial and banking community to submit an early petition for a national charter. On March 9, 1863, Philadelphia attorney Owen W. Davis wrote to Thomas W. Olcott, whom Davis erroneously believed to be the newly appointed Comptroller of the Currency based on local newspaper reports. "I heartily endorse the nomination and to ask your attention officially to an application forwarded Hon. S.P. Chase on February 25th for the benefit of the Act of Congress for an association which some of us wish to organize as the *first* in Phila."[29]

In a subsequent letter to Assistant Secretary of the Treasury George Harrington on April 17, Davis proposed organizational activities with a slightly different timeline:

> The act to provide a national currency first appeared in the daily papers on Saturday Feb 28. On Monday March 2, I and my associates made informal application to Gov. Chase. We presume we are entitled to style our association the "First" in Philadelphia. We have not forwarded preliminary certificate and copy of articles of association because we have been awaiting a reply. They will be forwarded however on Monday next and unless we hear from the Department that some other applicants have stepped in before us, they will be entitled "The First National Banking Association of Philadelphia Pennsylvania."[30]

Cooke and Davis selected Morton McMichael Jr., who had advanced the charter campaign with the Comptroller's office, as the planned bank's cashier. Although not yet 30 years of age, McMichael hailed from a family prominent in Philadelphia's business and social circles. His father, Morton McMichael Sr., owned the pro-Union *Philadelphia North American* and served as postwar mayor of Philadelphia.[31]

In mid-May the younger McMichael wrote to Comptroller of the Currency Hugh McCulloch seeking a meeting to discuss "necessary measures for putting into immediate operation the First National Bank of Philadelphia." McMichael conferred with McCulloch in Washington, then a few weeks later reported back to the Comptroller on progress in his bank's organizing efforts in Philadelphia. Following McCulloch's suggestion, McMichael confirmed that articles of association had been amended, his bank's board and officers duly elected, and first installments of capital stock paid. McMichael offered to come to Washington immediately with the required papers and bonds as soon as the Comptroller's office was prepared to issue the bank certificate necessary before the bank could commence business.[32]

Meanwhile, the Philadelphia institution's organizers secured space on the corner of Third and Chestnut Streets to house their bank while they impatiently awaited paperwork from the Comptroller allowing them to open their doors. On June 17 cashier McMichael again wrote to McCulloch, this time on printed stationery of the First National Bank of Philadelphia, "I am compelled to trouble you again by asking you whether I can obtain our Certificate by coming to Washington at this time."[33]

Early applicants under the new and untried national banking system commenced the process of incorporating without the benefit of precedent and while dealing with newly installed federal officers and regulators. Predictably, considerable delay and false starts in the application process—including evolving guidelines in the naming of institutions—raised hurdles for pioneer bank organizers. On July 13, 1863, just two days after the opening of the First National Bank of Philadelphia, the exhausted and somewhat exasperated bank president Owen Davis wrote to the Comptroller, "I hope that some modifications will be made next winter as many of the provisions are difficult to comply with and unless they are altered many will be deterred from organizing associations."[34]

Requirements for naming new national banking institutions frustrated one group of prominent citizens from Connecticut, who wrote to Secretary Chase in mid-March announcing their intention to form a bank under the act. They selected the name Commercial Bank of New Haven Connecticut and, upon receiving further instruction in proper procedure for application from one of Chase's underlings, chief bank organizer and New Haven mayor H. M. Welch responded to the Comptroller's office:

> If I understand the intention of the certificate as sent me it is that in establishing a bank in this city we must call it the "First National Banking Association of New Haven Conn." Now, we had adopted a name as following "The Commercial Bank of New Haven Conn." Our certificate preliminary to commencing banking is nearly ready, also our articles of association, and we propose to commence at once with a capital of $300,000. Must we adopt the name as proposed in the form sent me, or can we make use of the name as we have agreed upon. Please inform me, also how soon circulating notes can be furnished. PS: we supposed that under the Act of Congress, associations might adopt such name as they thought desirable for their locality.[35]

At the time of the Act's passage, Secretary Chase had insisted on a requirement that existing banks give up their original names and instead adopt new names under a sequential numbering system.[36] Although Chase eventually relented on the bank name requirement, the convention of naming new national banking institutions with numbers in sequence as First National, Second National, etc., in each city where such institutions installed themselves in business discouraged many established banks operating under state charters. These banks would be required to abandon their familiar names and adopt new national charters with a numbered identity and lesser distinction.[37]

Naming issues delayed the application of the New Haven entrepreneurs, who submitted their Articles of Association for "The First National Banking Association" New Haven, Conn. to Washington on May 2, 1863.[38] Comptroller McCulloch meanwhile had determined that banking institutions organized under the National Currency Act would be designated national banks and not national banking associations, and, according to news reports, applications for organizations already made would be returned for resubmission in proper form.[39] On May 25 a preliminary certificate and amended Articles of Association for "The First National Bank" of New Haven went to Washington. The Connecticut bank had hoped to open in early June and, in fact, by June 18 quietly began business taking deposits and writing drafts on New York in advance of receipt of the official certificate from the Comptroller's office.[40]

Charter No. 1, the first national banking charter issued by the OCC, went not to Connecticut but to Pennsylvania—to Jay Cooke and his associates.[41] On June 20, 1863, acting Comptroller of the Currency Samuel L. Howard affixed his signature and the seal of the Office of the Comptroller of the Currency to Charter No. 1 for First National Bank of Philadelphia.[42] That same day, First National Bank of New Haven received Charter No. 2, First National Bank of Youngstown Charter No. 3, and First National Bank of Stamford Charter No. 4. These four institutions were the first quartet of national banks chartered under the National Currency Act of 1863.[43]

These and other newly organized national banks, as planned, provided a ready market for war bonds, and Jay Cooke employed his promotional energies to encourage the organization of additional national banks, with a view to earning commissions for helping them raise the necessary capital. A Cooke-authored pamphlet entitled "How to Organize a National Bank under Secretary Chase's Bill," issued in the summer of 1863, outlined step-by-step instructions for organizing a bank and included sample legal forms and bylaws. Jay Cooke involved himself in founding three national banks under the 1863 act: First National Bank of Philadelphia, First National Bank of Washington, and Fourth National Bank of New York, which opened in March 1864 with $5 million in capital raised primarily through the efforts of Cooke.[44]

First National Bank of Philadelphia and First National Bank of Washington included many investors and Cooke associates from the banking house of E. W. Clark, where Jay Cooke had learned the banker's trade in his early years. Cooke also championed the organization of other national banks, such as one proposed in late 1863 at Frankfort, Pennsylvania, a suburb just seven miles from Philadelphia's city center. Writing to his brother Henry in Washington on January 14, 1864, Jay Cooke exhorted his sibling to "please see McCulloch and tell him that the parties are first order and all right in every particular."[45]

With its Charter No. 1 in hand, First National Bank of Philadelphia launched its business at 10:00 a.m. on Saturday, July 11, 1863, in quarters at the southeast corner of Third and Chestnut Streets.[46] The bank opened its doors just as the city's commercial district returned to normalcy after several tense weeks of rumors, military musters, and frantic preparations to defend the city from the Confederate forces that had crossed the Potomac into Pennsylvania on June 15. News of the retreat of Lee's Army of Northern Virginia from Gettysburg, immediately followed by the fall of the Confederate stronghold of Vicksburg, meant that First National Bank of Philadelphia could begin business in a general atmosphere of relief and jubilation.[47]

An item published in the *Philadelphia Press* on July 10 announcing First National Bank of Philadelphia's opening reminded readers, "this bank's Certificate or 'letter patent' dated June 20th, was the first issued by the

Comptroller of the Currency. The bank will be managed and transactions handled," the announcement continued, "in the same way as banks chartered by the state legislature." Bank president O. Wilson Davis and cashier Morton McMichael Jr. set the hours of business between the hours of 10:00 a.m. and 3:00 p.m., with discount days of Tuesday and Friday. The news item further stated that circulating notes of First National Bank of Philadelphia provided for under the National Currency Act were in preparation and would begin circulating in a few months. Until that time, the bank would use legal tender notes of the United States in transaction of business. "The stockholders are a large number of our wealthiest and most respectable citizens," concluded the column.[48] The original board of directors of the bank included O. W. Davis, W. S. Russell, James A. Wright, merchant Stephen A. Caldwell, coal and iron dealer George F. Tyler, Cooke & Company partner William G. Moorhead, banker Edward W. Clark, and Jay Cooke himself.[49]

Two days after opening, First National Bank of Philadelphia president Davis reported to Comptroller McCulloch that "so far our bank has been a success. Our deposits Saturday and today exceeded $10,000."[50] In its first mandated quarterly report published on September 30, 1863, First National Bank of Philadelphia reported loans and discounts of $211,099, capital stock paid in at $148,400, and total resources of $552,420.84.[51]

First National Bank of Philadelphia opened with initial capital of $150,000. Almost immediately after opening, its directors notified the Comptroller's office of their intention to increase the capital of their institution. In November 1863 the bank increased its capital to $500,000 and voted in Clarence H. Clark as president. Clark was a veteran banker who had begun his career under Jay Cooke's tutelage in his father Enoch Clark's firm, E.W. Clark & Company.[52]

Months after opening, the bank still awaited its assigned circulation of $5 and $10 national banknotes. "Is there any hope of our having any circulation by the 1st of January?" wrote an obviously exasperated cashier McMichael to Comptroller McCulloch on December 17.[53] On December 22 the bank's board voted to increase capital yet again to $1 million and submitted a request to the Comptroller's office for an additional $450,000 in circulating notes.[54] The directors of First National Bank of Philadelphia employed their $1 million in capital in the purchase of government bonds. By December 1863, the board had purchased $650,000 of the five-twenty bonds, with all but $100,000 deposited with the Treasury.[55]

Progress on producing the long-awaited uniform national bank currency was slow. Nearly six months after opening, First National Bank of Philadelphia had yet to receive any of its circulation. By late December, First National Bank of Washington had already received some of the newly styled $5 national banknotes, and Philadelphian Clark conveyed his disappointment in the quality of this currency:

> I hardly ever remember having seen a note of which the engraving appeared to be as inferior. The general appearance of the note is blurred,

there being nothing sharp in the engraving, and will be I think early photographed or otherwise counterfeited. ... The paper also appears to be very poor and likely soon to tear and wear out, thereby throwing on the department a serious expense in reprinting the notes, and on bank officers labor in signing them.[56]

When the shipment of his bank's $10 circulating notes arrived just before the New Year, Clark pronounced them "in every respect superior to the $5 issue" and reported that the bills met with general approval after being placed into immediate circulation.[57] As the new banknotes began to pass from hand to hand among Philadelphians, the *Philadelphia Press* on December 30 devoted a full ten column inches to detailing the design and appearance of the new circulating currency.[58]

At first the national banknotes competed with currency still issued by state banks.[59] Lingering uncertainty over acceptance of the new national bank currency worried First National Bank of Philadelphia's president Clark, who considered his bank's role as a newcomer among long-established institutions in the City of Brotherly Love when he confided to Comptroller McCulloch in January 1864, "There is no subject of more moment or interest to the National Banks, than the question, how will our notes be received by the old Banks."[60]

One month later, McCulloch and Clark conversed in Philadelphia about the Comptroller's plans for redemption of national banknotes at discount. Clark felt compelled to offer his advice on McCulloch's proposal to allow banks east of the Allegheny Mountains to redeem at ¼ percent discount and those west of the mountains at greater discount, up to ½ percent:

> I think, on mature reflection, you will be induced to change your mind on this point, first because the scheme of the National Banks, in theory, provided a "National currency to be of equal value everywhere." And any subsequent legislation should tend to perfect the scheme and not place the notes of certain Banks at a discount in other localities than where issued. Notes of all the Banks, from the fact of their being secured by U.S. Bonds, must be good, if anything is good, and their being made, especially, uniform in appearance, as well as in value, was for the purpose of making them equally current in all parts of the country. ... I want a "National Currency" in effect, as well as in name, and by compelling a par redemption in New York, which will not prove onerous to interior Banks, you will have it, but not without.[61]

The National Currency Act of 1863 was, by Comptroller McCulloch's own admission, an imperfect legislative act—ambiguous or silent on many details of reporting and operation. This was a situation that prompted new national bank officers and cashiers to frequently seek further instruction and clarification from the Comptroller's office. "Sir, herewith I send you a copy of the 'Press' containing statement of First National Bank as directed by the 24th section of the National Currency Act," wrote First National Bank of Philadelphia cashier Morton McMichael Jr. to McCulloch on September 2, 1863. "There is some obscurity in the wording of the sec[tion]. Does it contemplate a statement of the actual condition of the Bank at the time indicated, or the average for the month previous."[62] First National Bank of Philadelphia management also felt compelled to write the Comptroller's office inquiring about permission to close their institution on public holidays such as the Fourth of July, Christmas, and New Year's Day, as had been customary among private and state-chartered banks in their place of business.[63]

After one full year in business, First National Bank of Philadelphia issued its fourth quarterly report on July 5, 1864. It listed resources of $7,792,260, including $1 million in United States bonds to secure circulation and deposits and an additional $1,837,584 in government bonds and securities on hand.[64] The first report of national bank examiners remarked favorably on both the operations and the character of management and staff of the bank. Examiner W. Coombs recorded, "I cannot speak too highly of the perfect system under which the business of this bank is conducted, the urbanity of its President and Cashier, both with regard to their customers and in their intercourse with their subordinates, and the perfect accord among employees themselves."[65]

Business and industry in Pennsylvania and other northern states prospered during the wartime years, supplying materiel and arms to Union armies. The postwar years continued to be good for entrepreneurs such as Jay Cooke. Taking advantage of his financial and political influence, Cooke and his firm maintained its dominant position as underwriter of U.S. government bonds for a decade, holding that advantage for every year except 1862 until the spectacular fall of Cooke's empire in 1873. After the war, Cooke invested heavily in railroads and gained control of the Northern Pacific Railroad, which claimed land grants of 47 million acres across the northern plains. Cooke's firm sold Northern Pacific bonds with the same promotional zeal it had perfected in selling wartime government bonds. The Northern Pacific advanced steadily west, but in 1873 the railroad and its promoter, the mighty House of Cooke, went bankrupt, fueling the Panic of 1873.[66]

The value of Charter No. 1

First National Bank of Philadelphia took enormous pride in its status as the first bank chartered under the National Currency Act.[67] That status symbolized longevity and stability, characteristics of particular value to bank customers looking for a secure place to put their deposits. But early charters also came with uncertainties. The National Currency Act restricted national bank charters to 20 years. Thus, in 1882, after nearly two decades in business as one of Philadelphia's leading financial institutions, First National Bank of Philadelphia—like dozens of banks founded under the original 1863 legislation—faced the prospect of mandatory liquidation due to expiration of its original charter.

From the very beginnings of the national banking system, regulators and bankers alike recognized that the 20-year limitation on charters was a serious flaw, and that the most effective correction was legislation replacing the two-decade limit with a permanent charter. As the end of the initial 20-year charter period approached, management at First National Bank of Philadelphia placed increasing value on possession of Charter No. 1 and its singular distinction as holder of the earliest national bank charter. Since 1878 the bank had been imprinting its letterhead with a prominent shield graphic bearing the legend "National Bank No. 1."

As Congress weighed legislation on charter extension, cashier McMichael wrote to Comptroller John Jay Knox on May 18, 1882:

> Are we going to get the bill in time to save our re-organizing, or must we go through that excercize [sic]? We have the proxies of all our 179 shareholders—10,000 shares—but we don't want to lose our No. 1 if we can possibly help it. Perhaps we might retain it anyway; as we do the name. No one else can be No. 1 and it is a pity to lose the distinction. I have written to some of my friends in the Senate to ask them to expedite the bill there but of course so great a body as the Senators moves slowly. Can you give me an idea as to what the chances are of action early enough to serve us—we "run out" on June 14.[68]

The charter extension bill eventually passed but was signed into law too late for First National Bank of Philadelphia to avoid reorganization. On June 10, the bank's directors planned to organize a new First National Bank of Philadelphia, liquidate the old entity, and transferr its entire assets into the 1882 corporation. After closing out accounts at the end of the day on June 13, First National Bank would reopen under a new charter the following morning. In a June 6 letter relaying these liquidation and reorganization plans to the Comptroller's office, bank cashier McMichael added, "We are most anxious to retain our No. 1, and, if possible, I trust that favor may be awarded us."[69] On June 14, bank president George Philler wrote to the Comptroller and reiterated his hope that anticipated revisions to the National Bank Act would allow retention of early-issue charter numbers. "I hope Congress will soon pass the Extension bill and I think it would be well to add an amendment giving the banks that were obliged to re-organize the right to use their old numbers—what do you think of it and if favorably tell me how to proceed."[70]

First National Bank of Philadelphia continued in business without interruption but under newly issued National Bank Charter No. 2731 as of June 14, 1882. On that day, OCC bank examiner William P. Drew visited the bank's Chestnut Street quarters and reported, "The charter of this bank as 'No. 1' having expired today the bank was today reorganized as 'No. 2731' with the same stockholders, same directors, same officers and clerks, same assets, and same liabilities. The record here has been one of much prosperity, and its future is highly promising."[71]

Congress passed legislation on July 12, 1882, allowing a further 20-year extension of charters for banks incorporated under the 1863 act. A second extension of similar length was enacted once more in 1902.[72] National banks that had previously enjoyed low charter numbers could petition the Comptroller of the Currency to reclaim their old charter numbers. The Comptroller allowed petitioners to revert to early charter numbers if the institution could demonstrate a direct line of succession to the original charter holder of 1863.[73]

After the expiration of its 1882 extension, First National Bank of Philadelphia reclaimed Charter No. 1 on June 10, 1902.[74] In the decades that followed, the bank frequently touted its status as holder of the first national bank charter in its statements of condition, industry publications, advertisements, and letterhead. In a 1918 bank directory, First National Bank of Philadelphia exhorted readers to "Send Your Business to the First Bank Chartered under the National Bank Act."[75] The bank's condensed statement of condition for December 30, 1933, called attention to the bank's "Charter No. 1 – The First Bank Chartered Under the National Bank Act – Founded 1863." By this date the bank held assets in excess of $78 million.[76]

A depression-era display ad by First National Bank of Philadelphia in Polk's *Bankers Encyclopedia* of 1930 elaborated further on the bank's origins with a then-and-now comparison in ad copy. "1863: A Patriotic Duty prompted the organization [sic] of this ... the first bank to receive a charter under the National Bank Act." Juxtaposed with this historical statement was a statement of the bank's current business philosophy: "1930: A Civic Duty requires that we serve our community as well as the Nation along lines consistent with sound banking. Although mindful of its historical associations and enviable past record, this bank takes special pride in that it is organized, equipped, and conducted for the highest class service to its customers."[77]

During World War II, bank advertising regularly included the tagline "The First Bank chartered under the National Bank Act – Founded 1863."[78] Through the 1940s and extending into the following decade, First National Bank of Philadelphia also adopted a graphical representation of its unique charter status: a keystone symbol with "Charter Number One" inside, overlapping an oval 1st National logo and the bold statement in capital letters "THE FIRST BANK CHARTERED UNDER THE NATIONAL BANK ACT."[79] First National Bank of Philadelphia even designated "Firstbank" as its cable address.[80]

In June 1955 the directors of First National Bank of Philadelphia announced merger plans with The Pennsylvania Company for Banking and Trusts, an institution more than three times larger and Philadelphia's largest banking institution at the time.[81] This combination, effective September 30, 1955, created The First Pennsylvania Banking and Trust Company, the Commonwealth's first billion dollar financial institution, which operated under First Pennsylvania Company for Banking and Trusts' existing state charter. With the 1955 merger of First National Bank of Philadelphia into The Pennsylvania Company, National Bank Charter No. 1 was temporarily mothballed.

The Pennsylvania Company brought to the merger its own distinguished heritage, which dated back to The Bank of North America, founded in Philadelphia on December 31, 1781, as the nation's oldest commercial bank.[82] In recognition of this Revolutionary war era legacy and the opening of The Bank of North America in Philadelphia on January 7, 1782, The First Pennsylvania Banking and Trust Company's board authorized use of the phrase "banking since 1782" on appropriate advertising, letterhead, and forms. Thus, the merger of First National and The Pennsylvania Company not only combined two distinguished institutions, but the resulting merged entity embraced an even older historical identity, further embedding pride in heritage into the bank's marketing and brand identity. First Pennsylvania marked its 175th anniversary in 1956 by heralding its "contributions to the growth of our community and our country."[83]

In April 1974, First Pennsylvania Banking and Trust Company announced its intention to convert from a state charter back to a national charter. The bank was the main subsidiary of First Pennsylvania Corporation, a one-bank holding company formed in 1968 to enable First Pennsylvania to diversify into other financial services and businesses, In considering conversion, the Pennsylvania institution followed a number of prominent banks, including Chase Manhattan, Wachovia, and Wells Fargo, which had all converted from state to national charters in the previous decade.[84] The proposed switch of charters for First Pennsylvania coincided with a report by regulators in the Pennsylvania Banking Department and the Federal Reserve recommending a slowdown in First Pennsylvania Banking and Trust's growth—its assets had risen from $20 million to $43.3 million between 1968 and 1973.[85] In an article by the *Wall Street Journal* that speculated on management's motivations for readoption of a national charter, chairman John Bunting went on record stating that the decision in part came from the desire to expand beyond the state's existing geographic limitations on establishment of new branches and brushed aside speculation by the media over preference for federal versus state regulation.[86] In fact, First Pennsylvania, then the nineteenth largest banking institution in the nation, was already on the Comptroller's "watch list" for 1974. Comptroller of the Currency James E. Smith granted the national charter in June 1974, when the Philadelphia institution reclaimed its coveted Charter No. 1 designation and changed its name to First Pennsylvania Bank, NA.[87]

By 1980 the bank tallied $8 billion in total assets. But First Pennsylvania also had a large book of non-performing loans and a troubled securities portfolio, resulting in an open bank assistance transaction led by the Federal Deposit Insurance Corporation.[88] CoreStates Financial Corp. purchased First Pennsylvania Corporation and its Charter No. 1 designation in 1990, increasing the size of the CoreStates franchise by one-third and marrying the historic First Pennsylvania legacy to several other historic mid-Atlantic region financial institutions already a part of CoreStates.[89]

The distinction of holding Charter No. 1 passed to First Union Corporation in 1998 after that North Carolina-based institution acquired CoreStates. First

Union Corporation in turn merged with Wachovia Corporation in 2001, and the combined company, Wachovia Corporation, held Charter No. 1 as Wachovia Bank NA. Wells Fargo & Company acquired Wachovia Corporation in 2008 and in March 2010 consolidated the charters of Wachovia Bank NA, Wachovia Bank of Delaware NA, and Wells Fargo Bank NA under Charter No. 1.[90] Wells Fargo Bank NA currently operates under this honored charter number.

Banking has changed dramatically since Jay Cooke organized a group of Philadelphia's leading citizens to secure Charter No. 1 for First National Bank of Philadelphia on June 20, 1863. The reach of financial institutions and customer relationships today extends far beyond national borders to encompass global products, services, payment systems, and technologies. But even in a rapidly changing environment, there is still value in legacy, in the safety and security that longevity conveys and the confidence that an unbroken link to the past instills. Charter No. 1 is such a legacy link, as is our national banking system envisioned by Salmon P. Chase, championed by Jay Cooke and others, and evolved under the auspices of the Office of the Comptroller of the Currency for 150 years.

Notes

1 Herman E. Krooss, ed., *Documentary History of Banking and Currency in the United States*, vol. 2 (Chelsea House Publishers; distributed by Mainline Books, Bryn Mawr, PA, 1977), 1341–2.
2 Andrew McFarland Davis, *The Origin of the National Banking System*, National Monetary Commission, S. Doc. No. 61–582, at 22–23, 32 (1910).
3 Report of the Secretary of the Treasury on the State of the Finances, for the Year Ending June 30, 1861. (Washington, Government Printing Office, December 9, 1861), 18.
4 Richard Sylla, "Federal Policy, Banking Market Structure, and Capital Mobilization in the United States, 1863–1913," *Journal of Economic History* 29, no. 4 (December 1969): 659.
5 George A. Selgin and Lawrence H. White, "Monetary Reform and the Redemption of National Bank Notes, 1863–1913," *Business History Review* 68, no. 2 (Summer 1994): 207.
6 Ellis Paxon Oberholtzer, *Jay Cooke, Financier of the Civil War*, vol. 1 (Philadelphia: George W. Jacobs & Co., 1907), 329–35.
7 Bray Hammond, *Banks and Politics in America from the Revolution to the Civil War* (Princeton: Princeton University Press, 1957), 720–21.
8 Davis, *Origin of the National Banking System*, 33.
9 Milton E. Ailes, "National Banking System and Federal Bond Issues," *ANNALS* (American Academy of Political and Social Science) 36 (November 1910): 116.
10 Murray N. Rothbard, *A History of Money and Banking in the United States: The Colonial Era to World War II* (Auburn: Ludwig von Mises Institute, 2005), 123, footnote 103.
11 "$415 million" Rothbard, *History of Money and Banking*, 124, and Oberholtzer, *Jay Cooke*, 149.
12 Davis, *Origin of the National Banking System*, 42.
13 Rothbard, *History of Money and Banking*, 123.
14 Oberholtzer, *Jay Cooke*, 150–51, 158–60, 165.

15 Rothbard, *History of Money and Banking*, 132–3; Oberholtzer, *Jay Cooke*, 94.
16 Oberholtzer, *Jay Cooke*, 214.
17 Henrietta M. Larson, *Jay Cooke, Private Banker* (Cambridge, MA: Harvard University Press, 1936), 120.
18 Larson, *Jay Cooke*, 129–30.
19 Ibid., 329.
20 Hammond, *Banks and Politics*, 725.
21 Oberholtzer, *Jay Cooke*, 332–3.
22 Hammond, *Banks and Politics*, 725.
23 Larson, *Jay Cooke*, 138.
24 Oberholtzer, *Jay Cooke*, 335, 337.
25 Larson, *Jay Cooke*, 139.
26 Davis, *Origin of the National Banking System*, 115–16.
27 Ibid., 158–61.
28 Ibid., 163–4.
29 Owen W. Davis to Thomas W. Olcott, March 9, 1863, Office of the Comptroller of the Currency, "Division of Reports, Correspondence 1863–1901, Charters 1–7," file 1, box 1, Record Group (hereafter RG) 101, National Archives and Records Administration, College Park, Maryland (hereafter NARA-CP).
30 Owen W. Davis to George Harrington, April 17, 1863, file 1, box 1, RG 101, NARA-CP.
31 J. Thomas Scharf and Thompson Westcott, *History of Philadelphia*, vol. III (Philadelphia: L.H.Everts & Co., 1884), 1972.
32 Morton McMichael Jr. to Hugh McCullough [sic], June 2, 1863, file 1, box 1, RG 101, NARA-CP.
33 McMichael to McCulloch, June 17, 1863, file 1, box 1, RG 101, NARA-CP.
34 Davis to McCulloch, July 13, 1863, file 1, box 1, RG 101, NARA-CP.
35 H. M. Welch to Comptroller, April 15, 1863, file 2, box 1, RG 101, NARA-CP.
36 Bray Hammond, *Sovereignty and an Empty Purse: Banks and Politics in the Civil War* (Princeton: Princeton University Press, 1970), 345.
37 The Bank of North America in Philadelphia, for example, elected not to abandon the name it had held since its establishment as the nation's first commercial bank in 1781. When the Bank of North America did convert to a national charter in 1864, it was not then required to alter its historic name.
38 Rollin G. Osterweis, *Charter Number Two: The Centennial History of the First New Haven National Bank* (New Haven: First New Haven National Bank, 1963), 14.
39 *Philadelphia Press*, May 15, 1863.
40 Welch to McCulloch, June 18, 1863, file 2, box 1, RG 101, NARA-CP.
41 Osterweis, *Charter Number Two*, 14–15. The New Haven bank group deferred the honor of the first charter to Jay Cooke, who had so influenced and supported the establishment of the national banking system, according to the Connecticut bank's official centennial history
42 Charter No. 1, First National Bank of Philadelphia, Wells Fargo Corporate Archives, San Francisco, California.
43 "The First Ten National Banks," *The Bankers Magazine* 92 (January, 1916), 90.
44 Larson, *Jay Cooke*, 140–41.
45 Jay Cooke to Henry Cooke, January 14, 1864, file 1, box 1, RG 101, NARA-CP.
46 First National Bank of Davenport, Iowa, claimed to be the first national bank to open its doors, on June 29, 1863.
47 William L. Calderhead, "Philadelphia in Crisis: June–July, 1863," *Pennsylvania History*, 28, no. 2 (April 1961): 155.
48 *Philadelphia Press*, July 10, 1863.

49 "Charter Number One," undated publication of The First National Bank of Philadelphia, in the collection of the Hagley Museum and Library, Wilmington, Delaware.
50 Davis to McCulloch, July 13, 1863, file 2, box 1, RG 101, NARA-CP.
51 *Philadelphia Press*, October 3, 1863.
52 *Philadelphia Inquirer*, November 18, 1863.
53 McMichael to McCulloch, December 17, 1863, file 1, box 1, RG 101, NARA-CP.
54 Clarence H. Clark to McCulloch, December 22, 1863, file 1, box 1, RG 101, NARA-CP.
55 Larson, *Jay Cooke*, 140.
56 Clark to McCulloch, December 26, 1863, file 1, box 1, RG 101, NARA-CP.
57 Clark to McCulloch, December 30, 1863, file 1, box 1, RG 101, NARA-CP.
58 *Philadelphia Press*, December 30, 1863.
59 A 10 percent federal tax levied on state banknotes in 1866 soon reduced their issue.
60 Clark to McCulloch, January 7, 1864, file 1, box 1, RG 101, NARA-CP.
61 Clark to McCulloch, February 17, 1864, file 1, box 1, RG 101, NARA-CP.
62 McMichael to McCullough [sic], September 2, 1863, file 1, box 1, RG 101, NARA-CP.
63 Clark to McCulloch, June 29, 1864, file 1, box 1, RG 101, NARA-CP.
64 The 4th Quarterly Report of First National Bank of Philadelphia, file 1, box 1, RG 101, NARA-CP.
65 Report of Bank Examiner, September 5–6, 1864, Reports of National Bank Examiners, vol. 1, RG 101.
66 Rothbard, *History of Money and Banking*, 145, 156.
67 The OCC website names First National Bank of McConnelsville [Ohio] as the oldest national bank still operating under the same name and same OCC charter, Charter No. 46. http://www.occ.gov/about/what-we-do/history (accessed May 1, 2013).
68 McMichael to John Jay Knox, May 18, 1882, file 1, box 1, RG 101, NARA-CP.
69 McMichael to Knox, June 6, 1882, file 1, box 1, RG 101, NARA-CP.
70 George Philler to Knox, June 14, 1882, file 1, box 1, RG 101, NARA-CP.
71 Report of Bank Examiner, June 14, 1882. Reports of National Bank Examiners, vol. 1, RG 101.
72 Ailes, "National Banking System," 596.
73 "Getting Low Charter Numbers,"*United States Investor* 22 (August 12, 1911): 1.
74 *Banker's Magazine* 92 (1916): 90.
75 *Rand McNally Bankers Directory*, 1918, 1081.
76 First National Bank of Philadelphia Condensed Statement of Condition, December 30, 1933. Display ad published in the *New York Times*, January 2, 1934.
77 *Polk's Bankers Encyclopedia*, September 1930, 2076.
78 Advertisement, "Victory Begins at Home," *New York Times*, January 2, 1942.
79 Rand McNally, *The Banker's Blue Book*, 1950, 1270.
80 Ibid.
81 "Merger to Form Billionaire Bank," *New York Times*, June 24, 1955, 29.
82 Terrance A. Larsen, "CoreStates Financial Corp: Drawing Strength from History, Community and Diversity," address given at Newcomen Society of the United States Pennsylvania Meeting, November 21, 1992.
83 Annual Report of The First Pennsylvania Banking and Trust Company for the Fiscal Year Ended December 31, 1955, 6, in the collection of the Hagley Museum and Library, Wilmington, Delaware.
84 "Statement by California Superintendent of Banks James M. Hall Regarding the Proposed Conversion of Wells Fargo Bank to a National Charter," California State

Banking Department News Release, June 14, 1968, Wells Fargo Corporate Archives.
85 "Changing Charters: Did the Bank Switch Rather than Fight the Fed Examiners?" *Wall Street Journal*, April 26, 1976.
86 Ibid.
87 First Pennsylvania Corporation, Annual Report, 1981, Wells Fargo Corporate Archives.
88 "Managing the Crisis: The FDIC and RTC Experience", available at www.fdic.gov/bank/historical/managing/chron/1980/index.html (accessed September 6, 2014)
89 CoreStates Anniversary Dates, memo dated April 12, 1995, CoreStates collection, Wells Fargo Corporate Archives.
90 http://blogs.wellsfargo.com/guidedbyhistory/2010/05/end-of-an-era-and-continuation (accessed September 6, 2014).

5 E.T. Wilson and the banks
A case study in government regulation and service

Paula Petrik

Introduction

Whether the new national banking system succeeded or failed depended heavily on the supervision of individual national banks. That job was largely the responsibility of the Comptroller's examiners, who moved from one institution to the next, making sure the bank's business practices conformed to the growing body of law and regulation governing their behavior.

The job of the national bank examiner in the nineteenth century was probably most difficult in the states and territories of the American West. Traveling to remote locations, examiners were at the mercy of railroad connections that were slow and erratic. Such delays could leave the regulators stranded for days and allow bankers to anticipate (and prepare for) their arrival. In the classic O. Henry short story, "Friends in San Rosario," the "friends" were competing Texas bankers who by pre-agreement moved assets between them, enabling them to present a misleadingly healthy face to the story's examiner.

A related problem was that as one traveled from more- to less-settled areas, the law had less presence and less force. Where they were in conflict, community sentiment sometimes trumped written law. Communities with fewer banks naturally relied on them more heavily, and there was likely to be more resistance to supervisory action requiring a bank to curtail lending or, worse, to suspend its operations. Examiners had to be mindful of those circumstances.

In this chapter, Paula Petrik looks at just such a community: Helena, Montana, in the 1890s. The story of OCC bank examiner E. T. Wilson reveals resourcefulness required to deal with boomtown banks that sometimes skirted legal requirements. Petrik's story, drawing on a wide variety of local and federal documents, highlights the human dimension in overseeing the national banking system.

Paula Petrik, Professor of History and Art History at George Mason University, received a Ph.D. from the State University of New York-Binghamton and a Master of Fine Arts from the University of Montana.

Both historians and economists have discussed regulation, advancing arguments pro and con, theoretical and empirical, but they have paid little attention to rank and file regulators.[1] Bank examiners are a case in point. They are among those historical actors whose part in economic history has gone generally unremarked. If pressed, the man or woman on the nineteenth- or twentieth-century street would probably be at a loss to explain exactly what bank examiners did (or do) except to venture the obvious: a bank examiner examines banks. And to a great extent, "examines banks" would describe a bank examiner's work. Charged with determining a bank's soundness and fiscal health, bank examiners were (and are) the Comptroller of Currency's foot soldiers in the agency's program to ensure that banks lived up to their charters and complied with administrative law regarding loans, reserves, and management.[2] When a bank failed, an examiner often became a receiver, the person in charge of sorting out the bank's typically tangled affairs and recovering as much for the creditors, including the depositors, as possible.[3]

Eugene T. Wilson, the subject of this paper, was both a bank examiner and a receiver during his 30-year career with the Comptroller of Currency. Although he dealt with many banks and worked in several states, his connection with both the First National Bank and Merchants National Bank of Helena, Montana, after the Panic of 1893 provides a unique insight into the work and attitudes of the Comptroller of Currency's rank and file regulators. Wilson's story also complicates the narrative of regulation by showing how the Comptroller's regulators, whether as examiners or receivers, worked effectively within the limitation of their positions for the public good.

Born in Wisconsin in 1852, E. T. Wilson lived in a variety of western towns before beginning his professional life in Utah, where he had been employed by several mining companies. Moving to Washington Territory in the late 1870s, he became a merchant and newspaper publisher. Like many newspaper editor-owners, Wilson soon found his way into politics. In 1889, he was elected to the Washington Senate on the Republican ticket and became president *pro tem* during his second term. His growing reputation as an effective administrator and fiscal conservative brought him to the attention of the Republican Party's national leadership, who named him national bank examiner for the vast territory encompassing Idaho, Washington, and Montana in 1892. Shortly before the Panic of 1893, Wilson began the relationship with the First National and Merchants National Banks of Helena, Montana, that would preoccupy him for almost a decade.[4]

First National Bank, 1866–96

Almost from the day it was founded in 1866, First National had difficulties with its regulators. Examiners cited it for a variety of poor banking practices that included illegal overdrafts, loans to insiders, and poor record keeping. By 1890, First National was in very deep trouble. OCC examiner William Heald noted its many management deficiencies and its disregard for sound banking practices and banking law, citing excessive loans, loans to officers and directors, unsecured paper, and so forth. One good run on the bank, Heald concluded, would force its closure. Indeed, the run was not long in coming, and First National Bank suspended operations on July 27, 1893.[5]

With the support of several large depositors and the Office of the Comptroller of Currency, First National reopened in mid-January 1894. But it soon became clear that the bank had not learned from its near-death experience. E. T. Wilson, now the bank's OCC examiner, suggested to the agency that the management be replaced and, in short order, with the exception of ex-Territorial Governor Samuel T. Hauser, who retained the presidency in name only, all of the bank's staff was removed. Erastus D. Edgerton became vice president and managing director. By then, however, the region was entering the second phase of a classic double-dip depression, further eroding the bank's capital. On September 4, 1896, First National Bank closed permanently.[6]

Comptroller of Currency James H. Eckels appointed Edgerton as the bank's receiver. As the former managing vice president, Edgerton was a "friendly receiver." Drawing a receiver from among the bank's officers was common practice in nineteenth-century banking. A "friendly receiver" had advantages over an outsider. He knew the bank's records, its depositors, and its borrowers. For a variety of reasons, however, community sentiment shortly turned against Edgerton. Edgerton was among those who arrived in anticipation of the railroad in 1882, and Helena's pioneer residents viewed the newcomers as *arrivistes* who came to the city to cash in. More damaging were Hauser's covert efforts to undermine Edgerton's receivership via the bank's ownership of the *Helena Independent*. The *Independent* omitted recounting any of Edgerton's successes or First National's progress but reported in detail any criticism directed at Edgerton or the bank. Predictably, townspeople blamed Edgerton, and a grand jury quickly indicted him on multiple violations of banking law in December 1896, prompting his resignation shortly afterward.[7]

Stung by criticism of the OCC appearing in the Montana press, Comptroller Eckels resolved to make his own inquiry into the bank's second failure by sending Missouri examiner H. A. Forman to conduct a thorough, private evaluation of First National's books. Forman's report was damning. Evidence of long-term, gross mismanagement of the bank and its routine violations of banking law going back decades shocked him. He pointed the finger at bank managers, including former president Hauser, who he believed had "wrecked" the bank long before Edgerton's association with the firm.[8]

Forman's mere presence irritated Wilson, who felt that he was being second-guessed by Washington. "[I]t would seem to me that the Comptroller should have some confidence in you [A D. Lynch], Flynn, and myself," he wrote to Lynch, "and the sending of another to check up [on] our work is very depressing to say the least."[9] As First National Bank's examiner, Wilson also viewed the press criticism as an attack on his own integrity. Although he wished to answer his detractors, the Comptroller had directed Wilson to refrain from defending himself. Wilson aired his frustration to Lynch. Even if the Comptroller barred an individual defense, Wilson contended, an examiner should at least be able to defend the agency. "I should think the honor and credit of the bureau was at stake," he wrote.[10] Wilson need not have worried about Eckels's opinion; the Comptroller appointed Wilson receiver for First National Bank after J. Sam Brown, Edgerton's successor as receiver, resigned in September 1897.[11]

Merchants National Bank, 1882–97

Anticipating that the coming of the railroad would boost Helena's prospects, the brothers Hershfield—L. H. and Aaron—applied for and received a national bank charter in 1882. L. H. became the president of the new Merchants National Bank and Aaron the cashier. The two had previously run a private bank under the name Hershfield and Brother, which had been founded in 1868. Merchants National's performance initially pleased examiners. By 1887, however, the bank began to experience the same problems that characterized First National: overdrafts, low reserves, single-name notes, excessive loans, and large loans to the bank's managers. Despite its poor condition, Merchants National Bank managed to keep its doors open when First National and other banks suspended operations in July 1893. But the bank's circumstances continued to deteriorate. Paper remained long overdue, and excessive loans had ballooned in the absence of both principle and interest payments.[12] To conceal these problems, as later legal complaints alleged, the bank's management had begun cooking the bank's books. The bank's capital, according to the examiner, was more than wiped out. It was only a question of time, the examiner continued, until the bank would have to close.[13] Finally, on February 13, 1897, Merchants National Bank suspended operations, closing permanently in June. Among Helena residents and Montana journalists, rumors circulated that L. H. Hershfield's enemies, namely Hauser, had conspired to wreck Merchants National.[14] Meantime, Wilson had become its examiner-in-charge. He hoped that Hershfield would be able to raise enough capital to reopen the bank, but, when it became clear that was impossible, Wilson presided over its liquidation as its receiver.[15]

E. T. Wilson and the banks

As examiner and receiver of both banks in a rapidly declining local economy, Wilson knew that he faced a formidable task. At First National, he had to deal with the stubborn Samuel T. Hauser, its president; at Merchants National, his biggest problem was what he believed were violations of federal banking law by L. H. Hershfield and Thomas P. Bowman, who had replaced Aaron Hershfield as cashier in 1894.[16]

Wilson dealt circumspectly with Hauser in putting the bank's affairs in order. Wilson found that the previous receivers of First National had been careless and slothful caretakers of the banks' assets. First National properties stood empty, unkempt, and tax delinquent; the bank, moreover, lacked clear title to some of its assets. Wilson moved quickly on all fronts. "I am foreclosing right and left," he wrote in January 1898, shortly after he became receiver, "believing it is better for the bank to secure title in order that the redemption periods may expire as soon as possible. This, of course, only refers to property upon which we are compelled to pay the taxes and other expenses while the owners are receiving the benefits."[17] He also made progress in renting and repairing the bank's properties, although competition compelled him to make concessions on rental rates. He aggressively instituted suits for recovery, even to the point of suing Erastus D. Edgerton, a former First National officer and receiver.[18] He adopted the same approach with Merchants National, successfully reaching a compromise with the court on the damages levied against it in a case involving the theft of $10,000 from a safety deposit box.[19]

Despite his best efforts, Wilson made little progress in turning Merchants National's assets into cash. Comptroller Eckels approved Wilson's plan for raising additional capital and authorized a 100 percent assessment against stockholders, amounting to $100 per share of stock. For many, the assessment meant a minimum payment of $10,000. Collecting this obligation proved challenging. William C. Lobenstine of New York, a Merchants National stockholder, was representative of a certain type of conservative investor who did not try to evade responsibility—a trait Wilson admired and respected. When the Hershfield bank failed, Lobenstine was dismayed and questioned the receiver on a number of points but, once satisfied, Lobenstine set up a reasonable payment plan and made good on his commitment. But for every Lobenstine, it seemed, there were others who refused to honor their financial obligations or who resorted to legal subterfuge to avoid paying an assessment or making good a loan. In writing about the foreclosure of the Helena Power and Light Company in which his trust had an interest, Wilson noted with disgust the new style of bankers who used legal loopholes to dodge their responsibilities. "I am of the opinion," wrote Wilson of a defaulter who exploited the law to secure a slight advantage, "that he is running what we Westerners call a 'dead bluff,' but am not in the mood to be called. I feel more like seeing his bet and raising him out of his boots."[20] Likewise, Wilson had little respect, too, for those like R. H. Harlow, who had notes outstanding at all the Helena banks but on which he had paid neither interest nor principal. Harlow, one of the chief backers of the Montana Railroad, an enterprise that Wilson characterized as "a visionary project at best," hid his assets in his wife's name. Wilson was determined to "flush Harlow out" with legal proceedings to discover what property actually belonged to Harlow rather than to his wife.[21] Of another Helena high-flyer, C. K. Cole, who threatened to enter bankruptcy, Wilson wrote to a fellow banker, "If you know of any plan by which the sporty gentleman can be made to pungle, you will have my hearty cooperation. He is what I call a sorry specimen of the *genus beat.*"[22]

Wilson, however, reserved his greatest scorn for stockholders who attempted to evade their financial responsibilities through patently ridiculous excuses. Chief among them was L. H. Hershfield, who claimed that his stock holdings were really owned by his brother and, therefore, not liable for the assessment.[23] Another evasive stockholder, William Davis, maintained he was unaware that he owned the stock, although he had voted his shares and collected his dividends. Similarly, Wilson had little time for naive depositors, those who did not understand the rudiments of banking. "You have very few of the instincts of a gentleman," he wrote to Joseph Bergen, "and it would seem have not sufficient good sense to transact ordinary business and should apply for a guardian at once."[24] And he responded to an accusatory letter from the Odd Fellows Lodge in a neighboring town with stern advice: "If you will exercise a little common sense in this matter and also remember that no benefit could possibly accrue to me by attempting to beat your lodge out of its rights, it will be to your advantage."[25]

Wilson's assessment collection program at Merchant's National also led him to rethink the effectiveness of double liability—the provision that made bank investors liable for twice the value of their investments. For Wilson, double liability was impractical on two counts:

- The largest stockholders were the bank's officers and local stockholders, so there was little chance of collecting anything from them.[26] L. H. Hershfield's assessment, for example, amounted to $165,000, or 55 percent, of the total assessment figure; Hershfield, however, possessed no assets (or had placed them out of reach), so collecting his assessment was impossible. The onus of the assessment, as a result, fell on stockholders outside the bank's trading area, those like Lobenstine. A master of due diligence, Lobenstine noted that the last published report to the Comptroller "gave [the bank] a surplus of $70,000 and profits of $72,319.61."[27] With figures like these, he asked, how could Merchants National fail?
- The process of collecting the assessments prolonged the receivership and increased its costs. Faraway stockholders had to be located, contacted, and given reasonable time to meet their obligations. While double liability appeared to be a useful and prudential safeguard, it proved increasingly impractical and discriminatory as banking expanded its geographic reach and attracted investors from afar.[28]

Going to court

Despite naive, reluctant, and unsophisticated stockholders, borrowers, and depositors, by mid-1898, the receiverships had acquired all the easy assets, and Wilson turned to the more difficult problem of crooked bank officers. In April 1898, the grand jury indicted L. H. Hershfield, former president of Merchants National Bank; Thomas P. Bowman, its cashier; Aaron Hershfield, former president of State National Bank of Miles City, former cashier, and a major stockholder in Merchants National; and Leo G. Harmon of the Miles City concern. By December Wilson believed that he had acquired sufficient evidence to bring to the U.S. Attorney. Thomas Bowman had left his personal letterpress book behind and Wilson had found it.[29]

In a long letter to the Comptroller of Currency, Wilson outlined the case against the Merchants officers. As early as March 1896, according to Wilson,

Bowman had padded the cash accounts in order to deceive bank examiners about the condition of the cash reserves held by the bank. Such an action violated banking law, which mandated minimum levels of cash reserves for banks. Wilson, on a surprise visit, caught Bowman shuffling cash and negotiable paper around the accounts and promptly reported the incident to Hershfield. Hershfield, in turn, excused Bowman's action by claiming that Bowman "felt it to be his duty under existing conditions to make such a showing as would be encouraging to our city and allay any lack of confidence in the remaining banks." Hershfield went on to appeal to Wilson as a fellow banker "to so frame a report to the Honorable Comptroller as will relieve me from the humiliation of an extended explanation." In a thinly veiled offer of a bribe, Hershfield added that he would make it worth Wilson's while.[30] Wilson rebuffed Hershfield's explanation, believing that Hershfield was perfectly aware of the bank's cash position. Hershfield's defense of Bowman's action, Wilson continued in his letter to the Comptroller, was simply an acknowledgement that Merchants' management had been caught in a fiddle. When the receiver confronted Bowman, Bowman excused himself by claiming that his actions were "nothing more than other banks do" and that he was following general custom. Bowman, snorted Wilson, possessed "no knowledge of the acts of other banks other than from his imagination."[31]

Believing that an example should be made of Merchants' management in the interests of the banking fraternity, the general public, and the OCC, Wilson went forward with his efforts to prosecute the Hershfields.[32] His campaign, however, encountered trouble from the outset. In one instance, the trust's attorney most familiar with the case was prevented from presenting the trust's evidence by a ruling based on a technicality. Once the matter of the attorney had been resolved, additional rulings, in Wilson's view, suppressed evidence connecting the Hershfields directly with misuse of funds. Nonetheless, the U.S. Attorney managed to present one piece of damning evidence—a letter demonstrating the boldness of the bank's malfeasance. Bowman had reported to L. H. Hershfield in 1896:

> We were agreeably (?) surprised by the appearance of Mr. Flynn, bank examiner. I am getting along with him about as we usually do with these fellows, and he is not inclined to be suspicious. The only things that gave me any uneasiness were those notes in the cash box, but while Mr. Flynn was engaged with the teller I substituted a palmer [sic] note and attached Miles City, Philipsburg and Yellowstone bonds. I have not been separated from him 15 minutes since his arrival. He agreed with me not to report the notes to comptroller if I would not include them as cash in my report to the comptroller.[33]

Compounding the trust's difficulties was a judge who, in Wilson's opinion, did not understand banking, particularly the question of when cash was or was not really cash. And Bowman, whose case had been dismissed with the provision he would testify for the trust, "turned traitor and 'perjured himself like a gentleman.'"[34]

On August 24, 1900, Judge Hiram Knowles issued a directed verdict to the Hershfield jury for the defense. The prosecution, according to Knowles, had failed to provide sufficient evidence to substantiate the charges that Hershfield had *knowingly made or personally authorized* the false entries in the bank records or made false reports to the Comptroller. In his final remarks, however, Knowles suggested that the court of public opinion would render a different verdict. "[W]hile I shall instruct the jury to find Mr. Hershfield not guilty," he announced, "I doubt whether the public will consider that he was not guilty of making false entries in the books of the bank."[35] When the Hershfields and company went free, Wilson vented his frustration:

> I do not belong to the Department of Justice but am in the employ of the Bureau of Currency. My duty is to furnish the evidence, and I have it sufficiently strong to convict these people if they are properly prosecuted; but if the Attorney General of the United States sees fit to place obstacles in our way by preventing us from having the necessary assistance it does not seem as if there is much use in attempting to get justice in the courts.[36]

Wilson was discouraged: "For unsound reasoning and illogical conclusions, I think the charge of the court is not only entitled to the cake but [also] the entire bakery."[37] Refusing to dwell on his courtroom defeat, Wilson quickly turned his attention to another matter: the Helena Power & Light Company.

Defending the receiverships

Of all the assets Wilson managed in his two-bank portfolio, the Helena Power & Light Company was the only profitable enterprise. By 1901, largely as a result of Wilson's supervision in the previous year, the company was in the black. As a money-making operation with the promise of increased future profits, the company attracted the interest of T. A. Marlow, president of the National Bank of Montana, the third national bank in Helena and the largest of the three surviving banks. Marlow saw an opportunity to gain control of the company for pennies on the dollar. Via a series of legal maneuvers, Marlow and his associates arranged for a friendly receivership that would allow the Marlow group to "buy in" the property by purchasing the bondholders' interest at 37½ percent of face value. The Marlow receivership would then "sell out" the property to none other than the Marlow group.[38]

As a minority bondholder, Wilson had few options, but he resolved to secure a fair price for the trust's bonds:

- He began publishing all the Marlow's trust's transactions in the local newspaper, serving notice on the Marlow group that he planned to publicize its every move.[39]
- He bought time by winning an intervention in court against Marlow's receivership.[40]

- He used the intervention period to interest other bidders, among them the Butte Electric Company and the Chicago Underground Trolley Traction Company.[41]

Wilson's strategy was successful. C. H. Bosworth, an eastern businessman, agreed to form a syndicate and finance an offer of 60 percent of the bond's face value, but his organization wanted an option to buy the Marlow group's bonds.[42]

Although Wilson did not entirely understand Bosworth's desire for an option, he promptly went to Marlow and put the offer on the table, informing Marlow that other bidders were in play and that an outright offer was in the wings.[43] The group had two choices: counter the option offer with a firm tender equal to or greater than 60 percent of face value or let the deal go. Wilson also knew that the Marlow group did not have sufficient capital to "buy in" the property at more than 60 percent of face value. Wilson had Marlow cornered. Wilson remarked: "[Marlow] is very angry at me for making an effort to protect our interests and has asserted that he intended to teach me a lesson. Probably he will, but not until I have played my last card."[44]

On April 18, 1902, Wilson played his last card. He notified Marlow and his associates that he intended to bring a suit against them for fiduciary dereliction if the Marlow group attempted to dispose of the bonds under the option offer price. Playing on Marlow's fear of personal liability and public exposure, Wilson signaled his determination to make the individual members of the Marlow group responsible for any difference between the bonds' eventual sale price and Wilson's option price. Wilson's threats spurred Marlow to action; he offered Wilson, in his capacity as receiver, 60 percent of the face value for the minority bonds but gave Wilson a very short deadline. Although Wilson waited until the last possible minute for the Comptroller to make a counter offer, none was forthcoming. Wilson had no choice but to accept Marlow's proposal.[45]

Despite his weak position, Wilson had bested Marlow and had protected the trust's interests, realizing more than he had initially anticipated. When Wilson summed up his experience with the Helena Power & Light Company, he noted with disgust the new style of banker who used lawyers and legal ambiguities to make profitable deals. Wilson had much more respect for the "highway man who [took] his life in his hands when he [held] up a railroad train" than he had for the "financial freebooters" connected with T. A. Marlow and the National Bank of Montana. "The highwayman runs the risk of personal injury," wrote Wilson, "while these robbers protect themselves by the technicalities of the law."[46]

Managing the receiverships

During the same period that Wilson mounted his courtroom campaign against the Hershfields and dealt with the Marlow group, he dealt with both trusts' "slow assets," expensive properties requiring well-heeled buyers. One large group of slow assets consisted of properties such as the Hope, Ontario, and

Bear Gulch Mines. Enterprises such as mines had high, fixed-capital costs and needed to be operating to realize a profit. Not only did idle mines drain cash from the trusts, but they also needed constant attention to maintain them in salable condition. Wilson hired pump men to prevent flooding at the mines' lower levels and employed watchmen to forestall vandalism and theft. The trusts' mines were, moreover, precious metal operations whose easily extracted deposits had been exhausted before the 1893 panic. To achieve profitability, the properties required further development, necessitating additional capital investment. In consequence, Wilson had a variety of expensive white elephants on his hands.[47]

If maintaining the mines vexed Wilson, selling them drove him to distraction. The investors who held the properties jointly with the bank or who acquired an option were not up to the task. In reference to the Bear Gulch properties, Wilson cautioned the owners that they could not scramble around the countryside simultaneously offering options to a dozen people and hawking the real estate to a dozen others.[48] In the case of the Hope Mine, prospective buyers could not meet their contractual obligations and resorted to extra-legal means to come up with the cash. At one point, Hope Mine stock sold in New York without the brokers' knowing that the sellers did not have clear title to the property. The sellers, to make matters worse, became entangled in the infamous Boston & Montana litigation, the centerpiece of the War of the Copper Kings, which was then swamping the courts. As a result, parties attacked the Hope concern as a "bunco" scheme, and Wilson despaired of finding a suitable buyer should the group fail to consummate its deal.[49]

Another class of slow assets was the large parcels of real estate in several prospective town sites and additions to existing towns. The real estate boom in the late 1880s had persuaded many investors to buy anything that came to hand, and the would-be real estate moguls had purchased marginal land in anticipation of development that did not occur. Cities that expected to become duplicates of Denver platted extensive additions. County officials in several rival Montana towns subsequently approved excessive assessment on these new additions in order to retain or raise their city's classification and tax base. For county administrators, such a situation spelled higher salaries and increased patronage appointments; for the trusts, it meant that counties assessed trust properties at considerably more than their actual value, creating a tax burden for the trusts and a substantial loss at their liquidation. Wilson, for example, had "brought in" or gained clear title to 83 lots in the Black Eagle Falls Addition to Great Falls for $19,000, but he had been able to sell them for only $1,500.[50]

Still another class of assets occupied Wilson's attention. These odd lots included a newspaper whose liabilities exceeded its net worth; an opera house minus its piano; various cemetery lots; a ranch without sufficient water; partial ownership of a coal company; and title to the Helena Street Railway Company. None of these were small enterprises, and all required buyers with deep pockets. By July 1900, Wilson still held his portfolio of white elephants and still had the Hauser settlement to make.[51]

Two years after First National's failure and Hauser's written agreement to make good his financial responsibilities, nothing had happened. Hauser had managed to buy more time and stall Wilson, who could not afford to push Hauser into bankruptcy and stand in line with the rest of Hauser's creditors. Such rashness would have only served to dilute the trust's recovery. Wilson worked on his own to determine the extent of Hauser's liability but with little luck. Hauser's banking affairs were chaotic. No one, except perhaps Hauser himself, knew which notes he had signed as an accommodation for the bank or in his own right. Aware of Hauser's influence both locally and in Washington, Wilson refrained from public criticism and expressed his displeasure in private letters. Yet, just when Wilson had nearly given up hope of effecting a Hauser settlement, it occurred. Wilson's negotiations with the old capitalist were not pleasant. When Hauser dealt in six figures, he was magnanimous; when he dealt with the details, he claimed every personal advantage. In March 1901, nearly five years after First National closed, Wilson finished with Hauser. In the end, Hauser avoided paying the full amount of his liability. Although the final agreement was less than Wilson had hoped for, the Helena business community pronounced the settlement a good one.[52]

There were still legal and financial matters at Merchants National Bank to settle, but these, too, were finally resolved by time and circumstance. Aaron Hershfield's federal trials came to naught. His first trial ended in a hung jury. In the second trial, the government's star witness, Leo C. Harmon, was nowhere to be found. Without Harmon, who had turned state's evidence to avoid prosecution, the government had no case and the charges against Hershfield were finally dismissed.[53] L. H. Hershfield declared bankruptcy on debts of $498,469 and assets of $2,157 in June 1902.[54]

Closing the receiverships

In early 1903, Wilson finally closed the trusts. A syndicate, organized by William G. Conrad, James T. Stanford, and Thomas Curry, offered to buy the trusts' remaining assets for roughly $270,000 in November 1902.[55] On Wilson's advice, the Comptroller accepted the Conrad–Stanford Company's proposal, and Wilson prepared to end his Helena sojourn. Depositors in Merchants National Bank recouped approximately 68 cents on the dollar, while First National Bank customers recovered roughly 40 cents on the dollar. Business conditions generally had not improved. A wildcat strike at the smelter in East Helena resulted in the closure of the plant and unemployment for 600 workers. Real estate remained assessed at more than its real value, and few properties moved in the sluggish market. The city was broke, and its economy had flatlined; there was simply no capital available for any public or private investment.

As his trusts were drawing to a close, Wilson responded to one last depositor's questions regarding First National Bank. He pointed to three principal reasons for the collapse of the bank: the slump in the silver market, Montana's businessmen's inability to repay their bank loans, and the weak real estate market.

He concluded: "An institution like the First National Bank, active, energetic, and enterprising, willing to aid every enterprise that promised to build up the community, was overtaken in the cyclone of disaster and nothing human could save it, and I do not think that any human is, in justice, to blame."[56] With that, Wilson dutifully packed his records for storage; his work in Helena was finished.

Perhaps Wilson's last days as receiver prompted his charitable and politic response, or perhaps he thought nothing would be gained by rehearsing the details of the receiverships. Wilson's correspondence, however, suggested that the failures of the First National Bank and Merchants National Bank resulted from more than a "cyclone of disaster" and that there were responsible parties. Certainly, the collapse of the silver market and pressure on correspondent banks laid the groundwork for runs on the Helena banks. Nonetheless, corruption was the critical element in the banks' insolvency and subsequent failure. Had Hauser and the Hershfields maintained their banks' reserves, dealt with their bad paper, monitored the loans to officers, generally attended to business, and, most important, refrained from reckless and fraudulent practices, they might well have weathered the panic as other Helena banks had.[57]

Conclusions

Some scholars have argued that the Treasury secretaries of the post-Civil War period were politicized to the point of ineffectiveness and that the department and its bureaus, including the Comptroller of Currency, lacked sufficient numbers of mid-level professionals to formulate and implement policy. It is impossible to know to what extent E. T. Wilson typified the national bank examiner of his times. Nonetheless, his career, along with those of colleagues S. R. Flynn and A. D. Lynch, suggests that people like him—principled, skillful, and courageous—were not uncommon either.

In dealing with the rogue bankers of Helena during the 1890s, Wilson showed complete command of his business: he understood procedures of the courtroom as well as those of the counting house and demonstrated that he was a smart, savvy examiner and a sophisticated financier every bit the equal (and probably the better) of the bankers he was responsible for supervising. He also possessed an acute political sensibility; he knew when to flatter, when to bluster, and when to threaten. His correspondence reveals a fine sense of humor, often expressed in western idioms and poker metaphors.

Wilson's career underscores another important point: officials chosen for their positions for political reasons are not necessarily political animals once in office. As a national bank examiner, Wilson's allegiance was always, in his words, to the "bureau" rather than to a political party. There is evidence to suggest that neither political friendship nor animus ever guided Wilson's actions. Nor did he ever seek political advice or preference. Clearly, he believed that such political partisanship was incompatible with his oath as a national bank examiner. Throughout his government career, E. T. Wilson took the oath seriously and the idea of public service implicit in it.

Notes

1. Thomas K. McCraw, *Prophets of Regulation: Charles Francis Adams; Louis D. Brandeis; James M. Landis; Alfred E. Kahn* (Cambridge, MA: Harvard University Press, 1984), vii–ix. McCraw's book is one of the few attempts to discuss regulators, but he is more interested in agency or commission leaders than mid-level field personnel. See also, Cindy Sondik Aron, *Ladies and Gentlemen of the Civil Service: Middle-Class Workers in Victorian America* (New York: Oxford University Press, 1987). Aron's book deals with federal civil service workers who were mostly clerks or in similar jobs, positions lower on the occupational ladder than regulators in the various agencies. Aron's text does provide a sense of the problems faced by both groups of federal employees. By and large, the literature devoted to the history of regulation or regulators is thin.

2. Ross M. Robertson, *The Comptroller and Bank Supervision: A Historical Appraisal* (Washington, DC, 1995), 49–51, 65–6, 72. The Comptroller of Currency required that a national bank meet certain criteria. While there were a number of requirements pertaining to organizational membership, paid-up capital, and bonds on deposit, among others, one of the most important was maintenance of adequate reserves. After 1874, country banks such as the Helena institutions were obliged to keep a 15 percent cash reserve against their deposits: 5 percent in a Treasury redemption fund and the remaining 10 percent in the country banks' vaults, on deposit with correspondent banks, or a combination of the two. The reserves supported cash payments during financial crises when depositors demanded their money. There were other important rules for national banks. An institution could not make loans on real estate; could not lend a single borrower more than 10 percent of its paid-up capital; could not make loans to its officers; and could not purchase shares or bonds in another bank or corporation. As bank supervision evolved, the bank examiners also scrutinized the entirety of a bank's business: "the responsibility and prudence of its management and the total quality of its loans and its investment portfolio."

3. David A. Skeel, Jr., *Debt's Dominion: A History of Bankruptcy Law in America* (Princeton, 2001), 23–47; Henry Gabriel Tardy, John W Smith, Charles Fisk Beach, and William Atkinson Alderson, *A Practical Treatise on the Law of Receivers* (New York, 1897), 524–33; Henry Gabriel Tardy and John W Smith, *A Treatise on the Law and Procedure of Receivers*, Vol. 2, (San Francisco, 1920), 1285–436. Receivership is a form of insolvency in which a business attempts to reorganize its affairs or liquidate its assets for the benefit of its creditors with the help of a bureau- or court-appointed trustee or agent. Should a business appear salvageable, receivers manage, maintain, and rehabilitate its assets; should a firm appear beyond recovery, receivers liquidate its assets. Receivers are also charged with detecting any malfeasance and bringing to book any malefactors. By the Bankruptcy Act of 1898, bank receivership had evolved considerably, developing guidelines for different classes of creditors, defining a bank receiver's role and scope, and establishing legal precedents for a wide range of eventualities. Generally speaking, a nineteenth-century national bank receiver had greater latitude than his twentieth-century counterpart. A bank examiner acted as an officer of the federal government and operated in concert with both local courts and the U.S. Attorney rather than as an officer of the court who worked under the direction of the bench. Because a receivership was a species of trust, nineteenth-century receivers often referred to a receivership and themselves as a trust and trustees, respectively.

4. M. O'Connell and T.A. Martin, *State of Washington: Members of the State Legislature by Districts from 1889 to 1997 Inclusive (With Name Index)* (Olympia, Secretary of the Senate and Chief Clerk of the House of Representatives, 1997), 38, 40; *Progressive Men of Montana* (Chicago, ca. 1901), 490–91.

5 For a detailed discussion of the history of the First National Bank and its relationship with the Comptroller of Currency's office from its founding to E. T. Wilson's receivership, see Paula Petrik, "Parading as Millionaires: Montana Bankers and the Panic of 1893," *Enterprise & Society* 10 (2009): 732–41.
6 "A Bank Failure in Helena," *Daily Inter Mountain*, [Butte, MT], September 4, 1896; "Helena's Object Lesson," *Daily Inter Mountain*, September 5, 1896.
7 For community antipathy against newcomers, see Paula Petrik, *No Step Backward: Women and Family on the Rocky Mountain Mining Frontier, Helena, Montana, 1865–1900* (Helena, MT: Montana Historical Society Press, 1987), chap. 1; for Hauser's efforts, see "Rich Man Poor Man, Banker Man Thief: The Rise and Fall of Erastus D. Edgerton, 1886–1898" (*Montana, The Magazine of Western History*, 2017); "Helena Bank Failure," *Daily Inter Mountain* [Butte, MT], December 16, 1896.
8 H. A. Forman to J. H. Eckels, January 27, 1897, Bank #1642, Records of the Comptroller of Currency (hereafter ROCC), Examiner's Reports (hereafter ER), RG 101, National Archives and Records Administration, College Park, MD (hereafter NARA-CP). It seems reasonable to assume that Eckels wanted to understand what went wrong and when. As a result of Forman's report, Eckels and the Comptrollers who succeeded him became highly suspicious of S. T. Hauser and his claims.
9 E. T. Wilson to A. D. Lynch, January 5, 1897, Bank #1642, ROCC, ER, RG 101, NARA-CP.
10 Ibid.
11 "News of the State," *Ravalli Republican* [Stevensville, MT], November 17, 1897.
12 For a more detailed discussion of the history of Merchants National and its relationship with the Comptroller of Currency's office from its founding to E. T. Wilson's receivership, see Petrik, "Parading as Millionaires," 741–9.
13 Examiner's Report, March 4, 1896, Bank #2732, Merchants National Bank, ROCC, ER, RG 101, NARA-CP.
14 L. H. Hershfield to Chas. H. Peterson, February 3, 1897; see also Thomas P. Bowman, Letterbook, October 25, 1896, Merchants National Bank Records [hereafter MNBR], Montana Historical Society, Helena, Montana [hereafter MHS].
15 Petrik, "Parading as Millionaires," 755.
16 E. T. Wilson to E. D. Edgerton, January 26, 1898, First National Bank of Helena Records [hereafter FNBR], MHS.
17 E. T. Wilson to Goodrich, Whitney, and Hager, April 14, 1898; E. T. Wilson to Hoskin, Ogden, and Hoskin, April 5, 1898, both in FNBR, MHS.
18 E. T. Wilson to Charles G. Davies, July 8, 1898, MNBR, MHS.
19 Ibid.
20 E. T. Wilson to Frank W. Lewis, September, 27, 1898, MNBR, MHS. In this poker scenario, Wilson believed that his opponent was holding absolutely worthless cards and running a "bluff." Wilson responded that he was not "in the mood" to simply match the bet but would both match and raise the bet in order to force the other player to show his cards or fold. Either way, Wilson would win.
21 E. T. Wilson to William B. Ridgely, September 26, 1899, FNBR, MHS; see also E. T. Wilson to Charles G. Davies, April 30, 1898; E. T. Wilson to Julius Sands, February 22, 1898; E. T. Wilson to Charles G. Davies, February 23, 1898, all in MNBR, MHS.
22 E. T. Wilson to E. B. Weireck, January 1, 1899, FNBR, MHS.
23 E. T. Wilson to Charles G. Davies, March 15, 1899, MNBR, MHS. L. H. Hershfield had demanded his brother's stock to defray the costs of Aaron's divorce settlement and legal costs. Although L. H. Hershfield and his wife had instigated the divorce, Aaron Hershfield ended up paying for his relatives' folly.
24 E. T. Wilson to Joseph Bergen, February 22, 1898, FNBR, MHS.

25 E. T. Wilson to G. A. Ulrig, April 22, 1901, MNBR, MHS.
26 Macey, Jonathan R. and Geoffrey P. Miller. "Double Liability of Bank Shareholders: History and Implications," *Wake Forest Law Review* 27 (1992): 31–62.
27 W. C. Lobenstine to E. T. Wilson, February 14, 1898, MNBR, MHS.
28 Stockholder List, 1896, MNBR, MHS. Roughly 80 percent of the bank's stockholders resided outside the bank's trading area.
29 E. T. Wilson to Charles G. Davies, April 25, 1898, MNBR, MHS.
30 L. H. Hershfield to E. T. Wilson, October 8, 1896; E. T. Wilson to Charles G. Davies, December 20, 1898; see also Board of Directors of the Merchants National Bank to J. H. Eckels, all in MNBR, MHS. Merchants National already had experience with a dishonest employee. Shortly after W. C. Whipps, a Merchants bookkeeper, arrived at the bank he found Israel Sohlinger, the bank manager and Mary Hershfield's nephew, making erasures in Whipps's books. Whipps was furious: "Immediately, I went wild," he recalled. "I told him that he nor no one else could scratch or erase anything on a book I kept. . . . He knew that I was onto him and knew there must be something crooked. He was a crook, but it was not my business to watch him and I did not, though I was satisfied he was robbing that bank in some way all the time." As it happened, Sohlinger *was* robbing the bank. One day, Sohlinger, who held a high opinion of his abilities, "cut Mr. L. H. off at the pockets." Despite a family relationship, L. H. Hershfield fired Sohlinger at the end of the business day, and Whipps stepped into Sohlinger's position. Shortly, Whipps discovered that the original entry book, among other ledgers, was missing and surmised that Sohlinger had destroyed the books to cover his tracks. When he reported the disappearances, Aaron Hershfield hired a Chicago detective and recovered over $60,000. See Samuel William Carvoso Whipps, "Reminiscence," 1933, 98, MHS.
31 Ibid. Bowman's reputation in the community stood none too high either. Known by a particularly vile ethnic sobriquet, he had loaned money on his own account on stringent terms.
32 *U.S. v. Aaron Hershfield*, Case #337, United States District Court, Helena (1898); *U.S. v. Lewis Hershfield*, Case #338, United States District Court, Helena (1898); *U.S. v. Thomas P. Bowman*, Case #335, United States District Court, Helena (1898), RG 21, National Archives and Records Administration, Pacific Alaska Region, Seattle, Washington [hereafter NARA-Pacific]; see also, "Hershfield Trial," August 17, 1900; "Government Rests in Hershfield Case," August 18, 1900, all in *Anaconda Standard* [Anaconda, MT]. Aaron Hershfield was indicted on six counts of misapplication of funds or falsifying records in connection with his management of the State National Bank in Miles City; Lewis Hershfield, president of Merchants National Bank, was indicted on twenty-two counts of same charges; and Thomas P. Bowman, Merchants National Bank's cashier, was indicted on thirty-two counts of the same charges. A reader might properly ask: why the Hershfields and not Hauser and company? Wilson evidently believed that he had better evidence in the Hershfield case since he had literally caught Bowman "cooking the books." He was also mindful of Hauser's political influence both locally and in Washington as well as the mishandling of the earlier grand jury proceedings against First National Bank officers. In addition, on three separate occasions, First National officers and directors had successfully avoided or quashed indictments.
33 Quoted in "Government Rests in Hershfield Case," *Anaconda Standard* [Anaconda, MT], August 18, 1900.
34 E. T. Wilson to A. D. Lynch, August 27, 1900, MNBR, MHS.
35 "Hershfield Acquitted," *Great Falls Tribune* [Great Falls, MT], August 24, 1900; "Banker Is Acquitted, Not Evidence Enough," *Helena Montana Daily Record* [Helena, MT], August 24, 1900. Hershfield need not have worried. Few bank

officers went to federal prison at McNeil Island for violations of the National Bank Act. In fact, had Hershfield trafficked in white slaves or dealt narcotics, his chances for doing prison time would have been much better. See McNeil Island Penitentiary Intake Volume Index (microfilm portion M1619), RG 129, NARA-Pacific.
36 E. T. Wilson to Paul O. Fusz, November 28, 1899, MNBR, MHS.
37 E. T. Wilson to J. H. Eckels, August 27, 1900, MNBR, MHS. Despite Wilson's misgivings, Judge Knowles's ruling reflected contemporary thinking on fraud. Providing false statements, a species of fraud, required proof of intent and not its presumption. The government did not provide sufficient or convincing evidence that L. H. Hershfield had knowingly set out to deceive the Comptroller. Courts also took the economic conditions into consideration. See Paula J. Dalley, "The Law of Deceit, 1790–1860: Continuity Amidst Change," *American Journal of Legal History* 39 (1995): 405–42.
38 E. T. Wilson to Root & Clark, Attorneys-at-Law, October 31, 1901 and November 1, 1901, FNBR, MHS.
39 E. T. Wilson to William B. Ridgely, November 18, 1901, FNBR, MHS.
40 "They Want to Intervene," *Anaconda Standard*, December 1, 1901; E. T. Wilson to H. W. Turner, January 3, 1902, both in FNBR, MHS.
41 E. T. Wilson to H. W. Turner, January 10, 1902; E. T. Wilson to D. S. Bergin and C. H. Bosworth, February 21, 1902; E. T. Wilson to D. S. Bergin, March 21,1902, all in FNBR, MHS.
42 E. T. Wilson to William Ridgely, April 4, 1902, FNBR, MHS.
43 E. T. Wilson to H. W. Turner, January 3, 1902, FNBR, MHS.
44 E. T. Wilson to William B. Ridgely, April 15, 1902, FNBR, MHS.
45 E. T. Wilson to William B. Ridgely, April 22, 1902, FNBR, MHS.
46 E. T. Wilson to William B. Ridgely, July 8, 1902, FNBR, MHS.
47 E. T. Wilson to J. B. Southmayd, May 21, 1898; E. T. Wilson to G. M. Southmayd, May 21, 1898, both in MNBR, MHS; E. T. Wilson to E. D. Edgerton, January 19, 1899; E. T. Wilson to Harry Bush, May 14, 1899; E. T. Wilson to J. C. Vilas, July 11, 1898, all in FNBR, MHS. Later, Wilson also experienced the same difficulties with the mines in Merchants National's portfolio. Both the Euclid Mine and the Ontario Mine posed similar problems. See E. T. Wilson to Charles Dawes, February 6, 1901; E.T. Wilson to Charles Dawes, June 8, 1901, both in MNBR, MHS.
48 E. T. Wilson to Duncan Hunter, June 13, 1898, FNBR, MHS.
49 E. T. Wilson to Charles Davies, September 28, 1899, FNBR, MHS.
50 E. T. Wilson to E. W. Cullen, October 26, 1899; E. T. Wilson to Charles G. Davies, November 8, 1899; E. T. Wilson to Jay Anderson, May 16, 1900, all in MNBR, MHS.
51 E. T. Wilson to Charles G. Davies, June 14, 1899, MNBR, MHS; E. T. Wilson to Charles Davies, December 17, 1899; E. T. Wilson to J. W. Schofield, November 22, 1899; E. T. Wilson to A. D. Lynch, July 25, 1900, all in FNBR, MHS.
52 E. T. Wilson to A. D. Lynch, November 27, 1899; E. T. Wilson to Charles G. Davies, May 30, 1900; E. D. Edgerton to E. T. Wilson, May 19, 1900; E. T. Wilson to A. D. Lynch, March 23, 1901; E. T. Wilson to Charles G. Davies, January 25, 1901, all in FNBR, MHS. It is likely that Hauser settled his debts so suddenly because he had some assurance that he would prevail in the lawsuit over the Seven Devils mining claims in Idaho. Brought by Granville Stuart to recover his interest in the rich area, the suit pitted Stuart's claim that he had pledged his interest in the mine as mortgage collateral against Hauser's claim that Stuart's interest had been part of an acceptance or sale to offset Stuart's debt to First National Bank. Although both the lower and appellate courts found in Hauser's favor, it seems clear that Hauser had transformed Stuart's paper from a mortgage into a sale and betrayed his friend in the bargain. See Clyde Milner and Carol O'Connor, *As Big As the*

    West: The Pioneer Life of Granville Stuart (New York: Oxford University Press, 2009), 311–17.
53 "Hershfield Trial Called," January 11, 1901; "Case Against Hershfield," January 12, 1901; "Trial Was Concluded," January 13, 1901; "Harmon Indictment Dismissed," January 27, 1901; "No Verdict Reached," January 16, 1901; "Second Trial," May 7, 1901, all in *Anaconda Standard* [Anaconda, MT], MHS; Minute Book, US District Court, No. 4, November 4, 1901–May 18, 1903, 187, RG 21, NARA-Pacific.
54 "Bankruptcies," *New York Times*, June 28, 1902.
55 E. T. Wilson to William B. Ridgely, November 3, 1902, FNBR, MHS.
56 E. T. Wilson to D. C. Pearson, March 18, 1903, FNBR, MHS. When Wilson departed Helena, he took the train to Davenport, Washington, where he took up the receivership of the Big Bend National Bank. At Big Bend National, Wilson once more dealt with a felonious bank president and "cooked books." Just before World War I, he became vice president of the First National Bank of Tacoma, remaining there for the remainder of his career. Wilson "died with his boots on," suffering a heart attack on his way to work at the bank in November 1923. See "Financier Drops Dead," *Tacoma News Tribune* [Tacoma, WA], November 17, 1923. For E.T. Wilson's receivership of Big Bend National, see "Big Bend Bank Closes Doors," *The Spokesman-Review* (Spokane), November 26, 1904.
57 Three Helena banks, in fact, survived: Thomas Cruse Savings Bank, American National Bank, and Montana National Bank. The Cruse concern was chiefly a savings bank founded for the purpose of encouraging savings among the working class; it did not make large investments in speculative enterprises. It was also backed by the proceeds from the sale of five-sixths of the Drum Lummon Mine, some $1.5 million. The Montana National Bank survived because its financial well-being rested on the Charles C. Broadwater Trust. The American National Bank, chartered in 1890, associated with the Seligmans' New York banks and investment houses, simply had not been in business long enough to get into trouble.

6 Stabilizing the national banking system, 1864–1913

The role of bank examination

Eugene N. White

Introduction

In his first book, The Regulation and Reform of the American Banking System, 1900–1929 *(1984), Eugene N. White, professor of economics at Rutgers University and research associate of the National Bureau of Economic Research, discussed the rise of the Federal Reserve System and why the system, for all the benefits that came from it, proved no panacea for the structural problems besetting the U.S. banking system. In* The Comptroller and the Supervision of American Banking 1960–1990 *(1992), White focused on the Office of the Comptroller of the Currency's response to the dismantling of the restrictive rules put in place after the Great Depression and the effects of this deregulation on the banking system. In these books and other writings, White combined a solid grasp of economic theory with a historian's flair for narrative and analysis.*

In the following chapter, White looks back to the period of 1863–1900, the formative years for the OCC and the system of national bank supervision. Despite the recurring bank "panics" of the era, White finds that regulation and supervision made a significant difference in limiting losses to national bank customers. This, he contends, was mainly the result of provisions in the National Bank Acts that imposed double (as opposed to limited) liability on shareholders. Under these provisions, shareholders were not only at risk of losing their investment in the event of the bank's failure; they were further responsible for any difference between the liquidated value of the bank's assets and its obligations to depositors. This arrangement gave shareholders and managers extra incentive to conduct the bank's business in a safe and sound manner. Indeed, proposals to increase the liabilities of bank stakeholders as a safeguard against bank instability are still heard today.

White shows how OCC examiners helped to ensure that banks accurately measured the value of their assets and that failing institutions would be promptly closed. Although examiners achieved several notable successes in the banks they supervised (as shown in Paula Petrik's essay on Helena, Montana in this volume), White argues that it was too much to expect the modest staff of national bank examiners, whose territory often covered multiple states, to systematically root out fraud and mismanagement.

For historians, economists, and policy makers, correctly interpreting the National Banking Era, 1864–1913, is of critical importance for understanding the role of regulation and supervision in achieving financial stability. Created by the National Currency Act of 1863 and modified by the National Bank Act of 1864, at a time when there was no central bank, this regime, which might now be called a "micro-prudential" regime, supervised banks with a relatively light hand. A single federal regulator, the Office of the Comptroller of the Currency (OCC), supervised the largest and most important group of financial intermediaries—the national banks. Typically, it is viewed as a period of almost chronic instability, with frequent banking panics.[1] The last and perhaps most severe crisis, the Panic of 1907, induced Congress to begin a serious debate about banking reform that culminated in the passage of the Federal Reserve Act in 1913. To remedy the perceived defects of the existing system, a central bank was created with the intention of providing, as boldly proclaimed in the title of the act, "more effective supervision of banking."

This contemporary critique has rarely been challenged, leaving the lessons from the successes of the national banking system largely unappreciated. Even though the financial system was troubled by design defects, the national banks were safer and sounder than is conventionally believed.[2] By the end of the nineteenth century, and after 1907, the conduct of supervision by the Comptroller was regarded as best practice and many states began to more closely mimic the OCC's procedures.[3] Consequently, this study may be seen as an examination of best-practice nineteenth-century supervision, identifying its strengths and weaknesses and showing how the incentives given to the various bank stakeholders, combined with disclosure and examination, sharply limited the losses experienced by depositors, in spite of the frequent panics and crises.

An examiner's eye view of national bank regulations

Two key objectives of the National Currency Act were to establish a national "free" banking system that would provide a safe, uniform national currency and to create banks that would absorb some of the national debt. To do that, the law had to set up a properly monitored structure with incentives to guarantee that, in the event of a national bank's failure, noteholders would suffer no losses. Provisions for protecting the new currency with U.S. Treasury bonds and additional requirements for bank governance were designed to ensure that depositors and other creditors would suffer minimal losses.

The National Currency Act of 1863 was based on the states' experience with "free banking." The two common features of state free banking laws were a generalized act of incorporation for banks—making entry easy—and a bond-backed currency.[4] The motivation behind "free" incorporation was to remove the chartering of banks from state legislatures and democratize the provision of credit. If a state did not have a free banking act in the pre-1864 period, the right to open a bank could only be obtained by the granting of a special charter from the legislature. By the 1830s, this process had by and large become highly corrupt.[5] Setting up a system of general incorporation for banks led to an expansion of banks and credit, creating a more competitive banking market.

To ensure financial stability, the National Bank Act of 1864 employed what today would be termed micro-prudential regulation and supervision. It specified rules for corporate governance and regulations covering capital, reserves, banknotes, and loans and discounts. The intention behind controlling entry and exit by banks, the composition of their portfolios, and the incentives of their stakeholders was to limit risk, given that banknote holders, depositors, and shareholders were at an information disadvantage vis-à-vis the directors and managers who controlled decision-making at the banks. Supervision was also intended to overcome this asymmetry in information by forcing management to disclose the condition of banks at regular intervals. However, given that information about customers and bank activities was proprietary, disclosure policy was complemented by examinations that would analyze but not disclose proprietary information. These examinations not only ensured the enforcement of regulations, backed by penalties, but also sought to identify weaknesses that might precipitate insolvency.

To prevent the formation of banks that were too small to be viable, Section 7 of the National Bank Act set a minimum capital of $50,000 for banks in towns with populations under 6,000, $100,000 for banks in places where the population was between 6,000 and 50,000, and $200,000 for cities greater than 50,000.[6] Given the importance of protecting the means of payment, the issue of national banknotes was tightly controlled. An individual bank could only issue notes equal to 90 percent of the par value of the U.S. government bonds that the bank had bought and deposited, with each bank's total note issue limited to 100 percent of the bank's total paid-in capital.[7] To protect depositors, Section 31 of the act specified that country banks were required to have reserves equal to 15 percent of the total deposits and circulation, three-fifths of which could be held on deposit in a national bank in a designated reserve city, which was required to hold a reserve against deposits of 25 percent. In subsequent legislation, reserve city banks were ordered to hold a required reserve ratio of 25 percent with up to one-half held in national banks in one of the three designated central reserve cities.[8] In these cities—New York, Chicago, and St. Louis—all reserves had to be held in the vault. According to the National Bank Act, if a bank fell below its minimum reserve ratio, it could not make any loans or discounts or pay out any dividends until the minimum ratio was restored.

To control a bank's portfolio, Sections 28 and 29 of the National Bank Act circumscribed lending. Apart from real estate for the bank's buildings, a national bank could only hold the title to real estate under mortgage to secure debts for a maximum of five years. No loan to any individual or firm could exceed 10 percent of the bank's capital stock, and discounts were required to be for "bills of exchange drawn against actually existing values" and commercial or business paper actually owned by a person or firm. Usury laws of the state in which a national bank was domiciled limited the interest rate that banks could charge for loans.

Based on the experience of the state free banking laws, the National Bank Act (Sections 8 to 11) codified good corporate governance in the design of national banks by setting specific incentives for the various stakeholders. A minimum of five persons could form a national association, specifying in the organizational certificate the name and location of the projected bank, its capital stock, and the names and places of residence of the shareholders and their shareholdings. To enforce shareholder responsibility, Section 40 specified that banks must keep at all times "a full and correct list of the names and residences of all the shareholders in the association, and the number of shares held by each." This list was to be made available during business hours for inspection by any shareholder, creditor, or state official responsible for assessing taxes, with copies once a year to the Comptroller.

In a key provision of the National Bank Act (Section 12), double liability was imposed on shareholders who were "held individually responsible, equally and ratably" for any losses that the bank could not cover in the event of its failure. Thus, in addition to losing their stock in the bank, they could be called upon to make payments up to the par value of the stock they had owned. In a debate on the act in 1864, one of its proponents, Senator John Sherman, emphasized that double liability was intended to provide the creditors of the bank with protection by preventing "stockholders and directors of a bank from engaging in hazardous operations."[9]

After certifying the organizational certificate with a judge or notary public, the bank could begin operations once it had been examined and approved by the Comptroller. This process was straightforward, and charter applications were managed by correspondence rather than in person, with little discretion exercised by the Comptroller.[10] The affairs of the bank would be managed by a board of directors, and each director was required to own a minimum of 10 shares, which at a par value of $100 represented an investment of $1,000. At a minimum, directors of the smallest-sized national banks would together own 5 percent of the stock, giving them a substantial personal stake. One of the directors was to be elected president, with the directors appointing a cashier and other officers. Furthermore, following state free banking laws, directors were required by Section 9 to take an oath that they would "diligently and honestly administer the affairs" of the bank and would "not knowingly violate, or willingly permit to be violated, any of the provisions of this act."

To ensure compliance, the Comptroller had one major remedy: the authority to bring a suit in federal court to dissolve the bank. However, any director who participated in or assented to a violation would be held in "his personal and individual capacity for all damages which the association, its shareholders or any other person, shall have sustained in consequence of such violation" (Section 53). Thus, in theory, directors had substantial liability vis-à-vis the shareholders, helping to further align their interests. Penalties for officers and employees of a national bank were set by Section 55, where embezzlement, willful misapplication of funds, false bookkeeping, or other efforts to defraud a bank or deceive an examiner would be a misdemeanor with a penalty of imprisonment of five to 10 years.

Banks could begin operation with half of their capital paid-in but were obliged to complete its payment in five equal monthly installments after commencing operation. A national bank was expected to build up and maintain a minimum surplus of 20 percent from retained profits. Directors were given substantial discretion in paying out dividends. According to Section 33, a national bank could semi-annually declare a dividend, as the directors judged expedient. However, if losses reduced the surplus below the 20 percent minimum, no dividends could be paid until the surplus was restored. The Comptroller also had the option to close the bank if such a deficiency occurred. Thus, the Comptroller could shut down a bank before it technically became insolvent, thus limiting losses to depositors and other creditors. Section 38 further specified that no dividend could be paid if losses exceeded undivided profits, and no dividend could be greater than net profits less losses and bad debts. These detailed rules for the payment of dividends point to a concern with maintaining the integrity of the double liability provision for shareholders, which might be circumvented if funds were siphoned out of a bank via dividend payments to shareholders to cover and thus nullify their extended liability.

Both shareholders and the Comptroller had the power to close a national bank. If the shareholders were unhappy with the prospects of a bank, they could close it. Section 42 empowered shareholders to voluntarily close and liquidate a bank upon a two-thirds vote of the shareholders. After public notice was given in newspapers, noteholders and depositors would have a year to claim their assets, after which they would be handled by the U.S. Department of the Treasury. The Comptroller could suspend the operation of a national bank, pending its closure, if it engaged in any violation of the National Bank Act or refused "to pay its circulating notes ... and is in default" (Section 50). Except for fines for late reporting, there were no penalties that the Comptroller could levy except closing down a bank. When a bank was subject to closure, the Comptroller was directed to appoint a receiver to take possession of the books, records, and assets of the bank and collect all debts, dues, and claims and, upon court order, sell all assets and collect the shareholders' liability to pay the bank's obligations.

While the Comptroller was endowed with substantial authority to deal with delinquent banks, the National Bank Act set out disclosure requirements for national banks to enable the public to make more informed decisions about where to deposit their money. Banks were required to send the Comptroller a quarterly report of assets and liabilities on the first Mondays of January, April, July, and October and a limited monthly statement (Section 34).[11] Banks had five days in which to transmit their quarterly report to the Comptroller in Washington, DC, and were subject to a $100 fine for each day's delay in delivery after the five days.[12] Abstracts of these reports would then be published in a newspaper in the capital and in the town or region of the reporting bank. When it was realized that the fixed reporting dates led to "window dressing," the Comptroller complained to Congress, which in 1869 instituted the call report system. On four or five "call" dates, chosen by the Comptroller, national banks were obliged to report the condition of their balance sheets.

As banking is an information business, banks naturally regard much of their information on their activities and customers as proprietary. Yet a bank's true condition cannot be determined without this information, which is one reason the National Bank Act gave the Comptroller the authority to appoint examiners who would provide him with confidential assessments. The National Currency Act did not specify the qualifications for an examiner, except that, according to Section 54, an examiner could not examine any bank where he was a director or officer. An examiner was tasked to examine the directors and officers under oath and provide the Comptroller with a full and detailed report of the association's condition. As the Comptroller's eyes and ears, OCC examiners played a critical role in monitoring the condition of national banks and protecting the nation's banknote holders and depositors.

Examinations and examiners

Initially, national banks were examined once a year by a national bank examiner. But the adequacy of this regime was called into question in the mid-1890s. Weakened by a long-term deflation, the nation experienced three recessions in 1890–91, 1893–94, and 1895–97 with a severe panic in 1893 and a stubbornly high rate of unemployment.[13] In 1895, the balance of payments and budget deficits led to a run on the dollar, which was only staved off by an international loan from the Belmont-Morgan syndicate.[14] Populist agitation demanded that the gold standard, adopted in 1879, be modified or abandoned, with William Jennings Bryan, the Democratic presidential candidate, calling in 1896 for a return to bimetallism.[15] This prolonged economic instability weakened many banks, and there was a significant increase in the number of bank failures and a fall in the ratio of payments to proven claims to depositors and other creditors of failed banks. As seen in Figure 6.1, the percentage of national bank insolvencies in any year before 1890 was on average below one-half of 1 percent and only slightly above this for two years until the percentage rose sharply in the 1890s. Absolute numbers, shown in Figure 6.2, ranged between zero and 12 out of several thousand banks before 1890, then reached a peak of over 60 failures. Except for a few failures in the 1860s and 1870s that resulted in significant losses, the payout ratio for failed banks, also shown in Figure 6.2, averaged above 70 percent. During the 1890s, the payout ratio fell for several years to below 40 percent. These failures and depositor losses sparked congressional investigation of the OCC by the House Banking and Currency Committee (1893–94). This political pressure contributed to the OCC's decision to subject national banks to twice yearly examinations versus annual, even though it was difficult to expand its task force of examiners.

Stabilizing the national banking system 73

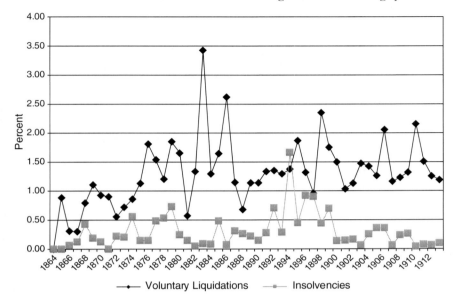

Figure 6.1 National bank insolvencies and voluntary liquidations 1864–1913.
Source: U.S. Comptroller of the Currency, Annual Reports (1865–1914), and White (2013).

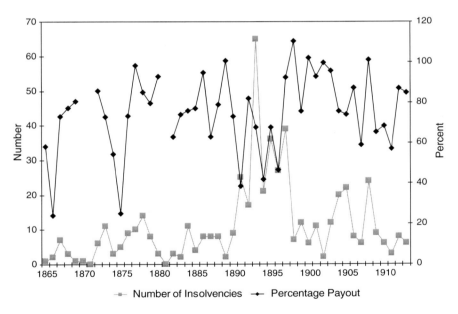

Figure 6.2 National bank insolvencies and payout ratios 1865–1913.
Source: U.S. Comptroller of the Currency, *Annual Report* (1918), and White (2013).
Note: The payout ratio is equal to the payments divided by the proven claims.

There is one more notable feature of Figure 6.1 that deserves close attention, though it has been largely ignored in most histories of this period: voluntary liquidations, brought about by a two-thirds vote of the shareholders to close down a bank. The rate of voluntary liquidations was twice as high as insolvencies. Given that shareholders faced double liability, voting to liquidate was a preemptive action to avoid assessments to pay a failed bank's creditors. The decision to liquidate placed an important brake on risk-taking.[16]

Although they were a vital link between the Comptroller in Washington and the banks across the nation, little is known about the national bank examiners. Even data on the number of examiners is sketchy. Table 6.1 presents some of the few numbers available. For only two years prior to 1902—1889 and 1896, when a single examination was required of each national bank—is the number of examiners available. Each of the examiners had to perform an examination roughly every three days, as the remainder of the time was taken up with travel and completion of the required forms to be sent to Washington, DC. The number of examiners was reported almost continuously between 1902 and 1911, when twice yearly examinations were required, and the table shows a steady increase in their numbers. However, the number of national banks was growing even faster, propelled partly by the Gold Standard Act of 1900, which reduced the minimum capital requirement to $25,000 for banks in the smallest towns, leaving the country bank examiner struggling to cover 20 percent to perhaps 40 percent more banks per year.[17]

Compensation of examiners was a contentious issue throughout the period. While the Comptroller's office expenditures were covered by congressional appropriations, national bank examiners were paid in the form of fees. The

Table 6.1 The examination workforce

Year	Number of national banks	Number of examiners	Required examinations per examiner
1889	3239	30	108
1896	3689	34	109
1902	4532	75	120
1903	4935	74	134
1904	5330	76	140
1905	5664	83	136
1906	6047	91	132
1907	6422	100	128
1908	6817	114	120
1911	7270	113	128

Source: U.S. Comptroller of the Currency, *Annual Reports* (1889–1913), Division of Reports, Weekly reports and vouchers of National Bank Examiners, 1896, RG 101, NARA-CP; and White (2013).

National Bank Act determined that examiners were paid $5 for each day of examination plus a fee of $2 for every 25 miles traveled. Beginning almost immediately, examiners complained that this compensation was inadequate. Some reported expenses that exceeded their income. In response to the Comptroller's complaints, the National Bank Act was amended in 1875 so that examination fees were based on the size of a bank and ranged from $20 to $75, with the Secretary of the Treasury setting the rates for the reserve city banks on the recommendation of the Comptroller.[18] For reserve city banks, those with capital under $100,000 paid a fee of $20; for banks with capital from $100,000 to $299,999, the fee was $25. For the next group of banks, with capital up to $399,000, $499,999, $599,999, and over $600,000, fees of $35, $40, $50, and $75, respectively, were charged.[19]

Expenses for travel and assistants, if any, were to be paid out of these fees. The intention of this form of compensation was to provide an incentive for examiners to control their expenditures. However, it also gave examiners an incentive to minimize their travel time and distances, making it easier for banks to track the movements of an examiner in the region. Comptrollers Henry Cannon (1884–86), William Trenholm (1886–89), and James Eckels (1895–97), among others, complained to Congress that this problem was undermining the value of examinations, especially for country banks; however, Congress failed to respond to their pleas.[20]

This issue erupted at the first conference of national, state, and clearinghouse examiners, which took place on July 8, 1912, in Brighton Beach, New York. Attendees came mostly from the northeast and mid-Atlantic states. The conference was chaired by Frank L. Norris, national bank examiner for Philadelphia. While there was discussion of examination methods and how to anticipate "the departure of frisky cashiers," the event was dominated by the:

> low rate of pay of the National Examiner working in the country, both from the standpoint of its inadequacy and from that of the corresponding menace to depositors, caused by the hurried way in which he must complete his task and get on to the next town, if he is to make enough to pay for his keep and traveling expenses.[21]

An example of the consequences of this problem was provided to the readers of the *New York Times* about the recent defalcation of an upstate New York national bank, where the loss of $350,000 "was the worst black eye the Government examining system had received in many years."[22] Reserve city and central reserve city national bank examiners, who had their pay determined by the Secretary of the Treasury, were believed to be well compensated, but the complaint was that country bank examiners were paid too little to guarantee effective examinations. While a national bank examiner of a country bank would receive $20 for an examination, much of this might be lost to paying assistant and travel expenses, whereas state bank examiners for New York state-chartered banks received $8 to $20 per day plus their expenses. The disparity was far greater when compared to the reserve city and central reserve city national bank examiners. The New York City national bank examiner received $3,630 for a bank with $25 million in capital and $300 million in assets.[23] It was estimated that the New York City examiner would be paid $50,000 annually and, after paying his six or seven assistants, office rent, and other expenses, would net $15,000 per year, which was three times the $5,000 salary of the Comptroller of the Currency.[24]

A further glimpse into the pressures facing the typical national bank examiner in the late nineteenth century can be gleaned from records at the National Archives that contain the cover sheets of the examination reports submitted by all examiners for one month in 1896.[25] Each cover sheet gave the date of submission and the city from which the reports were sent and listed the number of banks examined during the month with reports forwarded, the number of banks examined with reports not yet forwarded, and the total number of banks examined during the month. Those banks that were overdue to be examined were listed by name and location.[26] A summary of these cover sheets is provided in Table 6.2. Column 1 shows the state from which the examiner reported, and Column 2 gives the date that the reports were sent to the Comptroller's Office in Washington, DC. In the month of August 1896, 308 examinations were performed. If that level of productivity had been sustained, all 3,689 national banks in operation in 1896 would have been examined once.

Allowing for the inevitable delays in submitting a report after the examination had been completed, the data still shows that 155 national banks were overdue for an exam. Clearly, some examiners were falling seriously behind. For example, the first Colorado examiner did not submit any reports for the month of August and was 11 banks behind; the second Colorado examiner, while conducting seven examinations, forwarded six and was still behind schedule for five banks. In general, this fragmentary evidence confirms more general complaints about the heavy workload of examiners that caused them to occasionally conduct rushed, less than comprehensive visits.

Given the relatively small number of examiners assigned to cover a large number of often widely scattered banks and a poorly designed system of compensation, it is not surprising that examiners were often behind in their work. In spite of these problems, the safety and soundness of national banks may not have been seriously compromised, as they were also safeguarded by other examinations or audits imposed on the banks and the incentives provided to shareholders and depositors. It should be noted that many banks' board of directors conducted inspections, ranging from monthly to yearly, and some hired their own internal auditors to lead these "examinations." Some took a further step and hired an external auditor. For example, in 1904 the Philadelphia National Bank hired the Edward P. Moxey Audit Company to provide annual examinations. However, in 1909, when the Philadelphia Clearing House hired William M. Hardt as a special examiner to make detailed annual inspections of its members, the Philadelphia National Bank dropped its own external auditor.[27]

Stabilizing the national banking system 77

Table 6.2 Monthly National Bank Examination Reports, August 1896

State	Date	Banks examined/ reports forwarded	Banks examined/ reports not yet forwarded	Number of banks examined	Number of banks behind schedule
CA	9/1/1896	3	0	3	0
CO	9/1/1896	0	0	0	11
CO	9/1/1896	6	1	7	5
IL	9/1/1896	21	0	21	2
IL	9/1/1896	9	3	12	0
IL	9/1/1896	12	1	11	0
IL	9/1/1896	4	0	4	1
IN	9/1/1896	5	7	12	6
KS	9/1/1896	20	0	20	0
KY	9/1/1896	11	1	12	19
LA	9/1/1896	3	0	3	0
MA	8/31/1896	14	0	14	0
MA	9/1/1896	4	2	6	0
MD	8/31/1896	1	1	2	1
ME	9/1/1896	9	0	9	2
MO	9/1/1896	8	1	9	3
NA	9/1/1896	10	0	10	0
NB	9/1/1896	7	0	7	2
ND	9/1/1896	9	9	9	20
NY	9/3/1896	12	0	12	4
OH	9/1/1896	6	7	13	1
OH	9/1/1896	7	0	7	2
OR	9/1/1896	2	5	7	0
PA	9/1/1896	5	1	6	3
PA	9/1/1896	12	2	10	2
PA	9/1/1896	16	0	16	5
RI	9/1/1896	16	0	16	13
SD	9/1/1896	0	0	0	6
TX	9/1/1896	15	0	15	8
TX	9/1/1896	12	0	12	3
TX	9/1/1896	7	0	7	7
WA	9/1/1896	0	0	0	6
WA	9/1/1896	0	0	0	1
WI	9/1/1896	16	1	16	22
TOTALS		282	42	308	155

Reports and vouchers of National Bank Examiners, 1896, RG 101, Records of the Office of the Comptroller of the Currency, Division of Reports, National Archives.

The process of examination

A national bank examination in the late nineteenth century began with the surprise appearance of the regional bank examiner, lasting usually less than one day. Guiding him were instructions from the Comptroller. The first such instructions were issued by Comptroller Hugh McCulloch in 1864. These served only as guidelines because, as the Comptroller noted in his 1891 *Annual Report*, no "cast-iron rules, covering minute details, can be issued to examiners."[28] Minimally, the examiner would have carried with him his bank examiner's book, a leather-bound notebook provided by the OCC with pre-printed forms for assets, liabilities, and other key information about the bank with plenty of space for comments.[29] The first task of the examiner was to fill in a balance sheet for the day of the examination, which had the same information as the call report and would permit the examiner to note any substantial changes. He could then verify whether the required reserve ratio and other regulatory requirements were met.

After completing his examination (not until 1921 did the OCC have a female on the examination staff), he would meet with the board of directors and the president before departing. Later the examiner would fill in the official forms for the examination, and once a month he would send off a packet of completed examinations to the Comptroller's office in Washington, DC.[30]

The examiner would also provide a tally sheet of the banks that he had visited that month and what reports he was sending. Sometimes, his tally sheet would show that he had visited some banks but had not completed the reports. In Washington, DC, the Comptroller's office had a large staff of clerks to handle the inflow of several thousand annual reports and the Comptroller's correspondence with the banks. The reports were reviewed, and if the Comptroller deemed it necessary, he would send letters to the banks in which he might admonish the directors and/or the president, resulting in further correspondence.[31] As there were few legal remedies for violation of the National Bank Act's regulations, most of the Comptroller's efforts were directed at persuading the bank to conform to the law.

Visits by the national bank examiner were often viewed as adversarial events. The correspondence of the Comptroller with examined banks includes many letters that complain about examiners. However, some bankers saw value in an audit performed by an outsider. An OCC examination appears to have been viewed as a reasonably priced, nationally standardized audit. Furthermore, there was a belief among bankers that national bank examinations would help to ensure that problems at other banks in their city or region were addressed so that a failure would not result in panic, engulfing all banks. A competent national bank examiner was required for this task, and when a Philadelphia examiner—a Mr. Miller—did not seem up to par, the First National Bank of Philadelphia wrote a letter on May 5, 1869, to the Comptroller summing up the minutes of the Philadelphia Clearing House Association's May 1 meeting and describing the bankers' concerns:

The objection to Mr. Miller grows out of the recent case of the Fourth National Bank where he made the examination within thirty days of its failure and failed to discover any deflation in the accounts. The opinion of all Bank Presidents, perhaps save one in this city is that Mr. Miller is utterly incompetent to fill his position and ought not to be allowed to continue in it.[32]

Unfortunately, the Comptrollers' *Annual Reports* are largely silent on the general problems that examiners might have found: what, if any, regulations did national banks violate? How frequently did these violations occur? And how did the examiners and the Comptrollers respond to these violations? Surveying selected national bank examiners' reports deposited in the National Archives—the bank examiners' books belonging to A. Barton Hepburn—as well as selected bank histories reveals that, while national bank examiners usually found banks in good condition and in conformity with the law, it was not unusual for banks to have granted loans in excess of their legal limits or to have fallen below their legal reserves. These violations were hard to remedy.

Managing the required reserve ratios proved difficult for some banks. It seems fairly clear that banks frequently found themselves in the awkward position of being short of the required reserve ratio just as a visiting examiner showed up on their doorstep. The same held true for the call reports. In 1873 the First National Bank of Youngstown, Ohio, wrote to the Comptroller explaining that the call report requested of them on March 1 caught them "on a very unfortunate day." The bank pleaded that "We are *very seldom* below our reserve, although we have had a *very* stringent money market here for 5 months."[33] Although the Comptroller might admonish a bank in his correspondence, these deficiencies were most often treated as random fluctuations, and the harsh penalties—the only ones available—were not applied.

By the late nineteenth century, the growth of the bond markets offered banks a wider choice of investments, including marketable railways, mining, and manufacturing companies' securities. In examiners' notebooks and in the reports sent to the Comptroller, there is evidence of examiners dutifully marking these assets to market. The notebooks of A. Barton Hepburn, national bank examiner for New York City (1889–92) and Comptroller of the Currency (1892–93), reveal what was certainly best practice for examinations in the biggest cities. On July 29, 1891, Hepburn examined the Irving National Bank with $4.9 million in assets and $2.5 million in notes and bills discounts, which he characterized as "a good & well managed bank doing—mainly—a local business."[34] The bank's bond portfolio, consisting primarily of railways and some manufacturing companies, was carried on its books at $93,558 but he valued the portfolio at $89,405—not enough to make a dent in the bank's undivided profits, much less its capital and surplus.

More contentious was a national bank examiner's valuation of loans and discounts in a bank's portfolio, with arguments arising over determinations about a loan's prospects for repayment or whether it exceeded statutory loan limits. An 1887 report on the Merchants National Bank found $241,930 of bad debts as well as suspended and overdue paper, which, because it represented a major write-off, was discussed in considerable detail. But even small sums could induce an argument. For example, in 1874, the First National Bank of Youngstown sent a letter of protest to the Comptroller that the national bank examiner had declared $4,100 of good paper to be "worthless."[35] As there was often no market for much of a bank's paper, it was not easy to value. Perhaps the most difficult to value were loans on real estate. One frustrated participant at the 1912 New York bank examiners' conference "told of the necessity of looking up appraisals or having appraisals made in the case of all real estate security loans."[36]

It was not uncommon for banks to provide loans to an individual or firm in excess of the limit of 10 percent of a bank's capital, and such loans were clearly noted in the examiner's reports. What is surprising was the attitude of the banks and their response to criticism by examiners and the Comptroller's office. Nicholas Wainwright reported that in 1903 the Philadelphia National Bank, one of the largest and most prominent banks in Pennsylvania, with a share capital of $1.5 million, was criticized for loans in excess of $150,000. These were no minor or casual violations. The list of recipients of these loans included some of the most important industrialists and merchants of the day: Thomas Dolan, $200,000; John Wanamaker, $300,000; A. J. Cassatt, $250,000; C. A. Griscom, $215,000; Andrew W. Mellon, $250,000; W. C. Whitney, $500,000; P. A. B. Widener, $200,000; and William L. Elkins, $300,000. The board told the Comptroller bluntly that these loans were secured by good collateral and that "no individual, firm or corporation [would] be loaned at any one time on their single name paper a sum beyond 10% of the combined capital and surplus of this Bank or $350,000 except by special action of the Board."[37] The Comptroller challenged the Philadelphia National Bank, but the board of directors did not comply. When in 1905 a new examination again revealed excessively large loans and the Comptroller demanded an explanation signed by every board member, they responded that they interpreted the 10 percent capital rule to mean 10 percent of capital and surplus, "which is in our opinion in conformity with the Law."[38]

The Philadelphia National Bank was not the only bank to take this position. When a bank expanded its assets, the law required that it also increase its surplus and undivided profits—which together would be considered Tier 1 capital today. But the Comptroller adhered to a very strict interpretation of capital, limited to the initial share capital. Although banks had the option of raising share capital, most chose not to do so, as it would entail either a dilution for the existing ownership if there were new shareholders or an increase in their double liability if they bought the shares themselves. After waging a long lobbying campaign on Capitol Hill, bankers secured a change in the National Bank Act in June 1906, in which the loan limit was raised to 10 percent of capital and surplus, with no loan to exceed 30 percent of share capital.[39]

Compared to country and even reserve city banks, correspondent banks in New York City had a very different mix of assets, with a predominance of brokers' loans. After examining the Continental National Bank with $7.6 million in assets on June 19, 1891, Hepburn reported on the collateral backing its loans and bills discounted that accounted for $3.7 million. As a New York City bank, the Continental National provided substantial brokers' loans to brokerage houses that enabled them to finance their customers' purchases on margin and their own stock holdings. Against these loans, the bank held collateral valued by Hepburn at $8.0 million—a huge cushion—consisting of the bonds and stocks of railroads, manufacturing companies, public utilities, banks, and the U.S. government. The largest share of the collateral was $5.2 million in listed railway bonds. However, these brokers' loans were short-term loans, the bulk of which were to be paid within three months, thus limiting risk, and, while noting one problematic discount, Hepburn concluded, "This bank is clean & strong."[40]

A considerable portion of an examiner's report was given over to what would today be considered an evaluation of the governance of the bank. National banks typically had very flat management structures, with the directors taking an active role in the management of the bank and giving special oversight to loans and discounts. Elected by the shareholders, the board of directors elected the president—the CEO—from among their number to head the board, and they appointed a cashier—in effect, the CFO—who was not a member of the board.[41] Even as late as 1913, some large banks did not have additional officers, vice presidents, or assistant cashiers. The third page of an examiner's report listed the number and characteristics of the shareholders, as well as the names of the directors, the cashier, and the president. For example, the October 17, 1887, examination of the Merchants National Bank of Boston reported that the president, Franklin Haven, Jr., formerly the assistant treasurer of the United States at Boston, had been in office since January 1, 1884, and was "active and prominent in the management" of the bank. The cashier, Alonzo P. Weeks, had been a paying teller at the National Hide and Leather Bank of Boston before assuming his position at the bank on September 13, 1886. He was described as knowledgeable of "all the details of the bank's business and is a competent officer." The directors were described as "gentlemen of high character and standing. They meet twice a week for discounting, and examine the bank twice a year." The report went on to list the outside occupation of the directors, their shareholdings, and their liabilities to the bank. In the case of the Merchants National Bank, there were 1,216 shareholders who were described in a formula commonly found in examination reports as individuals associated with "savings banks, insurance companies, various societies, trustees, executors, [and] estates, [as well as] women and other persons."[42]

Examiners also paid close attention to the stock holdings of and loans to the directors and officers of the bank. The examination report of the Merchants National Bank showed that seven directors (including the president) held a total of 514 of the 30,000 shares outstanding. The directors and president, directly or through their firms, had borrowed $455,698, a relatively modest share of the $6,574,159 of total loans and discounts and secured with good collateral. The report also listed all 23 employees, their salaries, and the bonds they had to pledge. Many national bank employees were required to post security bonds. While the president of the Merchants National Bank, with a salary of $10,000, was not required to post a bond, the cashier, with a salary of $6,000, had a bond of $30,000, which reflected the cashier's access to the bank's assets. Almost all other employees, excepting the watchman, elevator boy, and laundress, posted bonds. The more senior positions were the paying teller, the receiving teller, the discount clerk, and the bookkeeper, who received annual salaries of $3,000, $2,200, $2,200, and $2,400, respectively, and posted bonds of $20,000, $10,000, $12,000, and $10,000, respectively. At the bottom of the pay scale at $600 each were the lowest-paid clerk and the assistant messenger, who were required to have security bonds of $5,000.

This monitored structure of salaries, security bonds, shareholdings, and loans helped to ensure that the directors and officers of the bank faced considerable downside risk if the bank were to fail. The bank's president had a loan of $15,000 from the bank, but he owned 171 shares, which at a par value of $100 left him with a potential maximum assessment of $17,100, or nearly twice his annual income, if the bank became insolvent. The director with the largest shareholding, T. Jefferson Coolidge, treasurer of the Amoskeag Manufacturing Company, owned 213 shares, a potential liability of $21,000. Cashier Weeks, who owned no stock and had borrowed nothing, had a security bond of $30,000 that was five times his salary.

Given these incentives, the presidents and boards of directors showed little patience with interference from the Comptroller. In the wake of the Panic of 1907, the Comptroller ordered national bank examiners to ask a set of specific questions of directors to assess their knowledge of their banks. The testy exchange between the Philadelphia National Bank president Levi L. Rue and bank examiner Frank L. Norris was recorded in the minutes of the board for 1908:

> NORRIS: How many of the Directors know the conditions of the Bank in all its details?
>
> RUE: All so far as condition of the Bank is concerned, but not as to clerical details.
>
> NORRIS: How many know nothing at all about the condition of the Bank?
>
> RUE: All the directors have a close knowledge of the affairs of the Bank as it is possible for men engaged in other active business.
>
> NORRIS: Have the directors full knowledge of the habits and general standing of the Bank's employees?
>
> RUE: It is impossible with upwards of 125 employees for the directors to possess full knowledge of the habits of the Bank's employees.[43]

After this examination, the affronted board wrote to the Comptroller to protest his right "to so interrogate its members."[44]

Appropriate expectations for supervision?

Although the public and Congress had relatively little tolerance for bank failures, as witnessed by the congressional hearings and pressure on the Comptroller to step up monitoring after the bank failures of the 1890s, the OCC lacked the resources and authority to vigorously police the national banks. The number of examiners was certainly modest and at times overstretched, leading many observers to conclude that examinations tended towards being cursory rather than thorough. Compensation of examiners exacerbated this problem, and the Comptroller had virtually no tools to discipline banks, except for suspension.

The OCC was certainly aware that it could not prevent bank failures, and Comptroller Knox wrote memorably in his 1881 *Annual Report* (p. 38): "It is scarcely to be expected, if a robber or a forger is place[d] in control of all its assets, that a national bank can be saved from disaster by the occasional visits of an examiner." This view changed little over the next twenty years, and at the 1912 examiners' convention, it was noted that "all examiners realize that so far as defalcations are concerned, the present system does not offer an absolute protection against loss."[45] While these statements reveal some frustration, they were also admissions that there were limits to what supervision could achieve. Yet the number of bank failures remained very small and the losses quite modest. Between 1865 and 1913, 540 banks were declared to be insolvent. Payments to depositors and other creditors totaled $146.9 million out of $191.0 million of proven claims, for a payout ratio of 76.9 percent. Total losses thus amounted to $44 million for this 50-year period.[46] In 2012 dollars, $44 million is approximately $1.2 billion, which was 0.3 percent of GDP in 1890. Compared with the much greater losses of the Great Depression (2.4 percent of GDP), the Savings & Loan Crisis (3.4 percent of GDP), and the Panic of 2008 (11.6 percent of GDP), the National Banking Era looks rather good.[47]

To explain this relative success, supervision needs to be seen as a complementary factor that supports and makes effective the incentives provided to stakeholders. The value of supervision certainly did not come from the enforcement of restrictive rules governing officers or the regulations imposed on banks, which were—as examinations revealed—violated, at times with impunity. For the depositors of national banks, published reports provided some information on the relative riskiness of these banks, making their banking choice more informed. But the shareholders were more central to ensuring that managers acted prudently. Double liability gave them extra reason to monitor directors and managers, and the public record of the shareholders reduced the likelihood that they would not have the resources or would shirk their added liability in the event of insolvency.[48] Directors who owned significant blocks of stock and had additional legal liability were perhaps even more sensitive to the potential of a failure. Given these incentives, the large number of voluntary closures—double the number of insolvencies as seen in Figure 6.1—may be appreciated as the response of shareholders and directors to close down banks that were unprofitable or weak before they became insolvent and saddled them with assessments to pay off the banks' depositors and other creditors. Generally, by guaranteeing good governance, rather than tough regulations, national bank supervision minimized losses during the National Banking Era.

Notes

1 For example, see Edwin W. Kemmerer, *Seasonal Variations in the Relative Demand for Money and Capital in the United States* (Washington, DC: National Monetary Commission, 1910); O. M. W. Sprague, *History of Crises under the National Banking System* (Washington, DC: National Monetary Commission, 1910); and Jeffrey A. Miron, "Financial Panics, the Seasonality of the Nominal Interest Rate, and the Founding of the Fed," *American Economic Review* 76, no. 1 (March 1986): 125–40.
2 For example, see Elmus Wicker, *Banking Panics of the Gilded Age* (New York: Cambridge University Press, 2000).
3 For details about the evolution of supervision by the states, see G. E. Barnett, *State Banks and Trust Companies* (Washington, DC: National Monetary Commission, 1911).
4 Hugh T. Rockoff, "The Free Banking Era: A Reexamination," *Journal of Money Credit and Banking* 6, no. 2 (May 1974): 141–67; Hugh T. Rockoff, "Varieties of Banking and Regional Development in the United States, 1840–60," *Journal of Economic History* 35, no. 1 (March 1975): 160–81; A. J. Rolnick and W. E. Weber, "New Evidence on the Free Banking Era," *American Economic Review* 73, no. 5 (December 1983): 1080–91.
5 Howard Bodenhorn, "Bank Chartering and Political Corruption in Antebellum New York. Free Banking as Reform," in *Corruption and Reform: Lessons from America's Economic History*, ed. Edward L. Glaeser and Claudia Goldin (Chicago: NBER and Chicago University Press, 2006), 231–58.
6 National Bank Act of 1864, available in Appendix C of Ross M. Robertson, *The Comptroller and Bank Supervision: A Historical Appraisal* (Washington, DC: Office of the Comptroller of the Currency, 1968). In 1900, to address competition from state-chartered banks, Congress lowered the minimum capital to $25,000 for new national banks in communities where the population was less than 3,000.
7 Bruce Champ, "The National Banking System: A Brief History," Federal Reserve Bank of Cleveland Working Paper 07–23 (December 2007), p. 7. In 1900, recognizing that these regulations were overly restrictive, the requirements were altered so that banks could issue notes up to 100 percent of the par or market value of the bonds, with a total note issue of up to 100 percent of their paid-in capital.
8 The Redistribution Act of 1874 required banks to keep reserves against deposits but not against circulation, though they had to maintain a 5 percent redemption fund with the Treasury that could be counted as reserves. The minimum legal reserve ratios were henceforth only calculated as a percentage of deposits. Champ, "The National Banking System," p. 14.
9 Quoted in Jonathan R. Macey and Geoffrey P. Miller, "Double Liability of Bank Shareholders: History and Implications," *Wake Forest Law Review* **27** (Spring 1992): 36.
10 U.S. Comptroller of the Currency, *Annual Report* (1881), 11.
11 The 1869 law permitted the Comptroller to call for special reports. Robertson, *The Comptroller and Bank Supervision*, 81.
12 A similar penalty applied if they failed to report the payment of a dividend within ten days.

13 National Bureau of Economic Research, "US Business Cycle Expansions and Contractions," available at http://nber.org/cycles/cyclesmain.html (accessed May 30, 2016).
14 Peter Garber and Vittorio Grilli, "The Belmont-Morgan Syndicate as an Optimal Investment Banking Contract," *European Economic Review* 30, no. 3 (June 1986): 649–77.
15 Hugh T. Rockoff, "The Wizard of Oz," *Journal of Political Economy* 98, no. 4 (August 1990): 739–60.
16 Benjamin C. Esty, "The Impact of Contingent Liability on Commercial Bank Risk Taking," *Journal of Financial Economics* 47, no. 2 (February 1998): 189–218.
17 Eugene N. White, *The Regulation and Reform of the American Banking System, 1900–1929* (Princeton, NJ: Princeton University Press, 1983): 22–23.
18 Robertson, *The Comptroller and Bank Supervision*, 76–7.
19 Robertson, *The Comptroller and Bank Supervision*, 78.
20 For details, see Robertson, *The Comptroller and Bank Supervision*, 76–79.
21 *New York Times*, July 9, 1912.
22 *New York Times*, July 9, 1912.
23 At this time, the fee structure for the central reserve city set by the Treasury was $90 for the first $1 million of capital and $10 for each additional $1 million, plus $10 for each $1 million of gross assets.
24 *New York Times*, July 9, 1912. The chief examiner for the New York Clearing House was paid a salary of $20,000.
25 RG 101, Records of the Office of the Comptroller of the Currency, Division of Reports, Weekly reports and vouchers of National Bank Examiners, 1896.
26 The state listed only refers to the state where the examiner sent his report. Examiners' territories were not contiguous with states' boundaries. For example, the examiner reporting from Rhode Island was Michael F. Dooley. From 1887 to 1899 he was the national bank examiner for Rhode Island and Connecticut. "Rhode Island and Providence Plantations Biographical," available at www.rootsweb.ancestry.com/~rigenweb/articles/133.html (accessed May 30, 2016).
27 Nicholas B. Wainwright, *History of the Philadelphia National Bank: A Century and a Half of Philadelphia Banking, 1803–1953* (Philadelphia: The Philadelphia National Bank, 1953), 167.
28 U.S. Comptroller of the Currency, *Annual Report* (1891), 26.
29 This description is drawn from the papers of A. Barton Hepburn deposited in the Archives of Columbia University.
30 The reports are found in Examiner Reports, 1864–1901, Division of Reports, Record Group 101, Records of the Office of the Comptroller of the Currency (hereafter RG 101), National Archives and Records Administration, College Park, Maryland (hereafter NARA-CP).
31 It does not appear that this was merely a pro forma collection of reports. On some examination reports, red check marks are visible, accompanied by initials, suggesting that the clerks or officers of the OCC closely inspected the reports and checked to make sure there was at least some compliance with regulations. The Comptroller's correspondence with each national bank is found in Division of Reports Correspondence, 1864–1901, RG 101, NARA-CP.
32 Letter to the Comptroller of the Currency, May 5, 1869, Charter 1, First National Bank of Philadelphia, Division of Reports Correspondence, 1864–1901, RG 101, NARA-CP.
33 Letter to the Comptroller, March 21, 1873, Charter 3, First National Bank of Youngstown, Ohio, Division of Reports Correspondence, 1864–1901, RG 101, NARA-CP.
34 Alonzo Barton Hepburn, Examiner's Book 1, July 29, 1891, Columbia University Archives, TN: 22586, Box 6, BibID 4078887.

35 Letter to the Comptroller of the Currency, March 21, 1873, Charter 3, First National Bank, Youngstown, Ohio, Division of Reports Correspondence, 1864–1901, RG 101, NARA-CP.
36 *New York Times*, July 9, 1912.
37 Quoted in Wainwright, *History of the Philadelphia National Bank*, 164.
38 Quoted in ibid.
39 Ibid., 165.
40 Alonzo Barton Hepburn, Examiner's Book 1, July 29, 1891, Columbia University Archives, TN: 22586, Box 6, BibID 4078887.
41 The post of chairman of the board only existed in a limited number of national banks late in the National Banking Era. The position of chairman of the board was created at the Philadelphia National Bank in 1907.
42 Merchant's National Bank, Examiner's Report, October 17, 1887, RG 101, Records of the Office of the Comptroller of the Currency, Division of Reports, Examiner Reports, 1864–1901, National Archives.
43 Quoted in Wainwright, *History of the Philadelphia National Bank*, 165.
44 Ibid.
45 *New York Times*, July 9, 1912.
46 Eugene N. White, "To Establish a More Effective Supervision of Banking: How the Birth of the Fed Altered Bank Supervision," in *The Origins, History and Future of the Federal Reserve: A Return to Jekyll Island*, ed. Michael D. Bordo and William Roberds (New York: Cambridge University Press, 2013), 29–30.
47 Ibid., 30.
48 Compelling payment after a bank failure remained difficult, and only 49 percent of shareholder assessments were paid in the 50-year period. White, "More Effective Supervision of Banking," 30.

Bibliography

Barnett, G. E. *State Banks and Trust Companies*. Washington, DC: National Monetary Commission, 1911.
Bodenhorn, Howard. "Bank Chartering and Political Corruption in Antebellum New York: Free Banking as Reform." In *Corruption and Reform: Lessons from America's Economic History*, edited by Edward L. Glaeser and Claudia Goldin, 231–58. Chicago: NBER and Chicago University Press, 2006.
Champ, Bruce, "The National Banking System: A Brief History," Federal Reserve Bank of Cleveland Working Paper 07–23 (December 2007).
Esty, Benjamin C. "The Impact of Contingent Liability on Commercial Bank Risk Taking." *Journal of Financial Economics* 47, no. 2 (February 1998): 189–218.
Garber, Peter, and Vittorio Grilli. "The Belmont-Morgan Syndicate as an Optimal Investment Banking Contract." *European Economic Review* 30, no. 3 (June 1986): 649–77.
Hepburn, A. Barton, Papers. Columbia University, Special Collections.
Kemmerer, Edwin W. *Seasonal Variations in the Relative Demand for Money and Capital in the United States*. Washington, DC: National Monetary Commission, 1910.
Macey, Jonathan R., and Geoffrey P. Miller. "Double Liability of Bank Shareholders: History and Implications." *Wake Forest Law Review* 27 (Spring 1992): 31–62.
Miron, Jeffrey A. "Financial Panics, the Seasonality of the Nominal Interest Rate, and the Founding of the Fed." *American Economic Review* 76, no. 1 (March 1986): 125–40.

National Bureau of Economic Research. "US Business Cycle Expansions and Contractions." Available at http://nber.org/cycles/cyclesmain.html (accessed May 30, 2016).

Record Group 101, Records of the Office of the Comptroller of the Currency. National Archives and Records Administration.

Robertson, Ross M. *The Comptroller and Bank Supervision: A Historical Appraisal.* Washington, DC: Office of the Comptroller of the Currency, 1968.

Rockoff, Hugh T. "The Free Banking Era: A Reexamination." *Journal of Money Credit and Banking* 6, no. 2 (May 1974): 141–67.

Rockoff, Hugh T. "Varieties of Banking and Regional Development in the United States, 1840–60." *Journal of Economic History* 35, no. 1 (March 1975): 160–81.

Rockoff, Hugh T. "The Wizard of Oz." *Journal of Political Economy* 98, no. 4 (August 1990): 739–60.

Rolnick, A. J., and W. E. Weber. "New Evidence on the Free Banking Era." *American Economic Review* 73, no. 5 (December 1983): 1080–91.

Sprague, O. M. W. *History of Crises under the National Banking System.* Washington, DC: National Monetary Commission, 1910.

U.S. Comptroller of the Currency. 1864–1929. Washington, DC: U.S. Government Printing Office.

U.S. Congress. *Hearings before the Committee on Banking and Currency, Reading System of Banking in the States and Territories.* 53rd Cong., 1st and 2nd sess. (1893–94).

Wainwright, Nicholas B. *History of the Philadelphia National Bank: A Century and a Half of Philadelphia Banking, 1803–1953.* Philadelphia: The Philadelphia National Bank, 1953.

White, Eugene N. *The Regulation and Reform of the American Banking System, 1900–1929.* Princeton, NJ: Princeton University Press, 1983.

White, Eugene N. "To Establish a More Effective Supervision of Banking: How the Birth of the Fed Altered Bank Supervision." In *The Origins, History and Future of the Federal Reserve: A Return to Jekyll Island*, edited by Michael D. Bordo and William Roberds, 7–54. New York: Cambridge University Press, 2013.

Wicker, Elmus. *Banking Panics of the Gilded Age.* New York: Cambridge University Press, 2000.

7 Founding the Fourth Branch
The Office of the Comptroller of the Currency

Jesse Stiller

Introduction

The National Currency Act of 1863 brought significant changes to the nation's financial, political, and government structure. Among them, as Jesse Stiller's essay explains, was the first independent federal regulatory agency—the Office of the Comptroller of the Currency. Stiller explores the circumstances surrounding the OCC's birth and how the intentions of the U.S. Congress were tested over the course of the agency's history.

Stiller is the OCC's Special Advisor for Executive Communications, a position that encompasses the role of agency historian and speechwriter for the Comptroller and other senior executives. He holds a Ph.D. from the City University Graduate School in New York City, where he worked under the supervision of the distinguished historian Arthur Schlesinger, Jr.

The views expressed in this chapter are those of the author alone, and do not necessarily reflect the views of the Office of the Comptroller of the Currency.

In his 1933 inaugural address, Franklin D. Roosevelt declared war on the Great Depression, asking Congress for executive power "as great as the power that would be given to me if we were in fact invaded by a foreign foe."[1] Congress complied. Over the next four years, federal spending rose 64 percent, 263,000 jobs were added in the executive branch alone, and three dozen new executive-branch agencies were created to carry out the president's program.[2]

Managing this expansion was a formidable challenge, as the 1933 White House lacked the resources to direct the process effectively. To coordinate the hundreds of programs and sub-programs that sprang up to implement the New Deal, the president had at his disposal dozens of clerks, personal assistants, and detailees from his executive departments. But there were at most a handful of high-level advisers who commanded his confidence and could legitimately claim to speak for the president. Without consistent, unified direction, executive-branch agencies frequently found themselves stepping on each other's toes and duplicating—or undermining—each other's work.

As his 1936 reelection campaign approached, Roosevelt felt compelled to address a growing perception that administrative disarray and the halting pace of economic recovery were not unrelated.[3] That summer he named three leading experts on public administration—Louis Brownlow, Luther Gulick, and Charles Merriam—to study the operation of the executive branch and, in particular, the president's executive office. The Brownlow Committee concluded that major changes in structure and procedure were needed to give the president administrative control commensurate with his responsibilities. The committee's report called for increased staffing, improved fiscal and auditing systems, rearrangement of the organization chart, and creation of the Executive Office of the President.[4]

None of these recommendations, however, touched on what the committee saw as a more fundamental threat to good government: the rise of what it called "a Fourth Branch" of government, the more than 100 "boards, commissions, administrations, authorities, corporations, and agencies" that performed various executive functions but, to a greater or lesser degree, answered to their own authority rather than that of the president.[5]

Several of these agencies, it noted, predated the New Deal. In 1883, Congress created the Civil Service Commission to build a merit system for federal employees—the first incarnation of the Fourth Branch, according to the Brownlow Committee. The second, it said, occurred in 1887, when the Interstate Commerce Commission was created to regulate common carriers.

Over time, the two became dozens. In 1933 alone, 17 agencies with independent characteristics were created either by congressional fiat or executive order. These agencies followed no single model of governance, representing almost as many combinations of powers, responsibilities, leadership, and funding arrangements as there were agencies. This diversity alone was enough to offend Brownlow and his colleagues, with their emphasis on regularity and orderliness. Their report blasted the Fourth Branch not merely as an affront to the principles of sound management, but also as an assault on "the basic theory of the American Constitution that there should be three major branches of the Government and only three."[6]

Brownlow's solution was simple: Congress should methodically merge each independent entity into the closest corresponding cabinet-level department, bringing all of them finally under direct presidential authority. But it was wrong to suggest that the Fourth Branch had arisen through inadvertence or error when, in fact, these agencies had been created deliberately to ensure that the people's business was done in the most professional way possible. In creating these agencies, Congress deemed the benefits of bureaucratic independence, expertise, and integrity to be worth the potential trade-offs in accountability, political inconvenience, and administrative complexity.[7]

Brownlow's account also missed a significant event in the history of the Fourth Branch. Two decades before the Civil Service Commission, in the midst of the Civil War, Congress had passed the National Currency Act, which established a new system of national currency, national banks, and a new federal agency, the Office of the Comptroller of the Currency, as their overseer. The new currency system aimed to provide both an infusion of funds into the beleaguered Treasury and a reliable money supply that would simultaneously promote patriotism and national commerce. The new banks were meant to be bastions of national authority, as well as collection and distribution points for the nation's financial capital. The new OCC was assigned the great responsibility—a responsibility that encompassed the work of the central bank and multiple financial regulatory agencies today—of administering this system, while developing and implementing laws and regulations aimed at ensuring public confidence in the banks that the OCC was empowered to license and supervise.

These goals were considered vital to the success of the Civil War effort, the post-war economy, and the permanence of the Union. Given the transcendent importance of those goals, Congress deliberately endowed the OCC with a broad structure that would enable it to operate independently—and a level of authority that no federal agency had possessed before. In making this break with the past, the NCA made a pivotal though mostly unrecognized contribution to the development of the modern administrative state.[8]

In recent years there has been a surge of scholarly interest in the evolution of the Fourth Branch, partly because of high-profile additions to its ranks. A key development in this connection was the Consumer Financial Protection Bureau (CFPB), a product of the Dodd–Frank Wall Street Reform and Consumer Protection Act of 2010. The CFPB's mission—and its independent structure—was controversial from the start. Dodd–Frank vested the CFPB's decision-making authority in a single director rather than a bipartisan board or commission, which would have been similar to the structure of the Federal Deposit Insurance Corporation (FDIC), the Federal Reserve, and many if not most other Fourth Branch agencies. Dodd–Frank placed the CFPB within the Federal Reserve, while specifically prohibiting the Fed from interfering in its rule-making and supervisory activities. It also provided that the CFPB would be funded not from congressional appropriations but rather from the resources of the Fed itself. The CFPB created by Dodd–Frank was then not just an independent agency, but also an independent agency within an independent agency, with two layers separating it from Congress and the public. At a time of broad distrust of government and doubts about government accountability, the CFPB was bound to become a lightning rod for renewed criticism of the Fourth Branch, and it did.

Yet, the structural features of the CFPB that so upset its detractors were little different from those assigned to the OCC more than a century earlier—a point sometimes emphasized by the CFPB and its defenders.[9] Like the CFPB, the OCC was organized to operate under a single agency head rather than a commission or board. The OCC was assigned an administrative home within the Treasury Department, with stipulations then and later that prevented the department from involving itself in the agency's decision making. And the NCA provided an independent funding mechanism for the most sensitive part of the OCC's work—the supervision of nationally chartered banks—to ensure that the agency would be free to do this work without concern about consequences for its appropriations and budget.

These provisions were intended to establish the OCC as a source of professionalism insulated from political intrigue and interference. No one said so on the record in the abbreviated congressional debate of 1863, which consumed no more than a few hours in both the House and Senate. That was all the time that a Congress beset by national crisis could afford to give it. "It is the misfortune of war," lamented Senator John Sherman, who was responsible for managing the bill in the upper chamber, "that we are compelled to act upon matters of grave importance without that mature deliberation secured in peaceful times." The quick process and lack of discussion virtually guaranteed that errors would go uncorrected—and that the importance of some of their work would make only a fleeting impression on history.[10]

What we do know about the thinking that gave rise to the NCA of 1863 comes largely from the discussion a year later, when Congress saw fit to revisit the banking issue and correct the inevitable oversights and mistakes. For colleagues who did not participate in the earlier debate, Senator William Pitt Fessenden (R-Maine) helpfully reminded them of the underlying, if unarticulated, principle Congress had embraced in the NCA. "It was felt," Fessenden recalled, "that this officer [the Comptroller] should be in a very particular degree independent of political changes and political considerations."[11] With his control over the nation's banking and money, he would wield enormous power—power that if suborned or misused could have catastrophic consequences.

The authors of the NCA understood the pernicious influence of politics in banking. Most states had required legislative approval for all bank charters, which opened the door to corruption that assumed epic proportions in states such as New York and Indiana (but then also led to reform in those and other states). Politicization made banks potentially less viable, less stable, and less useful to the communities they were supposed to serve. Their charters commonly required banks to undertake specific infrastructure investments, which led to the funding of projects that made little sense except on political grounds.[12] It is not surprising that some of the key leaders in the bid for a regulated national banking system—men such as Salmon P. Chase and John Sherman of Ohio, Zachariah Chandler of Michigan, and James Doolittle of Wisconsin—came from states where the relationship between politics and banking had been particularly troublesome. Their solution was to create a barrier between politics and banking, which is precisely what provisions of the NCA sought to achieve.[13]

Funding

The NCA provided two funding streams—one appropriated, the other independent—to support the OCC's operations. Its physical infrastructure was to be provided out of the Treasury's appropriation. Section 3 required Treasury to furnish the Comptroller with "suitable rooms in the treasury building." Because that building was not completed until 1868, the department wound up having to rent space around town for the Comptroller's use. The law also required that the Comptroller be provided with "safe and secure fire-proof vaults," two of which were added to the new Treasury building in 1864 for the Comptroller's specific purposes.[14]

The more important demand on Treasury resources was the task of starting up the new system of national currency. This was a labor-intensive proposition, involving the design, production, and distribution of the new currency, along with the collection and safekeeping of the government bonds deposited with the Comptroller as security. In 1870, this work consumed the energies of 74 clerks, copyists, and messengers, many of them women, whose salaries totaled $86,940. Another $54,000 of Treasury funds that year went toward the costs of such related items as dies, from which the notes were printed, and the paper they were printed on.[15]

Although these costs were not insignificant by the standards of the day, they were trivial by comparison to the income that the system produced for the government. The NCA assessed a tax of one percent on national currency, which, over a 50 year period, yielded revenues of more than $155 million. It can readily be seen, then, that the $21 million in OCC operating costs over the same period was more akin to an investment than an expense. Less easily calculated, though no less valuable, was the benefit that flowed from the lower interest rate the government paid for its debt as a result of the demand for bonds generated by national banks.[16]

Starting in 1875, the volume of national bank currency began to decline, as the economics of holding government bonds became less favorable to the banks. The public began to rely increasingly on checkable deposits rather than cash, and political support for the system began to wane. For these and other reasons, the last national bank notes were issued in 1935, their role largely filled by currency issued by the Federal Reserve. With that change, the Comptroller's currency functions were increasingly centered on the collection and retirement of the notes still circulating. Accordingly, the costs associated with those functions, which since 1913 were being absorbed by the Federal Reserve banks rather than the Treasury, steadily declined. By 1953, of a total agency budget of around $8 million, only $147,000 was attributable to currency operations.[17]

The rest of the budget, reflecting what had become the agency's exclusive mission, was earmarked for bank regulation and supervision, which has always been funded through assessments against national banks. Initially this was in the form of fees paid by banks to their examiners. Under section 51 of the NCA, OCC bank examiners were to be paid at the flat rate of $5.00 per day plus $2.00 for every 25 miles traveled. In 1875 this arrangement was changed so that examiners were paid according to a sliding scale based on the size of the bank's capital (later, its assets), to better reflect the time and complexity involved in its supervision. This made sense, but it did not address the basic flaw in a system that incentivized examiners to rush through examinations so as to get on to another bank and another fee. Not until 1914 were examiners placed on salary, which largely eliminated that tension.

There was some precedent for government agents to be paid by the business they inspected. In response to a rash of steamboat boiler explosions in the 1830s, Congress authorized inspectors to collect $5.00 per hull and $5.00 per boiler from the operators. But until the creation of the Steamboat Inspection Service in 1872, which placed the inspectors under a central authority, they were merely independent freelancers with a federal license to perform a professional service for their commercial customers at the customer's behest and expense. As for the steamboat operators themselves, they were free to hire an inspector and accept the inspection recommendations—or not. Nothing in the law compelled them to do so.[18]

By contrast, national bank examiners from the beginning were symbols of government authority whose findings carried the weight of law. There was nothing optional about national bank examinations. Section 51 called for examinations to take place "as often as shall be deemed necessary and proper," which section 21 of the Federal Reserve Act of 1913 refined to require that all Fed member banks (which by statute included all national banks) be examined "at least twice in each calendar years and oftener if considered necessary."

The standing arrangement for examiner compensation was intended to dispel any notion that they were self-employed contractors: national banks did not hand over the fees for examination and travel directly to the examiner, which would have been the simplest approach. Instead, banks remitted those fees to Washington, where examiners' claims for the amounts due to them were processed and payment issued.

Tenure and removal

The preamble of the NCA provided that the Comptroller "shall hold his office for the term of five years unless sooner removed by the President, by and with the advice and consent of the Senate." Within this single sentence were two significant breaks with previous practice: a fixed term of office for a presidential appointee and limits on the president's power to remove him.

There was some precedent for the fixed term. Before the postmaster generalship was converted into a cabinet-level position in 1829, the postmaster's tenure expired at the end of each congressional session—the rationale being that the office was too important a source of patronage to be entrusted to a single person for any longer than that. Here the fixed term was intended to prevent that person from enjoying the benefits of the job for more than two years—not to prevent him from being removed sooner.

In another case, in 1801, Congress empowered the president to appoint justices of the peace for the District of Columbia to five-year terms. The evidence is more ambiguous here, but Congress seems to have viewed these positions as akin to auditions for federal judgeships, with their lifetime tenure. Because these lesser positions were expected to go to lesser candidates, it was thought imprudent to entrust them with permanence until they had proved their integrity and competence. In this case, then, fixed terms provided a means for the executive branch to be easily rid of provisional incumbents found not to be up to the job.

Perhaps the best-known precedent for the fixed term involves the Tenure of Office Act, enacted in 1820 and repealed in 1835. It established a four-year term for certain presidential appointees, mostly Treasury Department fiduciaries such as customs collectors, land agents, disbursing officers, and paymasters previously removable only for cause. The legislation's authors argued that fixed terms were needed to promote financial accountability. Opponents claimed that the real goal was to get officeholders out of their jobs without having to fire them, so as to make way for a new crop of political loyalists. Either way, both in this case and in those relating to the Post Office and the DC judiciary, the goal was to give elected officials more control over patronage appointments and not less. In the NCA, Congress had the opposite goal: to impose a statutory limit on the president's removal power.[19]

That the Currency Act coupled the five-term term with the requirement that the president obtain the "advice and consent" of the Senate to remove the Comptroller suggests that Congress saw the two provisions as complementary parts of the plan to ensure the Comptroller's independence. The fixed term, it recognized, might be meaningless if there was nothing to stop the person appointed to the position from being removed without cause at any time. Of course, the provisions of the NCA did not rule out the possibility that a Senate friendly to the White House might concur in a politically motivated removal. But the "advice and consent" requirement would certainly make any such attempt more complicated.

By 1864, the improving military and financial picture had taken some of the pressure off Congress, allowing it to address its agenda at a more deliberate pace and to revisit legislation, such as the NCA, that might have benefited from greater deliberation the first time around. Some of the Currency Act's deficiencies were merely technical, and the first Comptroller, Hugh McCulloch of Indiana, addressed these issues in a revision submitted to Congress for its consideration.

What really nagged at lawmakers, though, was the "advice and consent" provision, which, upon reconsideration, they recognized had the potential to reignite one of the country's oldest constitutional controversies. In 1789, in the bill creating the Department of Foreign Affairs (later the Department of State), Congress had decided that the president had a preexisting constitutional power to remove executive officers. That was not an exclusive authority, for Congress could always legally remove executive-branch officials by terminating funding for the position, eliminating the relevant agency or department, or impeaching the incumbent. Nor was that authority universally subscribed to. Alexander Hamilton, among others, had argued that all officials confirmed by the Senate could be removed *only* with the consent of the Senate. Long after 1789, there remained a school of thought, albeit a minority, that Congress was within its constitutional rights to assert itself in removal actions—an opinion expressed, for example, in the Senate's 1833 decision to censure Andrew Jackson, in part for removing William Duane as his Secretary of the Treasury in 1833.[20]

Nonetheless, Senator Fessenden was correct when he conceded that the right to block a presidential removal was "a doctrine that has never been acceded to heretofore." The question was whether it was worth asserting in connection with the Comptroller's independence. Some members believe it definitely was. When Fessenden reported a new draft out of the Finance Committee with the "advice and consent" language expunged, Senator James W. Grimes (R-IA) demanded to know "what change has come over the spirit of the dream of the Finance Committee" to prevent the Comptroller "from being a mere political officer, as he doubtless will be, if he is to be turned out without any consultation with the Senate." Fessenden explained his constitutional concerns, but also offered a practical reason why the president should be free to deal with the Comptroller as he saw fit. Under the NCA, he pointed out, the Comptroller would "wield an immense power" over the national banking and monetary systems—power that, if he chose to use it unwisely, could "in the course of a very short time . . . produce the most disastrous effects." "It will be difficult to say," Fessenden concluded, "that the President should not have the power to remove him if he was found to be exercising the power of his office in that way" and to do so immediately if the Senate happened to be out of session.[21]

Senator Charles R. Buckalew (D-PA) sought to break the stalemate with an amendment giving the president power to remove the Comptroller "upon reasons to be communicated by him to the Senate." In this way, Buckalew explained, "we do not check the power of the President, but we limit his discretion" to remove the Comptroller without compelling reason to do so. That was essential, he added, so that the president did "not have combined in him all power over the purse of the country and the money affairs of the country further than it is absolutely necessary." For Buckalew, the removal provision was a means of reinforcing Congress's financial authority.

Some Senators saw the Buckalew amendment as tantamount to no removal restriction at all. What if the president refused to communicate his reasons for removal, asked Senator Jacob Howard (R-MI). "Would [the Comptroller] or would he not be actually removed? Would he remain in office because the president had not given reasons for his . . . removal?" Despite these questions, the motion carried, and President Lincoln signed the revised National Currency legislation on June 3, 1864.[22]

But would it have any practical effect on the Comptroller's independence or was it, as some Senators suggested, merely a face-saving acknowledgment of the president's unlimited authority to remove executive branch officials at will? Time would tell.

The removal power in practice

It took more than a century to get a definitive answer to the question. In 1961, President John F. Kennedy named James J. Saxon, a native Ohioan, to be Comptroller. Saxon had held a desk job at the OCC during the late 1930s until World War II took him away for five years of military intelligence work in Europe, North Africa, and the South Pacific. His OCC experience is probably why he declined Kennedy's offer of the far more visible position as Commissioner of Internal Revenue and asked for what he knew to be the more powerful and independent position as Comptroller—power and independence he was determined to use.[23]

Unfortunately, the job to which Saxon was appointed had an incumbent already in it. That person was Ray M. Gidney, the 17th Comptroller of the Currency. With Kennedy's election, Gidney's days in office were obviously numbered. He was a Republican, having been first appointed in 1953 and then reappointed to a second term as Comptroller by President Eisenhower in 1958. He was a septuagenarian in an administration that made much of youthful vigor. His policies—particularly his support of bank mergers—had offended powerful interests, including community bankers and their chief defender in Congress, House Banking Committee Chairman Wright Patman (D-TX). The anti-trust implications of those policies had also raised hackles at the Justice Department, soon to be headed by Robert Kennedy.

Gidney's exit to make way for Saxon was executed with comic ineptitude. At a press conference on the afternoon of September 20, Kennedy's Press Secretary Pierre Salinger announced that Saxon's name had been sent to the Senate for confirmation. When a reporter pointed out that Gidney was still on the job—and had two years left in his term—Salinger abruptly cancelled the news briefing. In the evening, Treasury issued a statement withdrawing Saxon's nomination and blaming the confusion on a "clerical error." Gidney was dumbfounded. "It is all news to me," was all he could say when questioned by reporters.[24] Later that evening he was summoned from home to the Treasury Department, where he and Secretary C. Douglas Dillon composed a resignation letter, to become effective on November 15. The next day, the president "accepted" Gidney's resignation, for which he was "most appreciative." Considering the potential for additional embarrassment had Gidney not chosen to go gracefully, the administration's appreciation was undoubtedly heartfelt.[25]

This was hardly the first time in history that the nation's Comptroller had stepped aside in response to presidential pressure. Some number of the early comptrollers yielded to that pressure, which was usually exerted when the White House changed hands. Of the first ten men to hold this position, only three served full five-year terms. Of the next seven, five immediately accepted senior positions in banking, which offered compensatory benefits.[26]

The "communication" provision was designed to protect those who refused to yield to such informal pressure, and Saxon was among those who did resist. No sooner had he moved into the office vacated by Gidney than he began using his power aggressively against the business and bureaucratic interests he viewed as obstacles to modernization of the banking system. That group included travel agents, insurance companies, and stockbrokers, who operated in markets sheltered from competition from banks. It further included the state banking commissioners, the Federal Reserve, the FDIC, the Securities and Exchange Commission (SEC), the Department of Justice, the Treasury Department, and the White House itself. Saxon viewed them all as defenders of a hidebound status quo. When the president of the American Bankers Association issued a public call for interagency harmony, Saxon turned on him, too: "You seem to regard the past thirty years of inaction in banking policy as an example of what can be accomplished through the 'coordination of effort' among the regulatory agencies."[27]

When Lyndon B. Johnson became president in 1963, all Kennedy appointees became vulnerable, and Saxon's enemies seized the opportunity, peppering the Johnson White House with letters demanding his removal. Some administrative officials weighed in with critical but more nuanced evaluations of Saxon's service and offenses. In a memo to Johnson dated March 19, 1964, for example, Treasury Secretary C. Douglas Dillon made it clear that he had no use for Saxon's methods, while acknowledging that he was "right in most of his basic objectives."[28]

Thus, in January 1965, in compliance with the "communication" clause of the NBA, a letter was prepared for Johnson's signature and submission to the Senate, stating that Saxon was being removed because "I no longer have full confidence in his ability to discharge his duties effectively and with the necessary coordination between his office and other agencies of government."[29] But there was reason to believe that this vague statement would not satisfy the Senate Banking Committee, whose chairman, A. Willis Robertson (D-VA), had long admired Saxon and shared his deregulatory agenda.[30] The White House's concern was that Robertson would respond by calling for public hearings, at which it would undoubtedly emerge that Saxon's chief misdeed was offending powerful interest groups in pursuing the mission of his office. Indeed, an attempt to oust him two years earlier, orchestrated by state banking officials, had backfired when he was summoned to appear before Patman's House committee to answer charges of overstepping his authority. If anything, Saxon emerged, as one newspaper put it, "stronger than ever," having turned on his not inconsiderable charm and his unarguable mastery of banking and banking law. He also received "a powerful assist from his opponents," who "so overstated their case against him" that their credibility was badly damaged.[31] With this history in mind, and with a mere 10 months remaining in Saxon's five-year term, his removal was ultimately judged to be more trouble than it was worth. Johnson never signed the removal letter, and Saxon served to the last day of his term, as he vowed he would.

Supporters of the communication requirement in 1864 had argued that, while it would not stop a president from removing a Comptroller for violating his oath of office, it would make the president think twice about removing that official for political reasons. The Saxon affair vindicated that argument.

The Treasury connection

The NCA provided that the Comptroller's office be "established in the treasury department" as "a separate bureau." So the OCC was both "in" the department and "separate" from it. These apparently contradictory provisions defined the novel concept of an agency that was a component of Treasury for many administrative purposes, but that set and implemented policy almost wholly apart from it. Indeed, that is a fair description of the OCC's status more than 150 years later.

A reference in the 1863 legislation offers further insight into what Congress meant for the Treasury–OCC relationship to be. Section 60 declares it the Comptroller's duty "to report annually to *congress*" [italics added] on the expenditures of the office and the condition of national banks, along with recommendations for "any amendment to the laws relative to banking by which the system may be improved." This pertained specifically to a written report, but it became more broadly applicable to testimony and other communications with Capitol Hill. How much consultation took place between the Comptroller and the Treasury secretary was entirely at the Comptroller's discretion.

Most of the other provisions of the NCA relating to the Treasury–OCC relationship had to do with the mechanics of the national currency system that the legislation created. The function required extensive coordination between the Treasury, which marketed the bonds national banks were obliged to purchase for the privilege of issuing circulating notes, and the Comptroller's office, which, as noted, was responsible for the mechanics of printing and distributing those notes.

The legislation also dealt with a function that, while fundamentally administrative, was far more consequential. The preamble of the Currency Act authorized the Secretary, rather than the Comptroller, to appoint a deputy comptroller and the office's clerical staff. Section 51 authorized the Comptroller to appoint bank examiners, subject to the Secretary's "approbation." Section 26 authorized the Comptroller, with the Secretary's "concurrence," to appoint "special agents" to investigate a bank's failure to redeem its notes. Section 41 empowered the Comptroller to appoint receivers, again, with a "concurrence" requirement.

These limitations on the Comptroller's appointments stemmed from a longstanding fear in Congress about concentrating patronage power within a single office. In worrying aloud about the law's unprecedented grant of power to the Comptroller and how that power might be abused, Senator Fessenden was speaking specifically about the banks and the money supply. But he and others were clearly concerned that the Comptroller might take improper advantage of his broad hiring authority. Giving the Secretary the final authority over hiring seemed to address that concern.

Having received that authority, Treasury Secretary Salmon P. Chase declined to use it. "Manage … the Bureau in your own way," he told the first

Comptroller, Hugh McCulloch. "When you need clerks, and as you need them, send their names to me and they will be appointed."[32] And "in no instance while I was Comptroller," McCulloch emphasized, "was an appointment made for the bureau which was not at my request."[33] For Chase, a diligent dispenser of patronage, such restraint was evidence of his own belief in the importance of the Comptroller's independence, as stipulated in the law he had been instrumental in framing. It also meant that McCulloch had to contend directly with pressure from office-seekers that would have fallen on Chase instead, which became a source of unending irritation to him.[34]

The power to appoint examiners, receivers, and other supervisory personnel remained both a burden and a blessing for future Comptrollers. Examiner positions were repeatedly exempted from the competitive civil service by executive orders, despite the insistence of the Civil Service Commission that they should be included.[35] For examiners, an informal hiring process prevailed for much of the twentieth century: junior examiners were recruited primarily from the ranks of bank employees upon the recommendation of OCC examiners who had worked with and observed them in the course of examinations. "It is not believed," one Comptroller declared, "that any other method of recruitment would be as satisfactory or would provide personnel of the same quality and competency."[36] But this approach also offered temptations that not all Comptrollers or elected officials could resist.[37]

Patronage pressures, among other factors, made McCulloch increasingly doubtful that the OCC would ever achieve the level of professionalism and independence that its duties demanded. That is why in his last annual report as Comptroller, he ventured a remarkable proposal. Congress, he argued, should cut all ties between the OCC and the Treasury Department and move the office to Philadelphia or New York City, closer to the most important national banks and far from the tumult of national politics. Freeman Clarke, McCulloch's successor, couched the proposal as an efficiency measure, predicting annual savings of $200,000 a year in shipping and travel costs.[38] But, for McCulloch, this was all about conducting the office's business in the most professional way possible. "It is of the greatest importance," he wrote, "that the national currency system should be independent of politics and freed from political influences."[39]

There is no evidence Congress considered this audacious proposal. It may already have had reason to regret that it had gone as far as it did to place the Comptroller's business beyond its reach. But McCulloch understood that operating in a political environment would make it more difficult for the Comptroller to supervise the national banking system in an objective, independent manner. Those who followed him into office would learn this for themselves.

Bank supervision meets politics: two case studies

Controversy between the Franklin D. Roosevelt White House and the independent federal banking agencies, of which there were three by 1934, fed the Brownlow critique of the Fourth Branch. One significant difference was that the newcomers, the Federal Reserve and the Federal Deposit Insurance Corporation, were not bound administratively to the Treasury, which narrowed the administration's influence. But the White House thought it *could* exert its influence over the OCC, and thereby influence the disposition of the nation's banking assets, the majority of which were held by national banks. A revival of bank lending was key to a sustainable recovery, and the OCC's assignment was to use its authority to get America's banks lending again.

Heading that effort would be Comptroller J.F.T. (James Francis Thaddeus) O'Connor, also known as "Jefty," who Roosevelt nominated in 1933. O'Connor, a North Dakota lawyer who had moved to California after the failure of a family-owned bank,[40] was among the most political of comptrollers. He cherished a personal relationship with the president, with whom he met regularly. He liked to consort with celebrities,[41] give entertaining press conferences, and use his appointment power to collect IOUs he hoped to call in at such time that he would run for higher office.[42] More importantly, from the administration's standpoint, O'Connor had an extensive network of contacts in the banking business he was expected to mobilize in support of the New Deal.

That bank lending had dropped off dramatically was beyond dispute. In 1934, total loans by commercial banks were about half of their level in 1930. There were many factors at work: weak balance sheets, fewer creditworthy borrowers, gun-shy lenders, and, last but not least, bank examiners determined not to allow anything resembling imprudent banking to happen again on their watch. Indeed, a Treasury Department study commissioned to sort out the finger-pointing found "conclusive evidence" that examiners were waging "a campaign against certain types of loans," especially long-term commercial and real estate loans, and were demanding that banks use current depressed market values in evaluating collateral. Bankers and examiners alike, the study found, were "obsessed with liquidity."[43] That was understandable in the wake of the recent bloodbath. But that mindset had to go away if the economy was to move forward.

The administration's assumption was that concerted arm-twisting would bring federal bank examiners into line and, through them, make credit more available. It soon became clear that this approach was overly optimistic. Career examiners, it turned out, took their independence every bit as seriously as the agency higher-ups. Practically speaking, it was extremely difficult for Washington-based managers to discipline or retrain employees operating hundreds or even thousands of miles away. An earlier Comptroller had divided the country into regions with local managers to better coordinate field operations, but distance, poor communications, and the fact that examiners were almost always in travel status frustrated these efforts. The typical examiner still considered himself as a free agent, accustomed "to operat[ing] largely on the basis of his own ideas, rules of thumb, and past experience," "doing things their way," as a staff report to Treasury Secretary Morgenthau pointed out.[44]

Thus, O'Connor met considerable resistance in carrying out the administration's directives. In response to complaints from bankers sent to Roosevelt—and passed on to O'Connor during their meetings—the Comptroller dashed off a paper to field examiners who, he said, seemed to "have lost sight of the President's recovery program and its relation to licensed banks," instructing them, in evaluating collateral, "not [to] apply liquidating values," but rather to apply the "fair values" likely to return when the economy recovered. Examiners, he directed, should review their recent examination reports and rewrite those that did not reflect this guidance. In March 1934, O'Connor issued another broadside to the field, directed specifically to examiners who "have not fully grasped the meaning" of the earlier guidance. O'Connor now ordered supervisory examiners to identify the recalcitrant examiners and provide retraining until each examiner understood that he was expected to be "as lenient as circumstances in each case will permit."[45]

If this were not enough—and it apparently wasn't—Secretary Morgenthau brought senior examination personnel from the OCC and other banking agencies to Washington in September 1934 for a conference (the first of several, as it turned out) and a good scolding. Then the examiners broke into smaller groups where they were assigned to think of ways to reduce the regulatory burden on bankers. Much of what they reported out would make for cosmetic changes only—an agreement, for example, that examiners would no longer use the term "slow" to describe delinquent longer-term credits—even though, in when these loans came due, "slow" was exactly what they were. Henceforward examiners agreed to dispense with adjectives altogether to rate loans, resorting instead to Roman numerals corresponding to categories of substandard assets.[46]

Predictably, none of this had much effect on lending. Only with the coming of World War II did bank lending rise to pre-Depression levels. Roosevelt continued to hear complaints from bankers about overly aggressive examiners, which drastically cooled his affection for O'Connor. During their one-on-one at the White House on October 3, 1934, Roosevelt hoped to entice O'Connor to leave office by extending him an offer of a position at the Federal Reserve Bank in San Francisco. It would pay him twice his Comptroller's salary of $12,000, the president was quick to point out, and return him to California, where he might pursue his political ambitions.[47]

O'Connor declined the offer. But his political position had greatly weakened, and Secretary Morgenthau, who distrusted O'Connor's relationship with bankers and resented his access to Roosevelt, took the opportunity to further reduce the OCC's independence within the administration. Late in 1934, Morgenthau presented O'Connor with a memorandum for his signature, under which the OCC would submit to Treasury all recommendations for appointments, all press releases, and all correspondence to the White House and other executive departments. Most importantly, Treasury demanded the disbandment of the Comptroller's legal staff, which would be reassigned to the Department.

"The raid is on," O'Connor noted tersely in his diary.[48] The only person who could stop it was Roosevelt, and, on September 11, 1934, O'Connor wrote a personal appeal for presidential support in blocking a plan that "will destroy the efficiency of my Bureau. Under my oath of office," O'Connor continued, "I cannot be party to the destruction of my Bureau of the Currency or the impairment of its efficiency. I would rather resign."[49]

Morgenthau did not abandon his plan to reduce OCC independence, and O'Connor did not resign until 1938, when he returned to California to run—and lose—in the gubernatorial primary. Roosevelt would later appoint him a federal court judge. But no sooner was he gone than Treasury promulgated a directive bringing OCC attorneys under the control of the Treasury chief counsel.[50] That arrangement remained in effect until 1989.[51]

Baltimore 1991

The challenge to OCC independence was greatly facilitated by O'Connor's replacement. Preston Delano, a distant relative of Roosevelt's, was a docile bureaucrat who was confirmed to office in 1938, a second time in 1943, and a third time in 1948, making him the second longest-serving Comptroller in history. This could not have been unrelated to his willingness to bow to the dictates of Morgenthau and his successors. He received some criticism for yielding too easily to the department's pressure, criticism that Delano rejected as a practical matter. "The Secretary of the Treasury," Delano wrote in his memoirs, "has so many guns and such authority ... that the Comptroller, if forced to the wall, has little choice but to follow the Secretary's wishes."[52] Saxon would no doubt have disagreed.[53]

The lesson, which was later reinforced by Saxon's tumultuous tenure in the 1960s, was that the best way to limit the independence of the OCC was to appoint lower-profile, more malleable people to fill the job. Saxon's successor, William B. Camp, a career bank examiner who was temperamentally his opposite, won his job in large part for that reason.

But the loss of Saxon-like leadership did not immediately translate into a less independent OCC. Instead, it hastened the power shift from Washington to the field examiners, a shift that was already evident in O'Connor's time. With improvements in communications and transportation in the years since, examiners who traditionally worked in near isolation and were likely to spend their entire OCC careers in a single location could take advantage of greater mobility and greater access to the agency's collective expertise. More frequent interactions, in turn, strengthened professional cohesion and resolve.

The banking crisis of the 1980s and early 1990s illustrated the growing power of career examiners. The crisis was largely rooted in the collapse of oil and gas prices, which triggered a major recession in the southwestern states. Between 1987 and 1989, 491 banks, including some of region's largest, failed. The crisis soon rippled beyond the energy sector to other areas of vulnerability, commercial real estate foremost among them. Attracted by large up-front fees and favorable changes to the tax laws, banks throughout the country had financed a big increase in retail and office space, in particular; in 1990, commercial real estate loans represented 27 percent of total bank assets, compared to 18 percent in 1980. Banks in New Jersey and New England, serving expanding high-tech and defense sectors, had exceptionally high exposures to these loans.[54]

These banks came under more intensive scrutiny from OCC examinations teams, comprising local examiners and veterans of Texas and Oklahoma brought in to assist. Their reputations preceded them: bankers who had not already been required to write down their commercial real estate loans anticipated that they would soon be forced to do so, possibly eroding capital to the point of insolvency. The failure of the $22 billion Bank of New England, a regional flagship, brought home these anxieties. Bank credit seemed to become harder to come by, and well-publicized anecdotes about otherwise sound borrowers being turned away contributed to a deepening psychology of capital scarcity.

To hear some bankers, this was all the examiners' own doing, and they demanded that the examiners' presumed political superiors do something about it. At a 1991 White House meeting with President George H.W. Bush and his top economic advisers, the powerful CEO of the North Carolina National Bank (soon to be NationsBank), Hugh McColl, put the issue in simplistic terms. "The problem you all have is that you think you are running this country, and you are not," he told the president and his men. "There is only one man running this country, and he is not in this room." He was referring to veteran OCC examiner Joseph Hooks, a veteran of the energy crisis now on assignment on the East Coast. "Hell, he's famous," McColl continued, warming to his subject. "He's the grim reaper. He marches into banks' real estate divisions and shuts them down." The best thing the president could do for the country, McColl offered, was to transfer Hooks to Alaska.[55]

All this had a distinct feel of 1934, except for one thing. Unlike O'Connor, Comptroller Robert L. Clarke defended the agency's examiners, who were now under attack from two sides: those who believed that the OCC had not acted quickly or decisively enough to close troubled banks, which magnified losses to the taxpayer-backed bank insurance fund; and those in the administration and in the banking industry who charged that tough supervision was responsible for a "credit crunch" that they believed was a major contributor to the national recession that began in July 1990. An unfortunate line in a Clarke speech referring to himself as the "regulator from hell," intended to be ironic, was interpreted as confirmation that examiners backed by their bosses were not only forcing banks to cut back on their loans, but were indifferent to the consequences of tight credit.

There was considerable doubt at the time about the validity of these charges, and subsequent research has discredited the notion that the tight credit and the recession of 1990–91 were cause and effect. No doubt a substantial number of sound borrowers were rejected by bankers whose sensitivity to credit risk had been heightened in their conversations with examiners. But studies have showed that what politicians were calling a credit crunch was primarily a drop in loan demand, as borrowers tried to work off surplus inventories, especially in commercial real estate and related fields during an economic slowdown.[56]

Nonetheless, in December 1991, the administration summoned some 500 senior bank regulators to Baltimore, where Treasury Secretary Nicholas Brady and other top officials delivered a "gentle chiding" about "too-tough" examination standards and the credit crunch.[57] Gentle or not, most examiners probably agreed with the FDIC examiner who rose from his seat to criticize Brady for telling them how to do their jobs. The relaxation of credit awaited the recovery in commercial real estate that did not occur until 1995.[58]

There is reason to think that the Bush administration's regulatory gambit in the 1990s was political theater more than anything else, intended to show that it would go to any length to revive the economy but without illusions that pressuring regulators would do much to accomplish that goal. Just months earlier, Secretary Brady had overcome the opposition of White House Chief of Staff John Sununu and convinced the president to nominate Clarke for a second term as Comptroller. That was a curious way of holding him accountable for the credit crunch.[59] The nomination was in part an expression of personal respect for Clarke, a Texan who had pulled no punches in dealing with failing banks and friendly bankers in his home state. Clarke's reappointment was also an expression of respect for the integrity and independence of the office and the new and existing laws that protected it. The Financial Institutions Regulatory Reform and Enforcement Act (FIRREA) of 1989 gave the OCC authority to provide its employees with pay and benefits comparable to those offered by the Federal Reserve and the FDIC, which were not subject to civil service pay ceilings. This freedom enabled the OCC to better compete with those agencies and the private sector to recruit and retain professional staff. Then, in the Riegle–Neal Interstate Banking and Branching Efficiency Act of 1994, Congress restored the OCC's legal authority revoked by Morgenthau in 1938 and instructed the Secretary of the Treasury never to "delay or prevent" any rule or regulation that the agency might issue. Thus, in important respects, the OCC emerged from the worst financial crisis since the Great Depression (a distinction later ceded to the 2007–9 crisis) with its independence not only intact, but also strengthened.

Conclusion

Since 1937, when the Brownlow Committee coined the term by which the independent agencies are collectively known today, there have been a number of attempts to enumerate and define the characteristics that qualify a federal agency as independent. One legal scholar focused on the central role of budgetary independence, arguing that "self-funded agencies are likely the most structurally ... independent agencies in the federal government."[60] Another offered a matrix of 50 structural characteristics, funding among them, arguing that an agency's independence can be measured in terms of how many of those characteristics it possesses.[61]

By either standard, the National Currency Act of 1863 created a new kind of government entity—one that belonged both to the executive and legislative branches, but that was dependent on neither. In an act of historic self-denial, Congress cut the OCC loose from its own budgetary controls, an arrangement that was only acceptable politically because the president and the Treasury Department were willing to accept significant constraints on their own authority over the Comptroller's actions. As the legislative history of the NCA and future enactments shows, Congress meant both to build on and break with the past in creating the agency that the OCC became.

What Congress did in 1863 was not completely without precedent. Nothing ever is. The founders of the national banking system drew on their own experience and the innovations of others in doing their work. That experience shaped the view that politics and sound banking were incompatible, and that a new kind of government entity was necessary for the nation to enjoy the benefits that safe and sound banks under federal authority would provide.

Notes

1 The text of the address is available at http://avalon.law.yale.edu/20th_century/froos1.asp (accessed May 30, 2016).
2 "Summary of Receipts, Outlays, and Surpluses or Deficits," at https://www.whitehouse.gov/omb/budget/Historicals, Table 1.1 (accessed May 30, 2016); U.S. Bureau of Labor Statistics, Handbook of Labor Statistics (Washington, 1942), p. 181.
3 Matthew L. Dickinson, *Bitter Harvest: FDR, Presidential Power, and the Growth of the Presidential Branch* (Cambridge, UK: Cambridge University Press, 1996), pp. 45–85, 91–92.
4 The President's Committee on Administrative Management, *Administrative Management in the Government of the United States* (Washington, D.C: U.S. Government Printing Office, 1937), pp. 3, 36. Cited hereafter as the *Brownlow Report*. Available at http://users.polisci.wisc.edu/kmayer/408/Report%20of%20 the%20Presidents%20Committee.pdf (accessed May 30, 2016). An assessment of the committee's work, prepared by a former member of the committee staff, is James W. Fesler, "The Brownlow Committee Fifty Years Later," *Public Administration Review*, 47:4 (July–August 1987), pp. 291–6.
5 *Brownlow Report*, pp. 29–30.
6 *Brownlow Report*, pp. 32–40.
7 *Brownlow Report*, pp. 31–3.
8 In one of the few references to the OCC in this context, the U.S. Senate website notes that Lincoln signed into law a measure granting independence to the "controller [sic] of the treasury." The "comptroller of the treasury," largely an accounting position, did exist, but only until 1817. See http://www.senate.gov/artandhistory/history/common/briefing/Nominations.htm (accessed May 30, 2016).
9 See David H. Carpenter, "The Consumer Financial Protection Bureau: A Legal Analysis," Congressional Research Service, CRS Report 7–5700, January 14, 2014, p. 12, fn. 65. See also Stacy Mitchell, "Why Republicans Hate Warren's CFPB But Love Another Bank Regulator," Institute for Local Self Reliance, March 18, 2011, available at http://ilsr.org/why-republicans-hate-warrens-cfpb-love-another-bank-regulator (accessed May 30, 2016).

10 *Congressional Globe*, 37th Congress, 3rd session, February 10, 1863, p. 840.
11 *Congressional Globe*, 38th Congress, 1st session, April 26, 1864, p. 1865.
12 Howard Bodenhorn, *State Banking in Early America: A New Economic History* (New York: Oxford University Press, 2003), pp. 85–6.
13 Fritz Redlich, *The Molding of American Banking: Men and Ideas* (1951; reprinted by Mansfield Center, CT: Martino Fine Books, 2012), v. II: 87, 104, 108.
14 "History of the Treasury Building," available at http://www.treasury.gov/about/education/Pages/edu_fact-sheets_building_history.aspx (accessed May 30, 2016).
15 *Report of the Comptroller of the Currency 1870* (Washington, D.C., 1871), p. xxvi–xxvi.
16 Thomas P. Kane, *The Romance and Tragedy of Banking: Problems and Incidents in the Supervision of National Banks* (New York: The Bankers Publishing Company, 1922), p. 21.
17 *Report of the Comptroller of the Currency 1953* (Washington, D.C., 1954), p. 30.
18 See Lloyd M. Short, *Steamboat-Inspection Service: Its History, Activities, and Organization* (New York: D. Appleton and Company, 1922), pp. 2–7. A case has been made that this was in reality the first regulatory agency of the Federal government. But it was not an "agency" in any sense, lacking as it did a central office, funding, a head, appointment powers, or a reporting relation to the rest of the government. See Robert Gudmestad, "The Horrific Accident That Created the Regulatory State," January 13, 2013, available at http://www.bloombergview.com/articles/2013-01-31/the-horrific-accident-that-created-the-regulatory-state (accessed May 30, 2016).
19 Carl Russell Fish, *The Civil Service and the Patronage* (New York: Longmans, Green, and Co., 1905), pp. 66ff; Richard J. Ellis, *The Political Development of the American Presidency* (New York: Routledge, 2012), pp. 310–11. In "The Removal Power of the President and Independent Administrative Agencies," *Indiana Law Journal*, 36:1 (1960), pp. 63–73, Reginald Parker suggests that the fixed term as conceived in the NCA represented a significant limitation on the president's removal power, because such a removal would "violate positive law."
20 Stephen G. Calabresi and Christopher S. Yoo, "The Oldest Debate in Constitutional Law and Why It Still Matters Today," in Calabresi and Yoo, *The Unitary Executive: Presidential Power from Washington to Bush* (New Haven, CT: Yale University Press, 2008), pp. 3–9. See also Brian J. Cook, "Subordination or Independence for Administrators? The Decision of 1789 Reexamined," *Public Administration Review*, 52:5 (September–October, 1992), pp. 497–503.
21 Extended extracts and discussion of the debate can be found in Kane, *Romance and Tragedy*, pp. 13–18.
22 *Congressional Globe*, 38th Congress, 1st session, April 26, 1864, p. 1865.
23 Joseph D. Hutnyan, "Jim Saxon's Death Revives Memories of the Exciting 1960s," *American Banker*, February 1, 1980, p. 4.
24 Richard E. Mooney, "Currency Chief Chosen—Name is Withdrawn, Then is Put Back," *The New York Times*, September 21, 1961, p. 1.
25 Ibid. "Gidney Accepts 'Error' Story," *Arizona Republican*, September 22, 1961, p. 3. An internal OCC memorandum to Gidney from OCC attorneys in the author's possession fills in important details. Gidney's resignation letter and the president's response are in the John F. Kennedy papers, President's Office Files, Treasury Department, September 1961.
26 The straight-to-a-bank employment option was foreclosed after the Glass–Steagall Act of 1933 imposed a two-year "cooling off" period before an outgoing Comptroller could go to work for a national bank.
27 Saxon to John Kelly, February 11, 1964, Confidential File FG 110, Lyndon B. Johnson Papers. A useful summary of Saxon's tumultuous tenure is in David M. Welborn, *Regulation in the White House: The Johnson Presidency* (Austin, TX: University of Texas Press, 1993), pp. 144–60.

28 Dillon to Kenneth O'Donnell, March 19, 1964, FG-110-5, LBJ Papers.
29 Katzenbach to LBJ, February 7, 1965, Ex-FG 110–15, LBJ Papers.
30 On the Saxon–Robertson relationship, see Box 190, Folder 9, A Willis Robertson Papers, College of William and Mary.
31 James R. Hambleton, "Saxon Knew His Battlefield," *American Banker*, May 10, 1963. See also "Drive to Dump Saxon Goes to Capitol Hill," *Chicago Tribune*, April 30, 1963, James J. Saxon Papers, JFK Library.
32 Hugh McCulloch, *Men and Measures of Half a Century* (New York: Scribner, 1889), p. 166.
33 McCulloch, *Men and Measures*, p. 166.
34 The McCulloch papers at the Lilly Library, Indiana University, contain multiple letters seeking OCC employment on the writers' or someone else's behalf. See, for example, William Findlay to McCulloch, Nov. 11, 1863.
35 OCC Memorandum, "Employment of National Bank Examiners and Assistant National Bank Examiners: History of the Relationship of the Comptroller's Office with the Civil Service Commission," n.d. (1951), OCC Historical Files.
36 OCC *Annual Report 1959* (Washington, D.C., 1960), p. 12.
37 In his oral history, William B. Camp, the 22nd Comptroller, recalled how he got his entry-level job at the OCC: by asking his congressman, the powerful Sam Rayburn, to intercede for him. Rayburn, Camp recalled, "merely picked up the phone and said to me, 'You go down there tomorrow and they will have a job for you.'" He did, and they did. "William Bacon Camp," Oral History Collection, LBJ Library, p. 2.
38 *Report of the Comptroller of the Currency 1865* (Washington, D.C., 1866), p. 12.
39 *Report of the Comptroller of the Currency 1864* (Washington, D.C., 1865), p. 64.
40 Treasury Secretary Morgenthau commissioned a "Special Report on J.F.T. O'Connor" to investigate allegations of misconduct about him. Box 369, Morgenthau Papers, FDR Library.
41 "O'Connor at League Hunt Breakfast . . . sat at a table with a galaxy of movie celebrities," including the 7-year-old Shirley Temple, "who helped serve O'Connor and other guests." Unattributed clipping in the O'Connor Diaries, Bancroft Library, University of California, Berkeley.
42 According to a knowledgeable insider, Morgenthau had lost confidence in O'Connor when it became clear that the Comptroller "was appointing receivers and counsel on purely political grounds." Entry for April 27, 1934, Charles S. Hamlin Diary, Library of Congress.
43 Charles O. Hardy and Jacob Viner, "Report on the Availability of Bank Credit in the Seventh Federal Reserve District" (Washington, D.C., Treasury Department, 1935), p. 20.
44 "Preliminary Report to Secretary Morgenthau on Bank Examinations," Box 215, Morgenthau Papers.
45 The examiner guidance (October 26, 1933, March 14, 1934, and an additional message dated December 19, 1934) is in Official File 21B in the Franklin D. Roosevelt papers.
46 "Drop in Loans Laid to Federal Rules," *The New York Times*, September 11, 1934, p. 1.
47 FDR to O'Connor, November 15, 1934, President's Personal File 1512, Roosevelt Papers.
48 Entry for September 10, 1934, O'Connor Diary.
49 O'Connor to FDR, September 11, 1934, Official File 21B, Roosevelt Papers.
50 "Comptroller's Legal Staff Put Under Treasury," *American Banker*, September 15, 1938.
51 Section 331 of the 1994 Riegle–Neal Interstate Banking and Branching Efficiency Act further stipulated that "The Comptroller of the Currency may act in the

Comptroller's own name and through the Comptroller's own attorneys" in enforcing and implementing banking laws, and that "The Secretary of the Treasury may not delay or prevent the issuance of any rule or the promulgation of any regulation by the Comptroller of the Currency.".

52 Preston Delano, *Leaves from a Comptroller's Notebook* (Washington, D.C., n.d.), p. 31.
53 "When James J. Saxon was Comptroller of the Currency, he would do something and the Treasury Secretary—his supposed boss—would learn about it the next morning in the Washington Post." "Comptroller Clarke Brings New Style," *National Journal*, 18:1 (January 4, 1986), p. 28.
54 FDIC, *History of the Eighties, Lessons for the Future. Vol I: An Examination of the Banking Crises of the 1908s and Early 1990s* (Washington, D.C., 1997). On banking problems in the Southwest, see pp. 291–336; on the commercial real estate crisis, see pp. 137–65.
55 Ross Yockey, *McColl: The Man with America's Money* (Atlanta, GA: Longstreet Press, 1999), pp. 410–14.
56 Kevin L. Kleisen and John A. Tatom, "The Recent Credit Crunch: The Neglected Dimensions," Federal Reserve Bank of St. Louis, 1992, available at https://research.stlouisfed.org/publications/review/1992/09/01/the-recent-credit-crunch-the-neglected-dimensions (accessed June 9, 2016); Ben S. Bernanke and Cara S. Lown, "The Credit Crunch," Brookings Institution, 1991, available at –http://www.brookings.edu/about/projects/bpea/papers/1991/the-credit-crunch-Bernanke (accessed 9 June 2016). Allan N. Berger, Margaret K. Kyle, and Joseph M. Scalise, "Did U.S. Bank Supervisors Get Tougher During the Credit Crunch?" National Bureau of Economic Research Working Paper 7689 (May 2000) available at http://www.nber.org/papers/w7689.pdf (accessed May 30, 2016).
57 Peter H. Frank, "Officials Ask for Leniency for Banking Industry," *The Baltimore Sun*, December 17, 1991.
58 On the credit crunch and the Baltimore conference, see John F. Bovenzi, *Inside the FDIC: Thirty Years of Bank Failures, Bailouts, and Regulatory Battles* (Hoboken, NJ: John Wiley & Sons, Inc., 2015), pp. 63–72.
59 On a party-line vote in November 1991, the Senate Banking Committee rejected Clarke's bid for reconfirmation, ostensibly on the basis of his performance, but also because Senate Democrats were unwilling to tie up the position for another five years with presidential elections looming.
60 Charles Kruly, "Self-Funding and Agency Independence," *The George Washington Law Review*, 81:5 (August 2013), p. 1733.
61 Jennifer L. Selin, "What Makes an Agency Independent?" Center for the Study of Democratic Institutions, Vanderbilt University, Working Paper 08–2013.

8 National bank preemption and the Financial Crisis of 2008

Raymond Natter

Introduction

In January 2004, the OCC issued rules on national bank preemption and "visitorial" (that is, examination and supervisory) powers. The rules were intended to codify case law dating back to 1819, when U.S. Supreme Court chief justice John Marshall ruled, in McCulloch v Maryland, *that the states may not impinge on the lawful exercise of Federal authority.*

But the OCC's action provoked controversy. The agency was accused of overstepping its constitutional limits by immunizing national banks from certain state laws, especially those concerned with consumer protection. The controversy sharpened during the financial crisis of the late 2000s, with the OCC's critics blaming the agency's preemption policies for allowing problems to fester in the subprime mortgage sector, where the crisis began.

In this essay, Raymond Natter explores the history of Federal preemption in banking and, in particular, its connection to the financial crisis. He concludes that the OCC's 2004 policies were well grounded in legal precedent, and that, in any event, these policies had little to do with the rash of bad mortgages that were originated largely by less regulated non-bank lenders.

Natter, formerly a deputy chief counsel at the OCC, is a partner in the Washington law firm of Barnett, Sivon, and Natter.

An overview of federal preemption

The Supremacy Clause

The foundation for the doctrine that federal law supersedes conflicting state law is found in the "Supremacy Clause" of the U.S. Constitution.[1] In 1819, in the landmark case *McCulloch v. Maryland*, the Supreme Court held that a Maryland law imposing a tax on a branch of Second Bank of the United States was preempted. The Court explained that, under the Supremacy Clause, the states have "no power, by taxation or otherwise, to retard, impede, burden, or in any manner control, the operations of the constitutional laws enacted by Congress."[2]

Express, field, and conflict preemption

The case law that followed the Supreme Court's decision in *McCulloch* established three ways in which a federal law may preempt state law:

- Congress may preempt state law by so stating in express terms.
- Preemption may be inferred when federal regulation in a particular field is so pervasive as to create a reasonable inference that Congress left no room for the states to supplement it. In such cases of "field preemption," the volume and complexity of federal regulations demonstrate an implicit congressional intent to displace all state law.
- Preemption may be implied when state law conflicts with federal law. Such a conflict arises not only when compliance with both federal and state regulations is a physical impossibility, but also where state law otherwise interferes with the federal enactment.

Thus, the Court has found preemption when the state law stands as an obstacle to the accomplishment and execution of the full purposes and objectives of the federal law, is unduly burdensome and duplicative, conflicts with the purposes of the federal law, or curtails or hinders a federal instrumentality.[3]

The National Bank Act

An overriding issue in any federal preemption question is congressional intent. As stated by the Supreme Court, "[t]he purpose of Congress is the ultimate touchstone in every pre-emption case."[4] "Did Congress, in enacting the Federal Statute, intend to exercise its constitutionally delegated authority to set aside the laws of a State? If so, the Supremacy Clause requires the courts to follow federal, not state law."[5] In making this determination, the courts will look not only at the language of the statute but also the overall structure and purpose of the legislation as a whole, including applicable legislative history, in order to reach a reasoned understanding of the way in which Congress intended the statute and its surrounding regulatory scheme to affect business, consumers, and the law.[6]

With this in mind, we turn to the National Bank Act, which provides for the chartering, regulation, and supervision of national banking associations. The Act is administered by the Office of the Comptroller of the Currency, a bureau within the Treasury Department. The OCC is headed by the Comptroller of the Currency, who is appointed by the President, with the advice and consent of the Senate, for a term of five years.[7]

Legislative history of the NBA

When the Civil War began in 1861, President Lincoln was faced with both military and financial challenges. The U.S. Treasury Department did not have the resources or income to meet the vast expenses associated with carrying on a war, and the government eventually had to resort to the issuance of notes, informally called "greenbacks," to finance its operations. However, public acceptance was far from complete, and these notes began to be traded at a considerable discount to the official price set for gold. In some western states, greenbacks were not accepted and trade continued in coin. Treasury Secretary Salmon Chase was particularly concerned about the impact of further issuances of greenbacks on the credit of the United States and the continuing damage it was causing to the economy.[8]

Equally disturbing was that the federal government had no control over state bank-issued notes, which were the primary circulating paper currency at that time. In his report to Congress in December 1861, Secretary Chase pointed out the problems with this system, including the fact that the weakest banks were responsible for some of the largest issuances of paper bills.[9]

In 1862, President Lincoln and Secretary Chase proposed to deal with both of these financial problems through the creation of a national bank system. National banks would be chartered by the federal government and required to hold U.S. Treasury bonds to back their notes. National Bank Notes were intended to circulate as currency, replacing the banknotes issued by the various state banks. On January 17, 1863, President Lincoln again urged that a system of federally charted banks be established to issue notes that would circulate as uniform currency. The President also noted that the continued issuance of circulating notes by "suspended" state banks would soon produce disastrous consequences.[10]

Congress responded to President Lincoln's pleas by enacting the National Currency Act. The legislation narrowly passed over the strenuous objections of many of the states concerned about losing their exclusive right to charter banks within their jurisdiction. The following year, the National Currency Act was revised and reenacted, and in 1874 Congress renamed the 1864 law the "National Bank Act."[11] However, the core features of the 1863 National Currency Act survived intact.

There can be no question that the National Banking System was intended to replace state banks as the source of paper currency in the United States and to operate distinctly from the existing state banks, and that it was established with the expectation that it would entirely replace the system of state banks.[12] Representative Samuel Hooper, who reported the bill to the House, stated in support of the legislation that one of its purposes was "to render the law so perfect that the State banks may be induced to organize under it, in preference to continuing under their State charters."[13] President Abraham Lincoln, in his annual message to Congress, stated that "[c]hanges from state systems to the national systems are rapidly taking place, and it is hoped that, very soon, there will be in the United States no banks of issue not authorized by Congress."[14]

As a consequence, there was considerable concern that the states would undermine the new National Banking System in order to protect state-chartered banks. The National Bank Act was drafted with this concern in mind.[15] Senator Sumner stated during the Senate debate that "[c]learly, the [national] bank must not be subjected to any local Government, state or municipal; it must be kept absolutely and exclusively under that government from which it derives its functions."[16]

Preemptive effect of the National Bank Act

The preemptive effect of the National Bank Act has been recognized repeatedly by the courts. As early as 1874 the Supreme Court stated:

> National banks have been national favorites. They were established for the purpose, in part, of providing a currency for the whole country, and in part to create a market for the loans of the general government. It could not have been intended, therefore, to expose them to the hazard of unfriendly legislation by the states, or to ruinous competition with state banks.[17]

In the following year, the Supreme Court reiterated that "the states can exercise no control over [national banks], nor in any way affect their operation except insofar as Congress may see proper to permit."[18] In 1896 the Court declared:

> National banks are instrumentalities of the Federal government, created for a public purpose. ... [A]n attempt, by a State, to define their duties or control the conduct of their affairs is absolutely void, wherever such attempted exercise of authority ... frustrates the purpose of the national legislation or impairs the efficiency of these agencies of the Federal government.[19]

In 1923, the Court held that a state's attempt to control the conduct of national banks was "void whenever it conflicts with the laws of the United States or frustrates the purposes of the national legislation or impairs the efficiency of the bank to discharge the duties for which it was created."[20] In *Franklin National Bank v. New York*, the Court determined that the NBA preempted a state law prohibiting a national bank from using the word "savings" in its advertisements, holding that the state law interfered with the authority of national banks to accept deposits.[21]

Recent case law affirmed the validity of these prior decisions. In its 1996 decision *Barnett Bank v. Nelson*, the Supreme Court held that a state law was preempted because it stood as an obstacle to the accomplishment of the purposes of the NBA. The Court reviewed the history of judicial construction of the NBA and found it is "one of interpreting grants of both enumerated and incidental 'powers' to national banks as grants of authority not normally limited by, but rather ordinarily pre-empting, contrary state law."[22] In 2007 the Supreme Court held, in *Watters v. Wachovia Bank, N.A.*, that state laws that would "significantly burden," "interfere," or "impair the exercise" of NBA powers were preempted.[23]

Although it is clear from the cases discussed above that the courts interpreted the NBA as having a broad preemptive effect, the case law is also clear that the

NBA does not occupy the field.[24] "Federally chartered banks are subject to state laws of general application in their daily business to the extent such laws do not conflict with the letter or the general purposes of the [National Bank Act.]"[25] The OCC agreed, explaining that the states retained power to regulate national banks in areas such as contracts, debt collection, acquisition and transfer of property, and taxation, zoning, criminal, and tort law. According to the OCC, application of these laws to national banks typically does not affect the content or extent of their federally authorized activities, but instead establishes the legal infrastructure that surrounds and supports the ability of national banks to do business.[26]

The OCC's preemption regulation

Preemptive effect of OCC regulations

As the agency charged by Congress with supervision of the NBA, the OCC oversees the operations of national banks and their direct operating subsidiaries. "To carry out this responsibility, the OCC has the power to promulgate regulations and to use its rulemaking authority to define the 'incidental powers' of national banks beyond those specifically enumerated in the statute."[27] However, the authority of the OCC is limited to the activities of the national bank and its direct operating subsidiary, and the OCC has no jurisdiction to affect the application of state law to a company controlling the bank (a "bank holding company") and the holding company's non-bank subsidiaries.[28] In other words, OCC preemption actions only apply to the activities directly performed by the national bank and—prior to the effective date of the Dodd–Frank Act—by the bank's direct operating subsidiaries.[29] The OCC's preemption determinations do not apply to any other entity in a banking organization, including activities conducted by the parent company or affiliated companies that are not national banks.

In *Fidelity Federal Savings and Loan v. de la Cuesta*, the Supreme Court established that federal regulations have the same preemptive effect as federal statutes. More recently, in *Geier v. American Honda Motor Co.*, the Supreme Court reiterated that agency regulations can preempt conflicting state law. Thus, OCC regulations have the same preemptive effect as the Act itself. Congress recognized the OCC's authority to issue regulations and other determinations with preemptive effect in the 1994 Riegle–Neal Interstate Banking Efficiency Act, which established notice and comment procedures for OCC preemption determinations. Congress again recognized that the OCC can preempt state law through regulations, orders, or "determinations" in the Dodd–Frank Act, which established procedures for, and judicial review of, OCC preemptive actions.[30]

Regulatory intent determines if a validly promulgated rule has preemptive effect. In *Williamson v. Mazda Motor of America*, the Supreme Court held that a Department of Transportation (DOT) automobile safety standard did not preempt a more stringent state requirement because the DOT rulemaking record disclosed no preemptive intent.[31]

Preemption prior to the 2004 regulation

Prior to 2004, the OCC issued a number of agency interpretive letters and legal opinions regarding the applicability of state law to national banks. These interpretations and legal opinions can be broken down into several categories.

The OCC preempted state laws that had the effect of protecting state-chartered depository institutions from national bank competition. For example, OCC regulatory actions preempted state laws that limited the ability of national banks to advertise their permissible business activities, establish branches within the state, operate offices within a certain distance from state-chartered bank home offices, locate ATM machines within the state, engage in fiduciary activities, and make particular types of loans.[32]

The OCC also preempted state laws protecting specific types of businesses from competition with national banks, including insurance agencies, securities firms, settlement attorneys, auto dealers, and even auctioneers. State attempts to assert licensing requirements or examination authority over national banks were also preempted.[33] State laws designed to provide enhanced protection for consumers are subject to preemption if they limit or restrict authorized bank powers. Such laws include state attempts to restrict or limit permissible fees and other non-interest charges, including service charges, fees on the use of ATM machines, consumer notices and disclosures, and similar laws.[34]

In a controversial decision in 2003, the OCC, following similar actions by the National Credit Union Administration and the Office of Thrift Supervision, determined that many provisions of the Georgia Fair Lending Act were preempted as to national banks. The Act contained restrictions on loans meeting statutory criteria and prohibited the use of certain features, such as negative amortization and balloon payments, in connection with these "predatory" mortgages. Consumer advocates opposed the OCC's action and argued that the OCC was preventing the state from protecting its citizens. The OCC, however, stated that it had no evidence that national banks were engaged in predatory lending practices. Further, the OCC noted that national banks could not engage in many practices associated with predatory lending without violating applicable regulatory guidance and supervisory standards. As discussed below, the OCC also decided to incorporate new anti-predatory lending rules in a formal regulation dealing with preemption more generally.[35]

OCC preemption regulation

Contemporaneously with the OCC's determination relating to the Georgia Fair Lending Act, the agency issued a Notice of Proposed Rulemaking (NPRM) to establish more generally the rules governing the applicability of state law to national banks. The final regulation, published on January 13,

2004, reviewed the judicial decisions on preemption under the NBA and, according to the preamble, attempted to distill the various formulations of when state law would be preempted into a concise test: state law may not "obstruct, impair or condition" national bank powers. The regulation then listed types of state laws that were preempted, as well as laws that were not preempted under this standard.[36]

The 2004 regulation included an anti-predatory lending provision that prohibited national banks from making consumer loans, including real estate loans, "based predominantly on the bank's realization of the foreclosure or liquidation value of the borrower's collateral, without regard to the borrower's ability to repay the loan according to its terms."[37] As explained in the NPRM, the requirement to underwrite a loan based on the borrower's ability to repay "reflects a bedrock principle of sound banking practices" and is consistent with the prior views of the agency that questioned the safety and soundness of consumer loans underwritten on the basis of the foreclosure value of the collateral.[38] The agency warned that "it is axiomatic that lenders following safe and sound lending practices will take reasonable steps to assure themselves and to verify that the borrower has the capacity to make scheduled payments to repay a loan, taking into account all of the borrower's obligations, including other indebtedness, insurance, and taxes, as well as principal and interest."[39] The final regulation, however, did not specify the means by which a bank could establish the financial capacity of the borrower and left that to the discretion of the bank, leading some to characterize the rule as "weak." The regulation also prohibited a national bank from engaging in any practice that would be deemed an unfair or deceptive practice under the FTC Act and regulations. The OCC stated that these provisions were intended to augment, not replace, other applicable predatory lending standards, including anti-predatory lending guidance previously issued by the OCC.[40]

The most significant criticism of the regulation was that the preemptive provisions went beyond judicial precedent, and that the standard "obstruct, impair, or condition" was not consistent with case law. Opponents of the regulation argued that *Barnett Bank* was the appropriate touchstone and that the Supreme Court applied a more stringent standard for preemption in that case than did the OCC. Some commentators focused in particular on the word "condition" as particularly aggressive and argued that any state regulation of a national bank would be viewed as an impermissible "condition" on national bank powers.[41]

The OCC's position, at least until 2011, was that the words in the regulation were "drawn directly from applicable Supreme Court precedents" and the OCC intended the phrase "obstruct, impair or condition" to be nothing more than "the distillation of the various preemption constructs articulated by the Supreme Court ... and not ... a replacement construct that is in any way inconsistent with those standards."[42] Comptroller John Hawke testified before Congress to this effect, and he further explained that the "key to determining the applicability to national banks of State laws ... is not the phrase 'obstruct, impair, or condition' but *rather the case law that underlies and supports that phrase* [emphasis added]."[43]

OCC regulation did not preempt all state consumer law

Despite the concern that the 2004 regulation effectively prevented the states from regulating any aspect of national bank activities, many state laws were found to be applicable to national banks under the preemption regulation. For example, state laws prohibiting fraudulent, unfair, or illegal acts or behavior have been deemed applicable to national banks. National banks also may be subject to state laws prohibiting "unfair or deceptive" acts or practices, including laws directed at deception, unfair business practices, and misrepresentation.[44]

State actions may be brought on the grounds that a national bank violated a common law duty of "good faith and fair dealing" with customers. Similarly, a national bank is subject to state law claims of "unjust enrichment." State laws relating to the right to collect a debt, as well as the regulation of debt collection practices, also have been found to be applicable to national banks. In *Epps v. JP Morgan Chase*, the court of appeals for the Fourth Circuit found that state laws requiring certain disclosures after an automobile was repossessed and prior to its resale were not preempted because such laws were part of the legal infrastructure establishing the bank's rights and obligations in collecting a debt. In *Cline v. Bank of America, N.A*, the court found that generally applicable restrictions on abusive collection practices do not interfere in any way with the purposes and objectives of federal law.[45]

Predatory mortgage lending

Beginning in 1999, 28 states adopted "anti-predatory lending" laws and regulations prohibiting "predatory" mortgage lending. The term "predatory" describes the use of abusive practices, including misinformation and manipulative sales techniques, to take unfair advantage of a borrower's lack of information about loan terms and their consequences. It should be distinguished from the term "subprime mortgage lending," which refers to mortgage loans made to borrowers with weakened credit histories and is often demarcated as mortgages made to consumers with a FICO credit score of 660 or less.[46]

Subprime loans do not necessarily have abusive terms, and until the downturn in the housing market beginning in 2007, the widely accepted view was that *responsible* subprime lending provided important public benefits by increasing credit availability and home ownership opportunities for lower-income consumers.[47] State anti-predatory lending laws never targeted subprime lending generally but instead were designed to eliminate the use of predatory practices. A comprehensive study by the Center for Responsible Lending analyzed 6 million subprime loans made in the 28 states with anti-predatory lending measures and concluded that these laws "are working well to prevent predatory mortgage lending, but ... also allow subprime credit not targeted by the laws to flourish."[48] The report noted that states with anti-predatory lending provisions "have struck an effective balance: Total subprime volume in states with [anti-predatory lending] reforms is similar to that found in states without significant protections."[49]

The OCC regulation issued in 2004 preempted state anti-predatory lending laws that had the effect of regulating the terms and conditions of mortgage loans made by national banks or their operating subsidiaries. In justifying this result, the OCC explained that the markets for credit products, including mortgages, were now national in scope, and the efficiency of national bank lending operations across state lines was impeded by having to comply with a multitude of requirements that differed state by state. According to the OCC:

> When national banks are unable to operate under uniform, consistent, and predictable standards, their business suffers, which negatively affects their safety and soundness. The application of multiple, often unpredictable, different state or local restrictions and requirements prevents them from operating in the manner authorized under Federal law, is costly and burdensome, interferes with their ability to plan their business and manage their risks, and subjects them to uncertain liabilities and potential exposure.[50]

The Comptroller touted this view publicly, stating in one speech:

> There is no question that national banks' immunity from many state laws is a significant benefit of the national charter—a benefit that the OCC has fought hard over the years to preserve. The ability of national banks to conduct a multi-state business subject to a single uniform set of federal laws, under the supervision of a single regulator, free from visitorial powers of various state authorities, is a major advantage of the national charter.[51]

Others argued that the OCC's preemption determinations were part of a race to the bottom, and that, by not providing a national standard comparable to the state anti-predatory lending laws, the agency's actions were intended to lure state banks into the federal system by offering a reprieve from the more stringent anti-predatory lending restrictions imposed by the states. The final report of the Financial Crisis Inquiry Commission discussed both views without reaching a conclusion.[52]

With respect to the consumer protection issues raised by the preemption of state anti-predatory lending laws, the OCC stated that predatory and abusive lending practices would not be tolerated and that, other than isolated instances, national banks and their subsidiaries have not been responsible for predatory lending activities.[53]

OCC regulatory response to predatory mortgage lending

Beginning in 2000, Comptroller Hawke raised an alarm about predatory lending practices in the mortgage lending area, which he called "a growing problem with national implications."[54] That same year, Comptroller Hawke announced that he would direct bank examiners to carefully review bank lending policies and practices to ensure that the only loans being made were those with a reasonable expectation of repayment without resorting to collateral. He also stated that examiners would look for abusive lending practices indicating an increased risk of racial discrimination.[55]

In 2003 the OCC issued an advisory letter warning national banks not to engage in predatory lending practices. The letter stated that a "fundamental characteristic of predatory lending is the aggressive marketing of credit to prospective borrowers who simply cannot afford the credit on the terms being offered."[56] As noted, in 2004 the OCC, as part of its preemption rule, prohibited national banks and their subsidiaries from lending "based predominantly on the bank's realization of the foreclosure or liquidation value of the borrower's collateral, without regard to the borrower's ability to repay the loan according to its terms," as well as other "abusive practices."[57] On January 31, 2005, the OCC issued legally enforceable mandatory residential mortgage lending standards applicable to national banks and their operating subsidiaries. These standards prohibit institutions from being involved, directly or indirectly, in mortgage loans involving abusive, predatory, unfair, or deceptive practices, including equity stripping and fee packing, loan flipping, refinancing of subsidized mortgage products, or encouraging a borrower to default. These standards also require a national bank or subsidiary to carefully consider the circumstances and the possibility of violating the prohibition on making abusive, unfair, or deceptive loans when a mortgage loan contains certain "high risk" provisions, such as negative amortization, balloon payments, prepayment penalties, or the absence of appropriate documentation of the borrower's ability to repay the loan. In May 2005, all of the federal banking agencies issued joint guidance on Home Equity Lending. This was followed, in 2006, by interagency guidance on non-traditional mortgages. This guidance also requires banks to assess the borrower's ability to repay the loan. In 2007, the OCC and the other federal banking agencies issued joint guidance on subprime lending, requiring that borrowers must be qualified for a loan using the fully indexed rate.[68]

Subprime mortgage lending

The effectiveness of the regulatory actions described above has been much debated. However, the available statistical evidence indicates that national banks and their subsidiaries did not play a significant role in the issuance of *predatory* loans and were not dominant in the origination of non-predatory *subprime* mortgage loans.[59]

The overwhelming majority of subprime loans were originated by state-regulated financial companies, which were outside of the scope of the OCC's preemption regulation. While some of the leading subprime lenders included bank holding companies and their non-bank subsidiaries, these companies were not regulated by the OCC and were not subject to the OCC's preemption rule or regulatory oversight. Since the OCC preemption regulation only applies to activities conducted by national banks and their direct operating subsidiaries, the regulation had no impact on any other affiliates, such as holding companies. Thus, the mortgage lending practices of holding companies and other affiliates remained fully subject to state law.[60]

More recently, an OCC review of subprime lending prepared for the Financial Crisis Inquiry Commission found that the vast majority of subprime lending was done outside of national banks in entities that were subject to state law. The same was true in the market for so-called Alt-A mortgages, which were mortgages originated without full documentation of the income and assets of the borrower.[61]

This conclusion is consistent with the mortgage lending activities of Countrywide Financial Corporation. Prior to its acquisition in 2008, Countrywide was one of the largest originators of subprime loans in the United States. However, almost all of its mortgages were originated by holding company units, which were not subject to preemption, and those units were subject to state regulation. For example, in fiscal year 2006, Countrywide's non-bank mortgage lending unit produced $421 billion of mortgages, while the national bank subsidiary produced only $23 billion of mortgages. In 2007 Countrywide converted its national bank subsidiary into a federal savings association, but the mortgage lending continued to be concentrated outside of the insured depository institution, with the state-regulated units producing $385 billion in mortgages and the federal thrift producing $18 billion in mortgages. Thus, preemption was not a significant factor in the origination of these loans, since Countrywide originated almost all of its mortgages in state-regulated entities. A review of securities filings for other large mortgage lenders revealed a similar pattern: the subprime originations were consistently located outside of the national bank or federal thrift units and housed in state-regulated mortgage departments.[62]

The role of state-regulated "shadow" financial institutions in unsafe subprime lending was recognized by the Treasury Department, which noted in its 2009 report to Congress that 94 percent of "higher-priced loans" to "lower income borrowers" were originated by non-depository institution lenders.[63] Congressman Barney Frank came to the same conclusion:

> Reasonable regulation of mortgages by the bank and credit union regulators allowed the market to function in an efficient and constructive way, while mortgages made and sold in the unregulated sector led to the crisis. At every step in the process, from loan origination through the use of exotic unsuitable mortgages to the sale of securities backed by those mortgages,

the largely unregulated uninsured firms have created problems, while the regulated and FDIC-insured banks and savings institutions have not. To the extent that the system did work, it is because of prudential regulation and oversight. Where it was absent, the result was tragedy for hundreds of thousands of families who have lost, or soon will lose, their homes and for those who invested in shaky and untested, even though highly rated, securities, and have been forced to take large losses and, in many cases, shut their doors.[64]

At least one major consumer group also acknowledged that the subprime lending originations were primarily occurring in state-regulated entities. In 2008 the Center for Responsible Lending published an "issue brief" finding that the Community Reinvestment Act (CRA), which is only applicable to national banks and other insured depository institutions, did not play a significant role in the mortgage crisis because "[t]he predominant players in the subprime market—mortgage brokers, mortgage companies and the Wall Street investment banks that provided the financing—aren't covered under CRA."[65] The issue brief went on to assert that "many banks shifted the most risky lending—the loans at the root cause of this current crisis—to affiliates *to escape CRA requirements and regulatory oversight.*"[66]

Prior to publication of the issue brief discussed above, the Center for Responsible Lending sponsored a detailed statistical analysis of 1.7 million subprime loans. This analysis found that mortgage brokers accounted for between 63 percent and 81 percent of all subprime loans in 2006. The study characterized these brokers as the "'engine' of the subprime market" and argued that, although all states license mortgage brokers, licensing alone—without substantive requirements—is inadequate to protect consumers.[67] The report also noted that banks are subject to more intense regulatory and supervisory oversight:

> Despite their integral involvement in mortgage transactions, there is scant regulation of mortgage brokers compared to traditional lenders. While banks, for example, are subject to regular oversight and regulatory examinations that scrutinize the quality and legality of the loans they originate, the regulatory reviews applicable to brokers are largely focused on ensuring that brokers meet certain bench marks in order to be licensed.[68]

Further, the report determined that, after matching loans for borrower characteristics, such as FICO scores and geographic area, subprime loans originated by mortgage brokers were significantly more expensive than similar loans made by traditional retail lenders, and that mortgage brokers originated four times the number of negative amortizing loans as traditional lenders and a "disproportionate share" of ARM loans and loans with prepayment penalties.[69]

Allen Fishbein, representing the Consumer Federation of America, testified that effective regulation of subprime lending is dependent upon the cooperation of state regulators and suggested that they adopt parallel guidance to that issued by the federal banking agencies. He noted that the participation of state regulators is "particularly crucial for subprime lending, since the lenders and mortgage brokers they supervise and license represent the majority of these originations."[70]

More current statistics support these views. A report accompanying Comptroller Dugan's testimony before the Financial Crisis Inquiry Commission states:

> Using the most reliable data available on nonprime mortgage lending, and accurately accounting for corporate organization and regulatory responsibilities, national banks and their subsidiaries subject to OCC supervision accounted for less than 15 percent of nonprime activity. ... In contrast, lenders supervised solely by the states accounted for well over half of nonprime lending; combining originations by those lenders with the totals for state-chartered banks reveals that nearly three quarters of nonprime mortgages originated at lenders that were wholly or partly the responsibility of state authorities. ... Moreover, the data show that subprime mortgages originated by OCC-supervised lenders have performed better than other subprime loans, with lower rates of foreclosure.[71]

This is not to say that national banks did not have a significant part in subprime lending activities in the mid-2000s. Some national banks made poorly underwritten subprime mortgage loans. National banks also played a role in funding loans made by non-bank lenders, through commercial loans, letters of credit, and the purchase of mortgage-backed securities. Many banks suffered losses as a result of these endeavors. National banks also assisted in the securitization process, for example by providing liquidity support. However, these types of commercial lending and investment activities were not the subject of state anti-predatory lending laws, which were directed at prohibiting predatory terms and practices in the origination of consumer mortgages.[72]

Did preemption inhibit state regulation of subprime lenders?

Another issue is whether federal preemption reduced the willingness of the states to adopt restrictions on state-regulated mortgage lenders. However, federal preemption did not prevent the states from adopting restrictions that were at least as stringent as those imposed on national banks. Indeed, Alan Fishbein of the Consumer Federation of America urged the states to do just that when he testified before Congress.[73]

In the states that did take action to restrict predatory lending, those actions were often successful. The Center for Responsible Lending found that in the states that adopted substantive protections, the state laws were "clearly working to clean up the subprime mortgage market."[74] For example, the study determined that "the proportion of loans in New Mexico with abusive terms was 38.5 percentage points lower than states without significant reforms."[75] In 2008 the Pew Charitable Trust released a study noting that "two thirds of all subprime loan applications are originated by mortgage brokers" but that only four states clearly established fiduciary duties on brokers. The study encouraged states to expand their role in regulating state-licensed mortgage originators.[76]

These studies demonstrate that preemption is not a bar to effective state regulation that can reduce lending abuses. Where states have acted with strong laws, they have been successful in curbing abusive practices.

Conclusion

In 1863 the National Bank Act established a system for the federal chartering and regulation of banking institutions, with the intent to have a national system supersede state banks. Efforts by the states to prevent this result—and to apply state restrictions to national banks—led to a continuing debate over the preemptive effect of the National Bank Act over the past 150 years.

Recently, preemption was put in the spotlight when some contended that the preemption regulations issued by the OCC contributed significantly to the risky mortgage lending practices that led to the financial crisis. In particular, it was argued that the OCC preempted state "anti-predatory" lending laws without providing an effective national standard to prevent abusive mortgage lending practices.

This study concludes that the underlying argument against preemption is not correct. National banks were largely prevented from engaging in predatory lending practices. The argument against preemption conflates predatory lending with subprime lending. The state anti-predatory lending laws were aimed at abusive lending practices, characteristic of only a fraction of the total subprime loans made. "Responsible" subprime lending was encouraged by both the states and the federal government as a means of increasing home ownership among lower income consumers. Unfortunately, once housing prices began to collapse, these "responsible subprime loans" began to massively default, initiating the financial crisis.

The overwhelming majority of subprime loans were originated by state-regulated and state-chartered entities, and these entities were not subject to preemption. Many conglomerates that had national bank subsidiaries chose state-regulated affiliates to originate subprime loans in order to avoid the more stringent underwriting standards imposed by the OCC.

The available evidence demonstrates that preemption was not a significant cause of the financial crisis and that the excesses in the subprime mortgage markets were largely the result of actions taken by loan originators that were not covered by the OCC's preemption rules.

Notes

1 U.S. Const. art. VI, cl. 2.
2 *McCulloch v. Maryland*, 17 U.S. 316, 402–3, 436 (1819). The First Bank of the United States was created by Congress in 1791 to handle the national debt that remained from the Revolutionary War and to establish financial order and credit for the United States. In 1811 the bank's charter expired. Second Bank of the United States was chartered in 1816 to help the nation recover from the debt and credit crisis following the War of 1812.
3 See, for example, *Jones v. Rath Packing Co.*, 430 U.S. 519, 523–24 (1977); *Island Park, LLC v. CSX Transp.*, 559 F.3d 96, 101 (2d Cir. 2009); *Chamber of Commerce v. Whitting*, 131 S.Ct. 1968, 1977 (2011); *Crosby v. National Foreign Trade Council*, 530 U.S. 363, 372 (2000); *Rice v. Santa Fe Elevator Corp.*, 331 U.S. 218, 230 (1947); *Air Transp. Ass'n of Am. v. Cuomo*, 520 F.3d 218, 220–21 (2d Cir. 2008); *Geier v. American Honda Motor Co.*, 529 U.S. 861, 869 (2000); *Florida Lime & Avocado Growers, Inc. v. Paul*, 373 U.S. 132, 142 (1963); *McCulloch v. Maryland*, 17 U.S. 316, 436 (1819); *AT&T Mobility LLC v. Concepcion*, 131 S. Ct. 1740, 1749–50 (2011); *Barnett Bank v. Nelson*, 517 U.S. 25, 31 (1996); *Hines v. Davidowitz*, 312 U.S. 52, 67–68 (1941); *Watters v. Wachovia Nat'l Bank*, 550 U.S. 1, 11, 13 (2007); *Anderson Nat'l Bank v. Luckett*, 321 U.S. 233, 248 (1944).
4 *Medtronic*, 518 U.S. at 485 (citing *Retail Clerks v. Schermerhorn*, 375 U.S. 96, 103, 1963).
5 *Barnett Bank*, 517 U.S. 25, 30.
6 *Medtronic*, 518 U.S. at 486; *Marquette Nat'l Bank v. First of Omaha Corp.*, 439 U.S. 299, 314–15 (1978); *Abdullah v. Am. Airlines*, 181 F.3d 363, 366–67 (3d Cir. 1999).
7 National Bank Act, ch. 106, 13 Stat. 99 (codified as amended in scattered sections of 12 U.S.C.).
8 Wesley C. Mitchell, *A History of the Greenbacks, with Special Reference to the Economic Consequences of Their Issue: 1862–1865* (University of Chicago Press, 1903), 10, 102–3, 135–46; First Legal Tender Act, Act of Feb. 25, 1862, ch. 33, 12 Stat. 345.
9 Jerry W. Markham, *Banking Regulation: Its History and Future*, 4 N.C. Banking Inst. 221–7 (2000); The Dep't of Treasury Dep't.: Rep. of Sec. Chase Rep. to Cong., Dec. 10, 1861, available at http://www.nytimes.com/1861/12/10/news/the-treasury-department-report-of-ecretary-chase.html?pagewanted=all (accessed May 30, 2016).
10 President Abraham Lincoln, Annual Message to Congress, Dec. 1, 1862, reprinted in Cong. Globe, 37th Cong., 3d sess., 2 (1863); Markham, *Banking Regulation*, 228; Special Message of President Lincoln on Financing the War, *Senate Journal*, 37th Cong., 3d sess., 121–22 (1863).
11 Act of Feb. 25, 1863, ch. 58, 12 Stat. 665; Statement of Senator Sherman in Cong. Globe, 37th Cong., 3d sess., 844 (1863); Bray Hammond, *Sovereignty and an Empty Purse: Banks and Politics in the Civil War* (Princeton University Press, 1970), 321–51; 12 U.S.C. §38, ch. 343, 18 Stat. 123.
12 John Wilson Million, "The Debate on the National Bank Act of 1863, *Journal of Political Economy* 2 (1893–94): 251, 267; Markham, *Banking Regulation*, 228; Annual Report of the Comptroller of the Currency, Nov. 28, 1863. In 1865 Congress imposed a tax of 10 percent on state bank-issued notes, which had the effect of making the issuance of such notes impractical (Act of March 3, 1865, 13 Stat. 469, 484, 1865). See also *Veazie Bank v. Fenno*, 75 U.S. 533, 538–39 (1869), for a more detailed description of federal attempts to restrict or eliminate the issuance of state bank notes through taxation.

13 See Representative Hooper's statement in Cong. Globe, 38th Cong., 1st sess., 1256 (1864).
14 President Abraham Lincoln, Annual Message to Congress, Dec. 6, 1864, in *Senate Journal*, 38th Cong., 2nd sess., 10 (1864).
15 Cong. Globe, 38th Cong., 1st sess., 1451 (1864).
16 See Statement of Senator Sumner in Cong. Globe, 38th Cong., 1st sess., 1893 (1864).
17 *Tiffany v. National Bank of Mo.*, 85 U.S. 409, 413 (1874).
18 *Farmers' & Mechanics' Nat'l Bank v. Dearing*, 91 U.S. 29, 34 (1875).
19 *Davis v. Elmira Savings Bank*, 161 U.S. 275, 283 (1896). Further, if the state law was not preempted, "confusion would necessarily result from control possessed and exercised by two independent authorities." See *Easton v. Iowa*, 188 U.S. 220, 231–2 (1903).
20 *First Nat'l Bank of San Jose v. California*, 262 U.S. 366, 369 (1923) (citing *Davis*, 161 U.S. at 283, 288, 290).
21 *Franklin Nat'l Bank v. New York*, 347 U.S. 373 (1954).
22 *Barnett Bank*, 517 U.S. 25, 31–3.
23 *Watters*, 550 U.S. 1, 3, 12–13, 21.
24 Ibid.; *Aguayo v. United States Bank*, 653 F.3d 912 (9th Cir. 2011); *Williams v. Wells Fargo Bank, N.A.*, No. 11–21233, 2011 WL 4901346, at *9 (S.D. Fla. Oct. 14, 2011).
25 *Watters*, 550 U.S. 6.
26 Bank Activities and Operations; Real Estate Lending and Appraisals, 69 Fed. Reg. 1904 (Jan. 13, 2004) (codified at 12 C.F.R. pts. 7 and 34) [hereinafter Preemption Final Rule].
27 *Martinez v. Wells Fargo Home Mortg.*, 598 F.3d 549, 555 (9th Cir. 2010).
28 Ibid. Hereinafter, the term "national bank" will include direct operating subsidiaries of the bank unless otherwise indicated in the text. As of July 21, 2011, the National Bank Act no longer preempts the applicability of state law to such subsidiaries. This will be discussed in more detail later in this chapter.
29 *Fidelity Fed. Sav. & Loan Ass'n v. De la Cuesta*, 458 U.S. 141, 153 (1982).
30 *Geier v. American Honda Motor Co.*, 529 U.S. 861, 884–85 (2000); *Aguayo v. United States Bank*, 653 F.3d 912, 919 (9th Cir. 2011); Riegle-Neal Interstate Banking and Branching Efficiency Act of 1994, Pub. L. No. 103–32, § 114; Dodd-Frank Wall Street Reform and Protection Act § 1044, 12 U.S.C.A. § 25b (2010); *Williamson v. Mazda Motor of Am.*, 131 S.Ct. 1131, 1139–40 (2011).
31 *Williamson v. Mazda Motor of Am.*, 131 S.Ct. 1131, 1139–40 (2011) (quoting Hines v. Davidowitz, 312 U.S. 52, 67, 1941).
32 Office of the Comptroller of the Currency, OCC Corp. Decision 98–07 (Jan. 15, 1998); OCC Corp. Decision 95–59 (Nov. 20, 1995). Prior to 1994, national banks had limited opportunity to operate branches across state lines, and branching within a state had to be on the same basis as allowed for state chartered banks. 12 U.S.C. § 36. The Riegle-Neal Interstate Banking and Branching Efficiency Act of 1994 authorized national banks to branch across state lines if certain conditions are met. Pub. L. 103–328; 108 Stat 2338 (1994). See also Office of the Comptroller of the Currency, OCC Interp. Ltr. No. 590 (June 18, 1992); Office of the Comptroller of the Currency, OCC Interp. Ltr. No. 939 (Oct. 15, 2001); Office of the Comptroller of the Currency, OCC Interp. Ltr. No. 789 (June 27, 1997); Office of the Comptroller of the Currency, OCC Corp. Decision 97–33 (June 1, 1997); Preemption Determination, 66 Fed. Reg. 28,593 (May 23, 2001); *Barnett Bank*, 517 U.S. 25 at 31–7.

33 Office of the Comptroller of the Currency, OCC Interp. Ltr. No. 749 (Sept. 13, 1996); *Clarke v. Securities Industry Association*, 479 U.S. 388 (1987); National Bank Charges, 66 Fed. Reg. 34,791 (July 2, 2001) (codified in 12 C.F.R. § 7.4002); Preemption Opinion, 66 Fed. Reg. 23,977 (May 10, 2001); Preemption Determination, 65 Fed. Reg. 15,037 (Mar. 20, 2000); Office of the Comptroller of the Currency, OCC Interp. Ltr. (Feb. 9, 1995); Office of the Comptroller of the Currency, OCC Interp. Ltr. (Feb. 4, 1992) (unpublished); *Baptista v. JPMorgan Chase Bank, N.A.*, 640 F.3d 1194, 1197–98 (2011), *cert. denied*, 2011 U.S. Lexis 5261 (Oct. 3, 2011).
34 *Monroe Retail, Inc. v. RBS Citizens, N.A.*, 589 F.3d 274, 283–84 (6th Cir. 2009); *Bank of Am. v. City & Cnty. of San Francisco*, 309 F.3d 551 (9th Cir. 2002); *Rose v. Chase Bank U.S.A., N.A.*, 513 F.3d 1032, 1037–38 (9th Cir. 2008). See, for example, 12 C.F.R. §§ 7.4008(b), 34.3(b).
35 National Credit Union Administration, 02–0649, Applicability of Georgia Fair Lending Act to Federal Credit Unions (July 29, 2002); Office of Thrift Supervision, P-2003-1, Preemption of Georgia Fair Lending Act (Jan. 21, 2003); GA Code Ann. §§ 7-6A-1 to 7-6A-13, *et seq*.; Preemption Determination and Order, 68 Fed. Reg. 46,264 (Aug. 5, 2003); Preemption Determination and Order, 68 Fed. Reg. 46,264, 46,265 (Aug 5, 2003). See also Comment Letter from the National Consumer Law Center to the OCC (Mar. 28, 2003), available at http://www.nclc.org/images/pdf/preemption/archive/032803_er.pdf (accessed May 30, 2016).
36 Bank Activities and Operations; Real Estate Lending and Appraisals, 68 Fed. Reg. 46119, 46120 (proposed Aug. 5, 2003) [hereinafter Preemption Proposed Rule]; Preemption Final Rule, 1916–17.
37 Preemption Final Rule, 1917 (codified at 12 C.F.R. §§ 7.4008(b), 34.3(b)).
38 Preemption Proposed Rule, 46,127; Preemption Final Rule, 1904.
39 Preemption Proposed Rule, 46,127.
40 Wilmarth, *Dodd–Frank Act's Expansion of State Authority*, 906; Preemption Final Rule, 1905, 1916–17 (codified at 12 C.F.R. §§ 4008(c), 34.3(c)); Office of the Comptroller of the Currency, Guidelines for National Banks to Guard Against Predatory and Abusive Lending Practices, OCC Adv. Ltr. 2003–2 (Jan. 7, 2003); Office of the Comptroller of the Currency, OCC Adv. Ltr. 2003–3 (Feb. 21, 2003).
41 Letter from Paul Sarbanes, Senator, U.S. Senate, to John D. Hawke, Comptroller, Office of the Comptroller of the Currency, Nov. 24, 2003; Arthur E. Wilmarth, Jr., "The OCC's Preemption Rules Exceed the Agency's Authority and Present a Serious Threat to the Dual Banking System and Consumer Protection", *Annual Review of Banking and Financial Law*, Vol. 23: 225–364, , 225, 249 (2004); *OCC's Proposal To Preempt Application of State Anti-Predatory Lending and Other Laws*, Center for Responsible Lending (Oct. 6, 2003).
42 Preemption Final Rule, 1910.
43 "Oversight of the Office of the Comptroller of the Currency," Hearings Before the House Committee on Financial Services, 108th Cong. 2d. Sess. (April 1, 2004), (letter submitted for the hearing record by Comptroller Hawke in response to questions posed by Representative Ron Paul).–
44 Kathleen C. Engel and Patricia A. McCoy, *The Subprime Virus: Reckless Credit, Regulatory Failures, and Next Steps* (Oxford University Press, 2011), 157–62; Bethany McLean and Joe Nocera, *All the Devils Are Here: The Hidden History of the Financial Crisis* (Portfolio, 2010), 146–7; *Martinez v. Wells Fargo Home Mortg.*, 598 F.3d 549, 555 (9th Cir. 2010); Office of the Comptroller of the Currency, Guidance on Unfair or Deceptive Acts or Practices, OCC Adv. Ltr. 2002–3 (Mar. 22, 2002); *Mann v. TD Bank, N.A.*, No. 09–1062, 2009 WL 3818128 (D. N.J. Nov. 12,

2009); *White v. Wachovia Bank, N.A.*, 563 F. Supp. 2d 1358 (N.D. Ga. 2008); *Jefferson v. Chase Home Fin.*, No. 06–6510, 2007 U.S. Dist. LEXIS 94652, at *2 (N.D. Cal. Dec. 14, 2007).

45 *Gutierrez v. Wells Fargo Bank, N.A.*, 730 F. Supp. 2d 1080 at 1122 (N.D. Cal. 2010); *Trombly v. Bank of Am. Corp.*, 715 F. Supp. 2d 290, 296 (D.R.I. 2010); *Williams v. Wells Fargo Bank, N.A.*, No. 11–21233, 2011 WL 4901346, at *9 (S.D. Fla. Oct. 4, 2011); *Aguayo v. United States Bank*, 653 F.3d 912, 919 (9th Cir. 2011); Office of the Comptroller of the Currency, OCC Interp. Ltr. No. 1082 (June 2007); *Opal v. Bate*, 454 B.R. 869, 878 (Bankr. M.D. Fla. 2011); *Epps v. JP Morgan Chase Bank, N.A.*, No. 10–2444 (4th Cir. Apr. 5, 2012); *Cline v. Bank of Am., N.A.*, 823 F. Supp. 2d 387, 399 (S.D. W. Va. 2011).

46 Wei Li and Keith S. Ernst, *The Best Value in the Subprime Market: State Predatory Lending Reforms*, Center for Responsible Lending 2 (2006) [hereinafter CRL 2006 Paper]; see, for example, 1999 N.C. Sess. Laws 332 (1999) (codified at N.C. Gen. Stat. 24–1.1A, 24–1.1E, 24–2.5, 24–28, 24–10.2); see Raphael W. Bostic, Kathleen C. Engel, Patricia A. McCoy, Anthony Pennington-Cross and Susan M. Wachter, "State and Local Anti-Predatory Lending Laws: The Effect of Legal Enforcement Mechanisms", *Journal of Economics and Business*, Vol. 60: 47, 2008. See also U.S. Department of Housing and Urban Development and Department of the Treasury, *Curbing Predatory Home Mortgage Lending* (2000), 16; Federal Deposit Insurance Corporation and Office of Thrift Supervision, *Expanded Guidance for Subprime Lending Programs, Board of Governors of the Federal Reserve System*, Office of the Comptroller of the Currency (2001), 1.

47 General Accountability Office, *Consumer Protection: Federal and State Agencies Face Challenges in Combating Predatory Lending* (GAO 04–280, Jan. 2004), 21–2.

48 CRL 2006 Paper at 2, 13.

49 Ibid., 13.

50 Preemption Final Rule, 1907–8.

51 John D. Hawke, Jr., Comptroller of the Currency, Office of the Comptroller of the Currency, "Remarks Before the Women in Housing and Finance" (Feb. 12, 2002), 2, available at http://www.occ.gov/static/news-issuances/speeches/2002/pub-speech-2002-10.pdf (accessed May 30, 2016).

52 Wilmarth, *OCC's Preemption Rules*, 274–75; The Financial Crisis Inquiry Commission, *The Financial Crisis Inquiry Report. Final Report of the National Commission on the Causes of the Financial and Economic Crisis in the United States* (2011), 111–13.

53 Preemption Final Rule, 1914. (Citing, among other authority, a joint HUD–Treasury study finding that predatory lending practices were largely confined to unregulated mortgage lenders, and the conclusion reached by all 46 state attorneys general that: "Based on consumer complaints received, as well as investigations and enforcement actions undertaken by the Attorneys General, predatory lending abuses are largely confined to the subprime mortgage lending market and to non-depository institutions. Almost all of the leading subprime lenders are mortgage companies and finance companies, not banks or direct bank subsidiaries.").

54 John D. Hawke, Jr., Comptroller of the Currency, Office of the Comptroller of the Currency, *Remarks Before the National Community Reinvestment Coalition, on Banks and Community Development* (Mar. 21, 2000), 77.

55 Statement of John D. Hawke, Jr., Comptroller of the Currency, Office of the Comptroller of the Currency, in *Predatory Lending Practices: Hearing Before the House Committee on Financial Services*, 106th Cong. (2000), 19.

56 Office of the Comptroller of the Currency, OCC Adv. Ltr. 2003–2 (Feb. 21, 2003). While advisory letters do not have the force and effect of a regulation, failure

to follow an advisory letter will subject a national bank to regulatory criticism and could lead to a downgrade in the institution's report of examination. As a result, advisory letters and similar informal guidance are often viewed by both examiners and regulated institutions as mandatory rather than discretionary instructions.

57 Preemption Final Rule, 1916–17, codified at 12 C.F.R. §§ 7.4008(b), 34.3(b) (2012)).
58 OCC Guidelines Establishing Standards for Residential Mortgage Lending Practices, 70 Fed. Reg. 6329, 6333–34 (Feb. 7, 2005) (codified at 12 C.F.R. pt. 30) (2012)); Credit Risk Management Guidance for Home Equity Lending, attachment to Joint Press Release, Office of the Comptroller of the Currency., available at http://www.occ.gov/news-issuances/bulletins/2005/bulletin-2005-22a.pdf (accessed May 30, 2016); Credit Risk Management: Guidance for Home Equity Lending, FDIC-PR-44-2005 (May 16, 2005); Interagency Guidance on Nontraditional Mortgage Product Risks, 71 Fed. Reg. 58,609 at 59,610–59,611 (Oct. 4, 2006); Statement on Subprime Mortgage Lending, 72 Fed. Reg. 37,569, at 37,571 (July 10, 2007).
59 As discussed above, the vast majority of subprime mortgage loans were not viewed by the states or the federal government as predatory, but rather were looked upon as a positive means to foster home ownership for lower income consumers. "Consumer Protections in Financial Services: Past Problems, Future Solutions: Hearing Before the S. Comm. on Banking, Housing and Urban Affairs", 111th Cong. (2009), 64; Wilmarth, *Dodd–Frank Act's Expansion of State Authority*, 901–3.
60 See Letter from John Dugan, Comptroller of the Currency, to Elizabeth Warren, Chair, Congressional Oversight Panel (Feb. 12, 2009).
61 *Subprime Lending and Securitization and the Government-Sponsored Enterprises: Hearing Before the Financial Crisis Inquiry Commission* (2010), Statement of John C. Dugan, Comptroller, Office of the Comptroller of the Currency [hereinafter Dugan, FCIC Testimony].
62 J. Dunbar and D. Donald, *Who's Behind the Financial Meltdown?* (May 6, 2009, updated Sept. 7, 2011), available at https://www.publicintegrity.org/2009/05/06/5449/roots-financial-crisis-who-blame (accessed June 9, 2016); Countrywide Financial Corporation, Annual Report (Form 10-K), 3, 23 (Mar. 1, 2007); Washington Mutual, Inc., Annual Report (Form 10-K/A), 34, 43 (May 22, 2008).
63 U.S. Department of the Treasury, *Financial Regulatory Reform, A New Foundation: Rebuilding Financial Supervision and Regulation* (June 17, 2009), 69–70.
64 Barney Frank, Op-Ed, "Lessons of the Subprime Crisis," *Boston Globe*, Sept. 14, 2007. Congressman Frank made the same point on the floor of the House; see Statement of Representative Barney Frank, 153 Cong. Rec. H13978 (daily edn Nov. 15, 2007).
65 Center for Responsible Lending, *CRA Is Not to Blame for the Mortgage Meltdown* (Oct. 3, 2008), 1.
66 Ibid. (emphasis added).
67 Center for Responsible Lending, *Steered Wrong: Brokers, Borrowers, and Subprime Loans* (Apr. 8, 2008) 3, 6–8.
68 Ibid., 6.
69 Ibid., 10–11, 14–18.
70 Statement of Allen Fishbein, Director of Housing and Credit Policy, Consumer Federation of America, in *Subprime and Predatory Mortgage Lending: New Regulatory Guidance, Current Market Conditions and Effects on Regulated Financial Institutions: Hearing Before the House Subcommittee on Financial Institutions and Consumer Credit*, 110th Cong. (2007), 10 [hereinafter Fishbein Testimony].
71 Dugan, FCIC Testimony, Appendix B.
72 Ibid., 9–11.
73 Fishbein Testimony, 9–10.

74 CRL 2006 Paper, 11.
75 Ibid., 12.
76 The Pew Charitable Trusts, *Defaulting on the Dream: States Respond to America's Foreclosure Crisis* (April 2008), 25, available at http://www.pewtrusts.org/en/research-and-analysis/reports/2008/04/16/defaulting-on-the-dream-states-respond-to-americas-foreclosure-crisis (accessed May 30, 2016).

9 The measure of a regulator
The Office of Thrift Supervision, 1989–2011

Paula Dejmek Woods

Introduction

No federal agency had a more tumultuous history than the Office of Thrift Supervision (OTS). Like the OCC, the Federal Reserve, and the FDIC, it was founded in response to financial crisis. Unlike the others, its assigned responsibility was to prop up a segment of the banking system that had just survived an existential crisis. The solution adopted by Congress was to alter the thrift industry itself, by giving it expanded, bank-like powers, while preserving its traditional mission of fostering home ownership.

It was a strategy that ultimately failed. The Dodd–Frank Act of 2010, passed to modernize the financial services industry, mandated the end of the Office of Thrift Supervision. The extent to which this failure owed to OTS action and inaction, as was sometimes charged, or, alternatively, to circumstances beyond its control, is the subject of Paula Dejmek Woods' essay. Dejmek Woods, a financial analyst, was among the hundreds of OTS employees who transferred to the OCC on July 21, 2011, when the provisions of Title III of the Dodd–Frank Act went into effect. Here she argues cogently that her former agency faced challenges which proved insurmountable in implementing a more permissive statutory framework, dealing with changes in the general economic climate, and working within the OTS's own resource limitations. She contends that the financial crisis that did OTS in illustrates the limitations of what she calls the political management of risk, under which OTS had limited authority to challenge or modify rules written by Congress. OTS became the scapegoat—unfairly, she says—for the failure of those rules to produce a safe and viable thrift industry.

The views expressed in this chapter are those of the author alone, and do not necessarily reflect the views of the Office of the Comptroller of the Currency.

Prelude

The thrift industry underwent important changes in the late 1970s and 1980s. Once almost exclusively a business of accepting deposits and making mortgage loans, thrifts increasingly experienced disintermediation (the diversion of funds from regulated financial institutions) as thrifts saw deposits flee to financial providers that were not subject to interest rate ceilings on savings. As a result, the number and size of passbook accounts, which had traditionally represented the major form of savings at thrifts, rapidly declined. In response, Congress enacted the Depository Institutions Deregulation and Monetary Control Act of 1980 (DIDMCA), which phased out Regulation Q, the Federal Reserve Board's instrument for setting maximum interest rates, and ultimately led to the deregulation of the S&L industry. By 1986, thrifts could pay a market return on savings, making them competitive in the marketplace.

The removal of interest rate ceilings was intended to give thrifts the means to fulfill their mission of providing funding for home purchases. Yet regulatory relaxation was a double-edged sword. Coincidentally, soon after Reg. Q lapsed, interest rates rose rapidly, and structural changes in the national and international economy led to instability in financial markets and in the financial services industry. Thrifts were especially vulnerable in parts of the country undergoing deindustrialization, where unemployment rates were especially high. This contributed to low profitability for thrifts and suppressed opportunities to raise additional capital.

Before the deregulation of financial markets began, the thrift's business model depended on low-cost retail deposits. Eventually, the thrift industry faced three major challenges:

- competition for deposits from other financial institutions;
- high interest rates that were creating substantial losses, and
- declining values of loans and other assets.

DIDMCA-mandated deregulation of only one side of the balance sheet led to greater interest rate risk as thrifts were locked into long-term fixed-rate mortgages funded with unstable short-term deposits. As a result, thrifts suffered major asset quality problems.

One of the goals of the Garn–St. Germain Depository Institutions Act of 1982 was to deregulate the asset side of balance sheets by enhancing the range of permissible investments. Fred Thompson, then a lobbyist for the Tennessee Savings and Loan League, is credited with helping author the bill, the full title of which was "An act to revitalize the housing industry by strengthening the financial stability of home mortgage lending institutions and ensuring the availability of home mortgage loans."[1] This measure enabled thrifts to offer adjustable-rate mortgage loans. As President Reagan explained:

> What this legislation does is expand the powers of thrift institutions by permitting the industry to make commercial loans and increase their consumer lending. It reduces their exposure to changes in the housing market and in interest rate levels. This in turn will make the thrift industry a stronger, more effective force in financing housing for millions of Americans in the years to come.[2]

State-chartered thrifts faced uneven deregulation as various states hastened to offer comparable investment powers. In some states, legislatures went beyond Garn–St. Germain and allowed state-chartered thrifts to make commercial loans and direct investments.

In encouraging thrifts to diversify their assets and funding bases, it was not Garn–St. Germain's intent to promote new lines of business and excessive risks. But that is precisely what happened. Accelerating asset growth became a common operational strategy for booking new assets at higher interest rates to mitigate the losses created by the rising interest rates offered on deposits. The acquisition of brokered deposits also gave rise to a flurry of higher-risk investments. For instance, the ability of thrifts to hold high-yield, below-investment-grade corporate debt securities ("junk bonds") was troubling because of the greater potential for these investments to sour.

Concerned about the impact of these policy changes on the thrift industry's safety and soundness, the industry's regulator, the Federal Home Loan Bank Board (FHLBB), raised capital standards and encouraged its subsidiary banks to adopt other measures designed to mitigate the effects of operating losses tied to market rates of interest.[3] Between 1981 and 1982, the nation's roughly 4,000 thrifts reported cumulative losses topping $8 billion. Losses due to mismatched interest rates on assets and liabilities combined with losses from nonperforming assets were frequently fatal. Eventually, these losses contributed to the failure of 455 thrifts with over $176 billion of assets in the 1980s.

Some of the key provisions of the Competitive Equality Banking Act (CEBA) of 1987 were designed to prop up the Federal Savings and Loan Insurance Corporation (FSLIC) and deal with the surge in thrift failures. But the damage had been done in the 60 months following the Garn–St. Germain Act. Hundreds of thrifts had failed, and an equal number required urgent assistance. Congress authorized $10.8 billion to be raised through the sale of bonds to be repaid by the thrift industry, with the monies to be used by FSLIC to close 47 thrifts in 1987. However, at the end of 1988, resolution costs were estimated to be $70–$90 billion.[4] Pressure on the system was exacerbated by the recession that afflicted many regions of the country, which contributed to declining asset values.

While these legislative actions narrowed the differences between the thrift and bank charters, the thrift charter continued to offer distinct advantages to organizers. For instance, unlike national banks, thrifts were able to open both interstate and intrastate branches without state law restrictions. Their federal preemption powers gave them expanded immunity from state legislation. Thrifts could establish service corporations to engage in any activity deemed reasonably related to thrift business, including real estate development, with appropriate capital reserves, whereas national banks were generally not permitted to engage in property management and development over an extended period.

Thrifts affiliated with diversified holding companies also had three distinct financial advantages:

- enhanced access to capital markets;
- diversification of liquidity sources; and
- lower costs of borrowing.[5]

Additionally, certain thrifts in a multiple holding company structure could sponsor, advise and distribute mutual funds.[6]

Despite these advantages, by the end of the 1980s the U.S. savings and loan industry was in full-blown crisis. As of December 31, 1989, FSLIC reported a deficit of $35.9 billion and was in serious need of recapitalization. FSLIC lacked sufficient funds to manage the growing number of troubled thrifts and close those for which there was no hope.

FIRREA

On August 9, 1989, President George H.W. Bush signed into law the Financial Institutions Reform, Recovery and Enforcement Act (FIRREA), which replaced the FHLBB with the Office of Thrift Supervision (OTS) as a newly created bureau, one of twelve in the U.S. Department of the Treasury. A new regulatory framework for thrifts was implemented to replace the structure that had served the thrift industry since the 1930s. Financial resources for member institutions would continue to be offered by the FHLBs, while regulatory oversight would become the primary function of this new government entity. FIRREA stripped away certain functions performed by OTS's predecessor. For example, it transferred the assets and liabilities of the FSLIC to a new deposit insurance fund, the Savings Association Insurance Fund (SAIF), operated by the FDIC. FIRREA redirected responsibility for oversight of the twelve FHLBs and the Federal Home Loan Mortgage Corporation which allowed the new OTS to focus directly on its role as the primary regulator for the thrift industry.

The overriding purpose of FIRREA was to restore waning public faith in the federal deposit insurance system, fund the cleanup of insolvent thrifts, impose stringent new capital and accounting standards on the surviving industry, and broaden enforcement powers of all federal banking regulatory agencies to effectively supervise troubled financial institutions. In writing the law, the House Banking, Finance and Urban Affairs Committee's frequently invoked the phrase "never again."[7] FIRREA also had the future health of the thrift charter in mind, mandating enhanced capital requirements coupled with fine-tuned accounting improvements to both eliminate misleading prior standards and to mitigate future financial downturns.

Under FIRREA, OTS became the nation's primary regulator of both federal savings associations and state-chartered thrifts insured by the newly created SAIF. It also regulated holding companies that owned thrifts and oversaw the acquisitions of thrifts by holding companies. OTS's mission was to foster public confidence in the thrift industry by ensuring the safety and soundness of the industry and compliance with all appropriate laws and to enable the thrift industry to adapt to changing economic environments.

OTS-governed institutions included those chartered as federal stock savings associations as well as those chartered as federal mutual savings associations. (Mutual savings associations are owned by their members, who provide the initial capital in the form of pledged savings. As no capital is issued, mutual savings associations have no shareholders.)

OTS structure

OTS launched in October 1989 with funding derived from fees and assessments levied on the thrifts it regulated, as provided in FIRREA. In addition to the establishment of OTS, and the SAIF at the FDIC, FIRREA also created the Resolution Trust Corporation (RTC) to manage the liquidation of failed thrifts and their assets. The OTS and RTC collaborated closely to ensure that insolvent thrifts were identified and promptly transferred to the RTC for resolution.

FIRREA decreed that OTS would be led by a single director appointed by the president and confirmed by the Senate to a five-year term. This was in contrast to the three-member FHLBB-appointed and confirmed board. By statute, the OTS director served on the FDIC board, was a director of the Neighborhood Reinvestment Corporation, and a member of the Federal Financial Institutions Examination Council (FFIEC). Congress intended to address any appearance of conflict of interest by separating the credit, insurance, and regulatory functions of the thrift industry's new regulator. Furthermore, this unitary regulatory was expected to be more independent of political influence than the former FHLBB, whose dual purposes—to promote the industry and safeguard its insurance fund—were viewed as incompatible.

The last chairman of the Federal Home Loan Bank Board and FSLIC, M. Danny Wall, became the head of OTS, but Wall's tenure was cut short by a congressional challenge to his official appointment. This was due to dissatisfaction with his leadership in the final years of his Bank Board stewardship, in particular with his management of the troubled Lincoln Savings and Loan Association. The FHLBB had backed away from its regulatory investigation of Lincoln, based in Irvine, CA, after five Senators intervened on its behalf. Lincoln Savings later collapsed in 1989 during Wall's tenure at the FHLBB, at a cost of $3 billion to the federal government. Ultimately, thousands of Lincoln's bondholders were defrauded and many small investors lost their life savings. While this congressional challenge was being sorted out, an acting director ran the OTS until Timothy Ryan became the first appointed OTS director confirmed by the Senate. He was sworn into office in April 1990.

Many new regulations, new examination procedures, and training protocols were also implemented in connection with this reorganization. An accreditation program consisting of rigorous educational requirements for thrift examiners and supervisors of the nation's thrift industry had already become fully effective in the transitional phase to OTS in September 1989. At the agency's inception, about 1,100 examiners and their supervisors were accredited as federal thrift regulators (FTRs) and many of the 900 remaining professional field staff were on their way to accreditation. Regulators who were not yet accredited could perform examination and supervisory functions solely in an acting capacity and only under the close supervision of a FTR, who was the signatory on OTS Reports of Examination.

OTS maintained its Washington headquarters at 1700 G Street NW. The agency consolidated the FHLB's 12 district offices into five regional offices in Jersey City, Atlanta, Chicago, Dallas, and San Francisco, locations chosen to reflect the geographic concentration of the thrift industry. Three-quarters of the agency's initial total complement of 3,379 employees were assigned to examination and supervision functions, and many of the others worked in various monitoring and corporate activities capacities, as well as in community affairs-related work.

OTS was the smallest of the federal financial institution regulators. It had the fewest employees and the smallest number of field offices, which made it especially reliant on programs to leverage staff resources and involve the industry in meeting its regulatory responsibilities. At its inception, the OTS regulated 2,616 thrifts, which held assets totaling $1.2 trillion. That translated into a ratio of 0.00001 percent of examiners for each dollar OTS regulated or just less than 0.5 accredited examiners for each OTS regulated thrift. All 1,100 accredited examiners had come from the defunct FHLBB that was itself widely viewed as woefully understaffed.

As Table 9.1 shows, OTS contracted even more rapidly than the thrift industry itself after 1989.

Table 9.1 OTS staffing ratios

	1999	1989
OTS staff	1,282	3,379
Regulated thrifts	1,103	2,616
Thrift assets (millions)	$863,312	$1,186,906
Total equity capital	$67,289	$52,137
Equity capital ratio	7.79%	4.39%
Net income	$8,240	($6,783)
Return on assets	0.98%	(0.54%)
Return on equity	12.18%	14.14%)

Regulatory developments after FIRREA

The early 1990s saw significant losses at FDIC-insured commercial banks. In 1991, in an effort to prevent the depletion of the deposit insurance fund, Congress passed the Federal Deposit Insurance Corporation Improvement Act (FDICIA), which required regulators to provide closer supervision to thrifts as well as to banks, and provided regulators with new tools to close failing institutions prior to the exhaustion of their net worth. Prompt corrective action (PCA) provisions established capital-based thresholds that required financial regulators to take specific actions against institutions that fell short. FDICIA had required regulators to intervene before a problem institution became insolvent, denying regulators the discretion to allow regulatory forbearance.

Pursuant to 12 USC 1467a(m),CEBA required all thrifts to be a Qualified Thrift Lender (QTL), which meant holding a majority of portfolio assets in mortgage-related financial products. FDICIA also brought about changes in one of the two qualifying QTL tests to liberate thrifts from a mandated concentration in mortgage-related finance options. The freedom to invest in a wider range of financial service options offered some relief from the competitive disadvantage under which thrifts otherwise operated under the restrictive QTL requirements.

Furthermore, FDICIA required all federal banking agencies to incorporate interest-rate risk into risk-based capital standards and to determine the capital treatment of purchased mortgage servicing rights. During the early 1980s, when interest rates rose to historic highs, the funding of long-term, fixed-rate mortgages with thrift deposits generated an inverted yield curve from the sharp drop in net interest margins. The result was negative net interest income for two years at U.S. thrifts after a decade-long period with net interest margins of approximately 1.5 percent.[8]

Thrift managers needed a tool to enhance their awareness of their sensitivity to interest rate risk. One pioneering OTS initiative provided them with interest rate risk exposure reports. The creation of the OTS Net Portfolio Value model (NPV) represented a novel risk-based regulatory approach to estimate the thrifts' market value of portfolio equity under various interest rate scenarios. Exposure reports were provided to management for tracking risk levels at their respective thrifts. The NPV model was the first such tool offered by a regulatory agency, and its framework, published on December 1, 1998, changed the monitoring of interest rate risk exposure. According to the *American Banker*:

> The NPV model for its time was one of the more advanced regulatory efforts focused on assessing interest rate risk to come out of a U.S. bank regulator, and was unique among regulatory efforts of this kind due mostly to the fact that the thrift charter's focus on mortgage-related assets was prone to interest rate risk.[9]

Further, the NPV impacted all full-service thrifts by requiring periodic reporting on detailed aspects of the balance sheet, incorporating a mix of interest rate shock scenarios. Ultimately, the NPV model was enhanced after 15 years of use to expand off-site monitoring capabilities for individual thrifts. While the model was later removed, in its day it met the pressing need to assess each thrift's exposure to interest rate risk, and, therefore, the exposure of the entire thrift industry.[10]

Industry climate

In 1992, OTS announced that the thrift industry had been profitable in each quarter of 1991. Coming after four years of large losses, this was a significant achievement. It marked the first time in six years that the industry would report consecutive profits in each quarter. Even more importantly, progress was being made in the cleanup of the remaining troubled thrifts. By 1993, the bulk of the problem thrifts had been moved to liquidation under the RTC. Only eight thrifts closed in 1993—the lowest number since 1979. This marked a clear sign of the industry's accelerating recovery.

Additionally, the early 1990s saw enforcement actions in the $300 million range against various individuals and accounting firms for violating OTS regulations and professional standards. OTS worked with both the Department of Justice and the Department of Treasury to pursue and punish individuals found to have contributed to individual thrift losses. A federal lawsuit seeking $275 million from the law firm that represented Charles Keating Jr.'s Lincoln Savings and Loan Association was settled. In addition, OTS sought $40.9 million in restitution from Keating and five other officers and directors of American Continental Corporation of Phoenix, AZ, for losses suffered by its subsidiary, Lincoln Savings. OTS also banned Keating for life from the banking industry.

As part of a joint settlement with OTS and the FDIC, the Grant Thornton accounting firm consented to the issuance of a cease and desist order and a payment of just under $10 million in restitution for audit failures in connection with a California thrift. In a similar case, the firm Deloitte & Touche was fined $312 million in connection with alleged accounting and auditing failures at five thrifts. These restitutions recovered some economic benefits derived from noncompliance and sent a strong signal to the thrift industry that illegal actions would not be tolerated.

OTS's early belief that informed directors needed to present a credible challenge led the agency to host educational directors' forums and to release two key publications: *Directors' Responsibilities Guide* and *Directors' Guide to Management Reports*, which emphasized to directors their fiduciary responsibility to exercise independent judgment in evaluating management's actions and competence. OTS also encouraged independent directors to schedule in-person visits with OTS regional staff to discuss their fiduciary responsibilities. These initiatives served as a vital link between thrift directors and the OTS in fostering the safety and soundness of each OTS-supervised institution.

One of the notable prototypes that OTS engineered was the OTS Matchmaker Program, whose aim was to pair capital-deficient institutions with prospective purchasers, who in turn would inject new capital into the insufficiently capitalized thrift. This program only involved acquisitions that required no federal assistance. An incidental benefit of the program was to preserve the franchise value of those problem thrifts and mitigate further deterioration. The thrifts that were targeted were undercapitalized but were deemed viable.

On June 30, 1995, a year ahead of schedule, the RTC ceased accepting failed institutions, and its functions were transferred to the FDIC. The Accelerated Resolution Program (ARP) that OTS had pioneered with the RTC was viewed as a noteworthy success, "one of the few federal agencies," as one academic put it, "that worked its way out of a job, finished its work and closed up shop."[11]

While few people welcomed the idea of the government assuming ownership of an institution by default of the underlying thrift, the results were undeniably positive. The FDIC estimated the cost of FSLIC resolutions during the 1980s to be almost $75 billion. It later estimated the final RTC resolution costs to be about $85 billion. Initial estimates of the cost to taxpayers had been as high as $500 billion, and the government was able to step in and out fairly quickly to help restore public confidence. The savings to taxpayers easily exceeded the costs of the program.[12]

Between 1989 and 1995, OTS transferred 744 failed thrifts with more than $392 billion in assets to the RTC for resolution.[13] In addition, more than 570 individuals were banned for life from the banking industry. In 1997, an independent academic study critiqued the Accelerated Resolution Program and concluded that favorable results had been achieved for the institutions involved as well as for the government.[14]

Regulatory burden

The regulatory cost of doing business as a thrift had always been greater than for banks. One academic study on the relative costs of stock and mutual thrifts found a "statistically significant difference between these two groups."[15] It was noted in this study that stock institutions operated at a lower cost point and that mutual thrifts were inherently more costly to operate. The fact that no commercial banks were organized as mutual institutions magnified the cost differential between the two.

New regulatory requirements added to the burden facing thrifts. Among other things, the Economic Growth and Regulatory Paperwork Reduction Act (EGRPRA) of 1996 included the Deposit Insurance Funds Act (DIFA). A major component of DIFA was to capitalize SAIF through a one-time special assessment on institutions with SAIF deposits. The after-tax contribution due from OTS thrifts was about $2.1 billion.

In addition, thrifts faced higher reporting expenses and corporate application fees, although the disparity was narrowed by FDICIA and FIRREA. The result of these actions was to achieve a closer parity between thrifts and banks for the costs of examination, audit, and assessments to the deposit insurance fund. FDICIA provisions required annual audits of banks by independent public accountants and full-scope, on-site examinations, expenses that thrifts were already incurring. However, thrifts still had to incur corporate application fees that could cost several thousands of dollars in a typical operating year while other types of financial institutions received a waiver on these expenses.

Thrifts were subject to the same reporting requirements as all U.S. depository institutions, but the typical size and condition of thrift institutions made the burden more onerous. In search of ways to lighten the load, the OTS was the first regulator to provide for electronic filing of mandatory quarterly financial reports. This innovation eliminated some unnecessary expenses and mitigated the regulatory burden that arose from the reporting and storage requirements that applied to thrifts.

In the late 1990s, OTS completed a comprehensive page-by-page review of its regulatory rulebook, and eliminated 7.8 percent of its regulations. OTS also became the first banking regulator to adopt a more straightforward communication style, and went on to rewrite 74 percent of its existing regulations to ensure their clarity.

Industry evolution

In 1997, for the first time in 17 years, there were no failed thrifts. That year, Ellen Seidman, the second OTS director, was confirmed by the Senate for a five-year term, and sworn into office. Seidman, a former senior counsel for the House Financial Services Committee, was a strong advocate of affordable housing. Her OTS tenure, therefore, was marked by an increased emphasis on community reinvestment while also keeping pace with the dynamic operating environment in which the thrift industry worked.

The exploding electronic and Internet banking segments that evolved in the 1990s brought new risks that demanded dedicated OTS personnel equipped with specialized knowledge in cybersecurity and other areas. In October 1998, the first new examiner hires at OTS in seven years, along with seasoned examiners, received specialized IT training. OTS was also the first federal financial regulatory agency to issue guidance on managing risk in the emerging Internet banking sector.

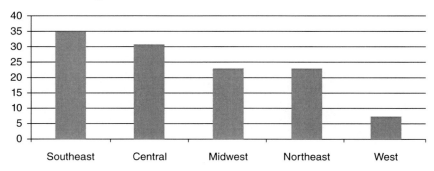

Figure 9.1 Number of *de novo* OTS regulated thrifts (1996–99).

OTS was also the first banking regulator to adopt rules addressing subprime and high loan-to-value lending, in which many thrifts were involved. Other product innovations, such as the increased use of credit scoring and asset securitization, also increased overall risk in the thrift industry, forcing the OTS to step up its field visitations and expand its off-site monitoring efforts.

The late 1990s saw an increase in mergers and acquisitions involving thrifts, which reflected the industry's improving reputation after the debacle of the previous decade. As figure 9.1 shows, the number of de novo (new) institutions was also increasing as organizing groups and their investors reacted to the improving prospects of the thrift industry.

After 10 years, the OTS could well take satisfaction in the improvement in the condition of the thrift industry. The industry's improved capital and asset quality and record profitability for three consecutive years were measurable signs of OTS's effectiveness. Adding to the record of success was the fact that there had been no thrifts failures in 1997, and not another one until 1999.

OTS had successfully led the thrift industry through the storm, more quickly and at lower cost than most observers had predicted. In addition, by taking record enforcement actions, it sent a strong message that malfeasance would not be tolerated. OTS had achieved a substantial and highly visible turnaround in the safety and soundness of the nation's thrifts. This transformation from the struggling financial sector it inherited into a vibrant and solvent thrift industry should be viewed as the legacy of OTS.

The agency's accomplishments served as the backdrop for its 10th anniversary. Few could have predicted, as Comptroller of the Currency John D. Hawke, Jr. observed, "the dramatic recovery of the thrift industry over that period which OTS has presided."[16] Treasury Secretary Lawrence Summers praised OTS employees for playing "no small part of a remarkable renaissance of the financial system."[17] President Bill Clinton thanked the agency for restoring "confidence in America's thrift industry" and for building "a sound regulatory and supervisory foundation for the nation's thrifts."[18] At the turn of the century, thrifts were experiencing more prosperity, stability and growth opportunities than at any time in the previous two decades.

Regulatory shift

Another major regulatory overhaul occurred in late 1999 with the enactment of the Financial Services Modernization Act, better known as the Gramm–Leach–Bliley Act, or GLBA. GLBA's main purpose was to repeal those parts of the Glass–Steagall Act of 1933 that separated commercial and investment banking and prohibited bank holding companies from underwriting insurance. For the first time, investment services could be offered, further eroding the lines between thrifts and commercial banks. The bipartisan passage of GLBA paved the way for larger and more integrated financial conglomerates, with all the profit potential—and risk—that entailed.

Even those who supported the legislation acknowledged the risks. Rep. John Dingell (D-MI) went so far as to argue that GLBA's liberalizations would eventually result in a bailout by the federal government. The new financial conglomerates, Dingell said, would be "too big to fail, so the Fed is going to be in and other Federal agencies are going to be in to bail them out."[19] His warning proved prophetic.

By the end of the 1990s, it was clear that GLBA was responsible for a pivot in the ownership of thrifts to diversified savings and loan holding companies (SLHCs). Many of the 119 de novo thrifts chartered between 1996 and 1999 were acquired by complex holding companies that included insurance companies, broker/dealers, fraternal benefit associations, and even a farm trade association. By the turn of the millennium, 29 percent of OTS-regulated thrift assets were held in SLHCs.

The competitive landscape for thrifts was also changing rapidly as the new millennium approached. Regulatory shifts, including those that stemmed from GLBA, meant greater competition, with various financial service providers now offering more generous terms on mortgage loans along with a wider array of loan products. This represented a significant swing from the days when thrifts originated two-thirds of the nation's mortgages.

The OTS was again called upon to meet these challenges with diminished resources. The relaxation of regulatory restrictions under GLBA should have prompted an increase in OTS supervision and supervisory resources. Instead, the agency entered this period of change under significant personnel constraints. During his tenure (2001–2005), OTS director James Gilleran cut one-quarter of OTS employees even though OTS supervised assets increased by 50 percent. In the mid-1990s, the Midwest region alone shrunk from approximately 800 employees to just 166. Nationwide, multiple OTS divisions were reduced or completely abandoned, and responsibilities were shifted. These measures left the agency short of the trained personnel it needed to effectively oversee the expanding and increasingly complex thrift industry. Thus, the OTS entered a new era in the history of thrift supervision with diminished capacity to monitor overall risks and set appropriate controls to mitigate them.[20]

The new millennium

During the early part of the 2000s, as the stage was being set for the subprime lending turmoil, a narrow approach to U.S. government regulation prevailed. Financial regulatory consolidation, free-market capitalism, and modest government involvement were very much in vogue. The OTS leadership's attempts to accommodate these sentiments meant that resource constraints would continue to be an obstacle in providing quality supervision.

The thrift industry was about to face another crisis. During the peak of the housing bubble in the middle of the 2000s, house prices increased by more than 70 percent after inflation. In some parts of the country, prices rose by more than 100 percent above historic trend levels. To take advantage of bubble-inflated prices, homeowners and investors sought funding, and the mortgage industry found creative ways to meet that demand, resorting to complex and risky financial instruments such as mortgage-backed securities and credit default swaps. This situation seemed to call for intensified supervisory rigor, but the spirit of regulatory relaxation persisted, and government regulators, in general, took a hands-off approach. This may have stemmed in part from political pressure under the Clinton and Bush administrations to conform to the Community Reinvestment Act (CRA).

Facing increasing competition from banks for their core residential lending business, thrifts found they needed to work harder to remain profitable. By 2007, thrifts were originating less than a quarter of the nation's home mortgages. Thus, they increasingly ventured into commercial lending, an area in which they generally had little experience due to prior regulatory prohibitions.

Combined with their particular vulnerability to housing downturns, thrifts were more affected than other financial providers by the economic downturn that began in 2007 and then spiraled into a full-blown global financial crisis. In response, the Emergency Economic Stabilization Act of 2008 (EESA) authorized the Treasury Department to spend up to $700 billion to purchase troubled assets and inject capital into the nation's banking system under the Troubled Assets Relief Program (TARP). TARP was later used to stabilize other volatile large institutions that were deemed to be systemic risks.

Not among those deemed worthy of saving were two of the largest OTS-regulated thrifts, IndyMac and Washington Mutual (WaMu). IndyMac, the largest thrift in the Los Angeles area and the seventh largest mortgage originator in the United States, became the fourth largest bank failure in U.S. history. The circumstances surrounding its failure led to the replacement of two top leaders at OTS and caused irreversible damage to OTS's credibility, especially after it was revealed that the OTS director in charge of the Western region had allowed IndyMac to backdate a capital infusion of $18 million from its parent company so that it would appear "well capitalized" in its securities filings

In February 2009, the Treasury Department's Office of Inspector General released a report citing laxity at the OTS for adding significantly to the $10.7 billion in losses sustained by the FDIC from the IndyMac failure, as well as the estimated $270 million in losses suffered by uninsured depositors. The report concluded that, despite its legal obligation to do so, OTS did not apply the Prompt Corrective Action penalties against IndyMac. Shortly thereafter, OTS Director John Reich resigned and, about a month later, amidst a continuing review of the backdating scandal, the new acting director, Scott Polakoff, was asked to step down.

WaMu was another story. At the time of its failure in September 2008, it was considered well capitalized, with 7.07 percent core capital and 12.44 percent risk-based capital. It was placed into receivership on the basis of liquidity concerns arising from the withdrawal of $16.7 billion in deposits during a nine-day bank run. In April 2010 testimony, acting OTS director John Bowman noted that WaMu's failure involved no cost to the Deposit

Insurance Fund. But he was particularly concerned about the inconsistencies in the way WaMu was treated in comparison to institutions such as Citigroup and Bank of America, which were arguably in worse shape and were kept alive through open bank assistance, which by law can only be granted to prevent failure. It was not, Bowman concluded, that OTS had poorly regulated the largest bank that failed, but rather that it regulated the largest bank that was "allowed to fail."[21]

The failure to afford WaMu the same treatment that other large financial institutions received during the crisis was a mistake, as some of the people who were involved later admitted. The then-Treasury Secretary Timothy Geithner has written that WaMu continues to haunt him. Its failure, he wrote, was "totally avoidable" and "unnecessarily intensified the crisis." It "sent a message to the world that the U.S. government was not seriously committed to defusing the financial crisis and containing the economic damage, even when it had the capacity to do so."[22] Yet it was OTS, rather than the officials who made the decision to allow WaMu's failure, that was held accountable.

With rumors of financial regulatory consolidation afloat, OTS made the unexpected decision to re-establish with minimal staffing its Chicago Central Regional Office, which had been closed for about six years. Subsequently, the OTS West Regional Office was permanently closed and its supervisory functions were abruptly transferred to the Chicago and Dallas OTS regional offices. The result was a mismatch between a short-handed agency and a burgeoning thrift industry.

2010 saw a net loss of 34 thrifts nationwide, reducing the number of OTS-supervised institutions from 765 to 731: 2 new thrifts were established, 18 thrifts failed, 8 converted to a bank- or state-regulated thrift, 5 were purchased by a bank, 4 merged into other OTS thrifts, and 1 thrift voluntarily dissolved. Nationally, the thrift industry was profitable in 2010, ending a three-year period of losses. But thrifts in struggling communities across the country fared much worse than their counterparts elsewhere.

Dodd–Frank brings major changes

The financial crisis gave way to a reputational crisis for the regulator of IndyMac and WaMu. Indeed, although each of the regulatory agencies came in for criticism, much of it deserved, the OTS seemed to suffer more heavily at the hands of the media and Congress. Much was made of one stunt in particular, in which OTS Director Gilleran, who had orchestrated the event, was photographed taking a chainsaw and other regulators taking garden shears to a pile of "regulations" bound in red tape. This picture lent credence to the belief that OTS policy was to grant thrifts extraordinary freedom to operate without regulatory intrusion.

Few were surprised, therefore, when ultimately it was OTS that was singled out for special attention in the Dodd–Frank Wall Street Reform and Consumer Protection Act, which was signed into law on July 21, 2010. Dodd–Frank brought the most dramatic changes in financial regulations since the reforms that followed the Great Depression. It called for the abolition of OTS and the transfer of responsibility for thrift supervision, chartering, and rulemaking to the OCC. OTS powers over state thrifts were transferred to the FDIC, and regulatory authority for thrift holding companies was transferred to the Federal Reserve Board.

The transition posed challenges for all of the concerned regulatory agencies. It required the FDIC, the Federal Reserve Board, and, most of all, the OCC to disrupt their own supervisory routines to accommodate the influx of new institutions while performing information technology system overhauls, integrating records administration systems, and preparing office space for the new employees about to join their ranks. The OCC also performed a formal cultural alignment assessment to facilitate the integration of the two workforces.

The integration, which took place on July 21, 2011, involved 642 thrifts with $906 billion in total assets. A total of 668 OTS employees also transferred into the OCC. Dodd–Frank provided each transferred employee with salary and benefits protections, and required OCC to ensure that each transferee received a position at a level similar to the duties and responsibilities they carried out prior to the integration. Pursuant to the law, the OCC submitted a report to Congress, dated July 20, 2012, detailing requested position reclassifications and its compliance with Dodd–Frank's requirements and safeguards.

Conclusion

It is entirely fitting that most post mortems on the financial crisis cite regulatory shortcomings as a contributing factor. The OTS bore its share of that responsibility. Allowing the IndyMac backdating, for example, was clearly a grievous error that not only increased the cost of that institution's ultimate resolution, but also cast widespread doubt on the competence and integrity of its regulator, raising questions about why it should continue to exist.

Several scholars have concluded, however, that, while OTS is not without blame for the recurring problems in the thrift industry, regulatory deficiencies were not a primary cause of the industry's troubles. One recent study that focuses on the distribution of government financial assistance shows that, although some institutions that held thrift charters were large enough to warrant bailout money, they did not receive it. Conversely, institutions that converted out of the thrift charters found that they received more bailout money than their size would have dictated. Data shows that thrifts underperformed banks only marginally. This should lead us to ask why dissatisfaction with the OTS was so much greater than with the other financial regulatory agencies, and why it was singled out for dissolution.[23]

The evidence adduced in this chapter raises questions about the connection between the OTS's performance over its 22-year history and the agency's fate and leads to the conclusion that OTS was hamstrung by a variety of internal and external factors in carrying out its mission. These included resource constraints, leadership instability and shortcomings, political pressures, and legislative actions that did little to make the thrift charter more viable while at the same time exposing thrifts to forms of risk for which they were unprepared. This is not to absolve the agency altogether, but rather to suggest that it was held to an unreasonable and inequitable standard of success.

Notes

1 Available at https://www.fdic.gov/regulations/laws/rules/8000-4100.html (accessed May 30, 2016).
2 Ronald Reagan, "Remarks on Signing the Garn–St. Germain Depository Institutions Act of 1982," October 15, 1982.
3 Deborah Cohen and Robert Freier, *The Federal Home Loan Bank System*, The Office of Finance Federal Home Loan Banks,1980, available at http://babel.hathitrust.org/cgi/pt?id=mdp.35128000844587;view=1up;seq=7;size=75 (accessed May 30, 2016).
4 Administrations [sic] Plan to Resolve the Savings and Loan Crisis, Joint Economic Committee First Session Hearing, 101st Congress, 1st session, Jan. 18, 1989–Feb. 23, 1989, 447–50.
5 "Holding Companies in the Thrift Industry," OTS Background Paper, April 1997, p. 7.
6 Aline J. Henderson, Julie L. Williams, and Harris Weinstein, "Some Attributes of the Thrift Charter" Department of the Treasury, Office of Thrift Supervision. April 10, 1992.
7 H.R. Rep. No. 101–54(1), 101st Congress, 1st Session 310, *reprinted* 1989, *United States Code Congressional and Administrative News,* 86, 106.
8 National Bureau of Economic Research, available at www.nber.org/c11490.pdf (accessed May 30, 2016).
9 "Has OCCs Ability to Monitor Interest Rate Risk Been Compromised?" October 30, 2012.
10 Ibid.
11 "Looking for Lessons from Agency that Mopped Up 1980s Thrift Mess," *The New York Times*, September 18, 2008.
12 Ibid.
13 See http://www2.fdic.gov/hsob/hsobRpt.asp(accessed May 30, 2016).
14 Roger D. Stover, "Early resolution of troubled financial institutions: An examination of the accelerated resolution program," *Journal of Banking and Finance* 21, 1997.
15 Dr. James M. Sfiridis and Kenneth N. Daniels, "The Relative Cost Efficiency of Stock versus Mutual Thrifts: A Bayesian Approach," *The Financial Review* 39, 2004.
16 A Decade of Accomplishment, Department of Treasury, Office of Thrift Supervision 1989–99.
17 Ibid.
18 Ibid.
19 John Dingell. *House Session* (Flash) (Television production). Washington, DC: C-SPAN. Event occurs at 03:02:11. Program ID 153391–1, November 4, 1999.
20 "Holding Companies in the Thrift Industry," OTS Background Paper April 1997, p. 8.
21 John Bowman, Acting OTS Director, "Testimony on Wall Street and the Financial Crises: The Role of Bank Regulators Before the Permanent Subcommittee on Governmental Affairs." United States Senate, April 16, 2010.
22 Timothy F. Geithner, "Stress Test," May 2014.

23 Dain C. Donelson and David Zaring, "Requiem for a Regulator: The Office of Thrift Supervision's Performance During the Financial Crisis," *North Carolina Law Review,* 2011, available at http://www.nclawreview.org/documents/89/5/zaring.pdf (accessed May 30, 2016).

Index

Accelerated Resolution Program (ARP) 137
Act of February 25, 1862 10
Alt-A mortgages 119
American Banker 135
American Bankers Association 97
American Bank Note Company 22, 23
American Continental Corporation 136
Amoskeag Manufacturing Company 82
anti-predatory lending laws 116–22

bankers: buying Federal debt 7; greenbacks to meet reserve requirements 14; national bank examinations 78
Bankers Encyclopedia 44
bank examiners 50; adversarial events 78–9; appointing 72; attacks on 103–4; balance sheet 78; bank examiner book 78; board of directors and president of bank 78, 81–2; civil service 99; compensation 74–5, 92; expenses 75; failed banks 51; falling behind in examinations 76; findings 93; first conference of 75; governance of bank 81; imprudent banking 100; independence 100; instructing 101; instructions from Comptroller 78; jobs of 51; listing employees, salaries, and bonds 82; loans 103; low pay for 75–6; national bank regulations 68–72; process of examination 78–82; rating loans 101; retraining 101; role of 67–84; salary 75–6; stock holdings 81–2;
tally sheet of banks visited 79; tracking movements of 75; valuation of loans and discounts 79–80; Western states and territories 50; yearly bank examination 72
bank holding companies and state banking law 113
banking: Civil War 1, 4; controversy with White House 99–101; crisis (1980s and early 1990s) 102–4; disposition of assets 100; dual banking system 3; federal chartering and regulation of 122; as local business 2; politics and 1, 91; practices and standards 1
banking system 4; deregulation effects 67; obstacles to modernization 97; public confidence in 1
banknote industry 22–4, 26
banknote reporters 8–9
banknotes: last year of issue 92; paper containing colored fibers 24; seven-thirties 34
Bank of New England failure 103
The Bank of North America 45
banks: assets and surplus and undivided profits 80; banknotes 34, 69; bonds 14, 34, 92; capital accumulation 4; charters i, 68–9, 91; condition of 69; credit 68–9, 103; economic instability 72; high standards for 2; interest 14; legal tender notes 22; lending dropoff (1934) 100; limiting size and power 2; mergers 96; Michigan commissioners 3;

Index 147

minimum capital 69; national debt 68; politics and 99–102; required reserves 69; retail and office space 102–3; scrutiny of 103; soundness and fiscal health 51; suing 55–7; supervision 1, 3, 69, 135; unit banking 2; World War II lending rise 101
Banks of the United States (BUS) 2, 8, 34
Barnett Bank v. Nelson 112, 115
Bear Gulch Mine 59
Belmont-Morgan syndicate 72
Bergen, Joseph 55
board of directors of banks 70–1, 76, 81–2
bonds: national banks 35; redemption of currency 33
bond-secured currency 8, 14, 33
Boston & Montana litigation 59
Boston Daily Advertiser 23
Bosworth, C.H. 58
Bowman, John 141–2
Bowman, Thomas P. 53, 55–6
Brady, Nicholas 104
bronzing 23
Brown, J. Sam 53
Brownlow, Louis 89, 100
Brownlow Committee 89, 104
Bryan, William Jennings 72
Buckalew, Charles R. 95
Bunting, John 45
Bureau of Construction of the Treasury Department 22
Bureau of Engraving and Printing (BEP) 20
Bush, George H.W. 103, 131–2
Butte Electric Company 58

Caldwell, Stephen A. 40
California and chartered banking 32
Camp, William B. 102
Cannon, Henry 75
Cassatt, A.J. 80
Center for Responsible Lending 116, 120–2
central bank 9, 68
Chandler, Zachariah 91
chartered banking 32

Charter No. 1: First National Bank of Philadelphia 39; First Pennsylvania Banking and Trust Company 45; First Union Corporation 45; temporarily mothballed 44; Wachovia Corporation 46
Chase, Salmon P. 1, 6, 20, 46, 91; authority to hire assistants 98–9; banknote industry 23; banknotes 16; bonds 24; Chief Justice of the Supreme Court 16; Civil War 9–11, 16; Comptroller's independence 99; debt management 16; former governor of Ohio 33, 34; government printing office 21; greenbacks 111; Jay Cooke and 34–6; national banking system 33, 35, 111; national banks 38–9; national currency 7, 11, 22–3, 33, 35; presidential election of 1860 and Lincoln 6; Secretary of the Treasury 6' state banking system 33–4
Chase Manhattan, 45
Chicago Underground Trolley Traction Company 58
Civil Service Commission 89, 99
Civil War: 150th anniversary of 1; banking changes 1; banking legislation 4; beginning of 33; cost of financing 1, 15; demand notes 9–11; fall of Vicksburg 39; federal expenses and revenue 15; gold 21; greenbacks 9–11; national currency 6–7, 22; National Currency Act 89–90; national debt 34; precious metals 34; retreat of Lee's Army 39; state banknotes 21; war bonds 22
Civil War-era tender note 10
Clark, Clarence H. 40–1
Clark, Edward W. 40
Clark, Enoch W. 34, 40
Clark, Spencer M. 20; banknote companies 26; Bureau of Construction of the Treasury Department 22; government bonds and notes 27; hydrostatic press 24; national banknotes 24–5; national currency 23–4, 26

Clarke, Freeman 99
Clarke, Robert L. 103–4
Cline v. Bank of America 116
Clinton, Bill 139
Cole, C.K. 54
Commerce Commission 89
The Commercial Bank of New Haven Connecticut 38
commercial banks 1
Community Reinvestment Act (CRA) 120, 141
Competitive Equality Banking Act (CEBA) (1987) 131
The Comptroller and the Supervision of American Banking (White) 67
Comptroller of the Currency 36, 110; authority to hire assistants 98–9; bank examiners 98; dividing country into regions 100; failed banks 98; fixed term 93–4; independence 94, 95; national banking and monetary system 95; removing from office 95, 96–7; reporting to Congress 98; Treasury connection to 98–9
conflict preemption 110
Congress: bank failures 83; Banks of the United States (BUS) 8; bank supervision 2–3; bond issues 10; cabinet-level departments 89; congressional intent 110; demand notes 10, 34; Depository Institutions Deregulation and Monetary Control Act (DIDMCA) (1980) 130; Federal Deposit Insurance Corporation Improvement Act (FDICIA) 135; House Banking Committee 96; national banking policy pre-Civil War 1; Office of the Comptroller of the Currency (OCC) 99; paper money 10; private property in hands of banks 2; removal actions 94–5; state banks 3; thrift regulator 133
Conrad, William G. 60
Conrad-Stanford Company 60
Consumer Federation of America 120, 121

Consumer Financial Protection Bureau (CFPB) 90
Consumer Protection Act (2010) 90
consumer protection and anti-predatory lending laws 117
Continental Bank Note Company 22, 26
Continental National Bank 81
Cooke, Henry 32, 35–6
Cooke, Jay 32, 40, 42, 46; E.W. Clark & Company's Philadelphia banking house 34–7; Jay Cooke & Company 35; national banks 39; national currency system 35–6; relationship with Chase 34–5
Cooke-Chase Bill (1863) 39
Coolidge, T. Jefferson 82
Coombs, W. 42
CoreStates Financial Corp. 45
correspondent banks 81
Countrywide Financial Corporation 119
credit, increasing availability 116
currency 8–9; gold 21; protecting with Treasury bonds 68; state-chartered banks 21, 33
Curry, Thomas J. 4, 60
customs taxes, 9

Davis, Owen Wilson 36–7, 40
Davis, William 54–5
Delano, Preston 102–4
Deloitte & Touche 136
demand notes 9–11
Department of Foreign Affairs (1789) 94
Department of Justice 97, 136
Department of Transportation (DOT) automobile safety standard 113–14
Deposit Insurance Funds Act (DIFA) 137
Depository Institutions Deregulation and Monetary Control Act (DIDMCA) (1980) 130
Dillon, C. Douglas 96, 97
Dingell, John 140
Directors' Guide to Management Reports 136
Directors' Responsibilities Guide 136
District of Columbia justices of the peace 93, 94
Dodd-Frank Act (2010) 129; thrifts 142–3; Wall Street Reform 90, 113
Dodge, Edward, 34

Dolan, Thomas 80
Doolittle, James 91
double liability 55, 70, 83–4
Drew, William P. 43
dual banking system 3
Duane, William 95

Eckels, James H. 52, 54, 75
Economic Growth and Regulatory Paperwork Reduction Act (EGRPRA) 137
Edgerton, Erastus D. 52, 54
Edward P. Moxey Audit Company 76
Elkins, William L. 80
Emergency Economic Stabilization Act (EESA) (2008) 141
Epps v. JP Morgan Chase 116
Erb, Richard 12
E.W. Clark & Company 34–6, 40
Executive Office of the President 89
express preemption 110

failed banks 72; bank examiners 51; banking crisis (1980s and early 1990s) 102–4; Bank of New England 103; Congress 83; directors and officers 82; Great Depression 83; noteholders 68; Savings & Loan Crisis 83; special agents 98; value of currency issued by 8
federal banking law 53
federal bonds 8
federal customs duties 34
federal demand notes 10
Federal Deposit Insurance Corporation (FDIC) 45, 90, 97, 133, 143; not bound administratively to Treasury 100; Savings Association Insurance Fund (SAIF) 132
Federal Deposit Insurance Corporation Improvement Act (FDICIA) 135
federal employees merit system 89
federal government: issuance of currency 9; state bank-issued notes 111–12
Federal Home Loan Bank Board (FHLBB) 131
Federal Home Loan Mortgage Corporation 132

Federal Institutions Examination Council (FFIEC) 133
federal preemption 109–10
Federal Reserve 97; Consumer Financial Protection Bureau (CFPB) 90; currency 18, 92; Treasury Department and 100
Federal Reserve Act (1913) 68, 93
Federal Reserve Bank 101
Federal Reserve Board 143; Regulation Q 130
Federal Reserve System 67
Federal Savings and Loan Insurance Corporation (FSLIC) 131–2
federal savings associations 4
Fessenden, William Pitt 91, 95
Fidelity Federal Savings and Loan v. de la Cuesta 113
field preemption 110
financial crisis (2008) 109–22
Financial Crisis Inquiry Commission 117, 119, 121
Financial Institutions Regulatory Reform and Enforcement Act (FIRREA (1989)) 104, 132–3; federal deposit insurance system 132; regulatory developments after 135–6
financial markets instability 130
financial providers deposits 129–30
Financial Services Modernization Act 139–40
First Bank of the United States 12
First Bank of the Washington, DC 27
First National Bank (1866-1896) assets 53–4; depositors 60; failure 52, 61; mismanagement 51–2; reasons for collapse 60–1; receiver 52; regulators 51–2; renting and repairing properties 54; reopening (1894) 52
First National Banking Association of New Haven Conn 38
First National Bank of New Haven Conn 39
First National Bank of Philadelphia 39–40, 40; bank examiners 42, 78–9; Charter No. 1 national bank 32–46; charter restriction 42–3; closing on public holidays 42;

150   *Index*

depression-era display ad 44; finding location for 37; Firstbank cable address 44; government bonds 40; investors and associates from E.W. Clark 39; merger with The Pennsylvania Company for Banking and Trusts Company 44–5; national banknotes 40; new charter number 43; opening 39–40; organizing 37–8; reclaiming original charter number 44; reorganization 43; World War II advertising 44
First National Bank of Stamford 39
First National Bank of Washington, DC 26, 39
First National Bank of Youngstown 39, 79–80
First Pennsylvania Bank, NA 45
First Pennsylvania Banking and Trust Company 45
First Union Corporation 45–6
Fishbein, Allen 120–1
fixed term 93–4
Flynn, S.R. 61
Forman, H.A. 52
Fourth Branch of government 89–90
Fourth National Bank of New York 39
Frank, Barney 119–20
Franklin National Bank v. New York 112
free banking 2–3, 8
free banking acts 68–9
"Friends in San Rosario" (O. Henry) 50

Garn-St. Germain Depository Institutions Act (1982) 130–1
Garsson, Robert M. 4
Geier v. American Honda Motor Co. 113
Geithner, Timothy 142
Georgia Fair Lending Act 114
Gidney, Ray M. 96
Gilleran, James 140, 142
Glass-Steagall Act 139
gold 21
gold standard 72
Gold Standard Act (1900) 74
Goodwin, Doris Kearns 6
government bonds 92
government printing office 21

Gramm-Leach-Bliley Act (GLBA) 139–40
Grant Thornton accounting firm 136
Great Depression: failed banks 83; federal spending 88; Fourth Branch of government 89–91
greenbacks 9–11, 21, 111; banknote industry 23; circulation of (1864) 34; creating market for 14; inflationary 16; legal tender 34; New York banknote companies 22; poor public acceptance 111
Grimes, James W. 95
Griscom, C.A. 80
Gulick, Luther 89
Gwynn, Stuart 24

Hamilton, Alexander: federal money 9; First Bank of the United States 12; National Currency Act 12; officials confirmed by the Senate 94
Hardt, William M. 76
Harlow, R.H. 54
Harmon, Leo G. 55, 60
Harrington, George 37
Hatch, George 23
Hauser, Samuel T. 52–3, 60
Haven, Franklin, Jr. 81
Hawke, John 115, 118
Hawke, John D., Jr. 139
Heald, William 51–2
Helena Independent 52
Helena Power and Light Company 54, 57–8
Helena Street Railway Company 59
Hepburn, A. Barton 79, 81
Herschfield, Aaron 53, 55, 60
Herschfield, L.H. 53–6
Herschfield and Brother Bank 53
Home Equity Lending 118
home ownership opportunities 116
Hooks, Joseph 103
Hooper, Samuel 11–12, 35, 111
Hope Mine 58–9
House Banking, Finance, and Urban Affairs Committee 132
House Banking and Currency Committee (1893-94) and Office of the Comptroller of the Currency (OCC) 72

Index

House Banking Committee 96
Howard, Jacob 95
Howard, Samuel T. 20, 22, 39
"How to Organize a National Bank under Secretary Chase's Bill" pamphlet 39
Hubbard, Bryan 4
Huntoon, Peter 1
hydrostatic printing 23–4, 26

implied preemption 110
IndyMac 141, 143
interest rates 130
investments 130
Irving National Bank 79

Jackson, Andrew 8, 95
Jay Cooke & Co. 34–5, 42
Johnson, Lyndon B. 97

Keating, Charles, Jr. 136
Kelley, Alfred 12, 13
Kennedy, John F. 96
Kennedy, Robert 96
Knowles, Hiram 56
Knox, John Jay 43, 83

Legal Tender Act (February 1862) 35
legal tender notes 21; circulating 22; federal debt 15; market for 8, 16; reserves in national banks 16; *versus* demand notes 10
Lincoln, Abraham: Civil War 110; on national banks 111; National Currency Act (NCA) 1, 12, 36; Salmon P. Chase as Chief Justice of the Supreme Court 16
Lincoln Savings and Loan 133
Lobenstine, William C. 54–5
Lynch, A.D. 52, 61

Marlow, T.A. 57–8
Marshall, John 109
McCulloch, Hugh 13, 20, 78, 103; authority to hire assistants 99; banknote companies 26; banknotes 25, 27; charter applications from bank organizers 22; Comptroller of the Currency 13–14, 21; Continental Bank Note Company 26; First National Bank of Philadelphia 37; greenbacks 23; national currency 21, 22, 26–7; National Currency Act (NCA) 94; Office of the Comptroller of the Currency (OCC) 99; practical limits of nationalization 20–8; State Bank of Indiana 13; Treasury Department 25–6
McCulloch v. Maryland 109, 110
McMichael, Morton, Jr. 37, 40, 42–3
McMichael, Morton, Sr. 37
Mellon, Andrew W. 80
Merchants National Bank (1882-1897): assets 54; bad debts 80; bank examiners 53; depositors 60; directors and president's loans 81–2; employees posting bond 82; federal banking law violations 53; legal and financial matters 60; management 53, 56; national bank charter 53; parties responsible for collapse 61; problems 53; shareholders 81; stockholders 54; suspending operation 53; Wilson outlining case against 55–6
Merchants National Bank of Helena, Montana 51
Merriam, Charles 89
Michigan commissioners inspecting banks 3
mines 58–9
Montana Railroad 54
Moorhead, William G. 40
mutual savings associations 133

Nash, Paul 4
National Bank Act (NBA) (1864) 4, 6, 110; bank examiners 72, 75; corporate governance 69–70; double liability 67, 70, 71; federal chartering and regulation of banks 122; legislative history 110–11; lending 69; loan limit 80; minimum capital for banks 69; national bankers 15; national banking system 68; national banks 71–2; national debt 68; Office of the Comptroller

of the Currency (OCC) 110; origins 6–18; preemptive effect of 112–13; redefining relationships 4; required reserves 69; revising and renaming National Currency Act to 3; violation of regulations 78
national banking association 36–7
National Banking Era (1864-1913) 68
national banking institutions 38–9
national banking system: delays and false starts in 38; national currency 68; opposition to 33–4; process of incorporating 37–8; replacing state banks 112; stabilizing 67–84
National Bank Note Company 22
national banknotes: bronzing 23; circulating as currency 111; control over 69; delays in delivery 25; final designs 24; forging 23; hydrostatic printing 23–4; printing 23, 25; redemption at discount 41; state banks' currency 41
National Bank of Montana 57
national banks 4, 89–90; anti-predatory lending provision 115–16; authority to bring suit in federal court 70–1; bank examiners 50, 68–72, 75; beginning operation 71; board of directors 70, 76; bond markets 79; bonds 15, 35, 111; branching power 2; call reports 79; cashier 81; Charter No. 1 32–46; charters 20, 36, 42–4, 70, 111; closing 71; Community Reinvestment Act (CRA) 120; competition with 114; corporate succession 17; disclosure requirements 71–2; dividends 71; employees posting security bonds 82; examination fees 75; examinations or audits 76; external auditors 76; failed 82; Federal oversight 17; financial capacity of borrower 115; flat management structures 81; government securities as collateral 1; growth 25–6, 74; insolvencies 72; interest rates 69; issuing notes 69; key leaders for 91; legal tender notes as reserves 16; loans 79–82; minimum surplus 71; mortgage loans 117; national currency 25–6; New York banking arena 22; organizational certificate 70; organizing 39; penalties for officers and shareholders 70–1; popularity 4; predatory lending practices 114; preemption 109–22; president 81; process of examination 78–82; quarterly reports 71–2; regulation and supervision 92; reserve ratios 79; safety and soundness 68; Southern states 9; stakeholders 70; stand-alone unit banks 17; standards 117; state-chartered banks 114; state laws 112–13, 116–17; stock holdings 81–2; subprime loans 121; supervising 68; Supreme Court on 112–13; suspending operation of 71; twice yearly examinations 72; voluntary liquidations 74; war bonds 39
National Credit Union Administration 114
national currency 20, 89–90; administering 17; bankers and investors 3; banknote companies 21, 22–3, 25; banknote paper 24; banknotes 40–1; bonds 7, 8; bronzing 23; Bureau of Engraving and Printing (BEP) 20; Civil War 7; constitutionality 16; design ideas for 23; dry printing method 24; failure to deliver 20; federal supervision 8; flaws 17; gold standard 72; hydrostatic printing 23–4; interest 14; legal tender notes 22; legislation 7; origins 6–18; producing 23, 40; security 3; shortcomings 17–18; starting up 92; struggle for 24–7; tax 92; uniform and reliable 6, 68; urgent need for 21–2; volume decline 92
National Currency Act (NCA) (1863) 1, 4, 6, 12, 68, 89–90, 105; charters 36, 42; Comptroller of the Currency 13–14; Congress 36, 111; depoliticizing banking 2; federal oversight 17; federal regulatory

agency 88; free banking acts 68–9; fundamental principles 12; imperfect legislation 41–2; long view 15–18; national banks 17, 39; national currency 92; New York law 12; Office of the Comptroller of the Currency (OCC) 90, 91–3; Ohio law 12; oversights and mistakes 91; passage i, 11–14; political opposition 17; postwar future and 1; redeemable currency 7; revising 3, 95, 111; state banking 2, 12; technical deficiencies 94; Treasury-Comptroller's office relationship 98–9; Treasury revenue 15; unit banking 2

National Hide and Leather Bank of Boston 81

nationalization, practical limits of 20–8

NationsBank 103

Neighborhood Reinvestment Corporation 133

Net Portfolio Value (NPV) 135–6

New Deal, 88–9

New York: banknote companies 27; state banks 33

New York City correspondent banks 81

New York Clearing House Association 22, 25, 27

New York Free Banking Act (1838) 12

New York Times 75

non-bank financial institutions 3

Norris, Frank L. 75, 82

North Carolina National Bank 103

Northern Pacific Railroad 42

Notice of Proposed Rulemaking (NPRM) 114–15

O'Connor, James Francis Thaddeus 100–2

Office of the Comptroller of the Currency (OCC) i, 4, 68, 88–9; *Annual Report* 78, 79, 83; Baltimore 1991 102–4; bank examiners 78; bank failures 83; bank regulation and supervision 92; Charter No. 1 33; Congress 99; deputy secretary 98; dissolving banks 70–1; employee pay and benefits 104; fire-proof vaults 92; funding for 90, 91–3; House Banking and Currency Committee (1893-94) 72; legal authority 104; limiting bank independence 102; National Bank Act (NBA) 110; national banks 3, 71, 83–4, 90, 100, 113; national currency 3, 21, 90, 92; Notice of Proposed Rulemaking (NPRM) 114–15; operating independently 90; politics 91; predatory mortgage lending 118; preemption regulation 113–16; recommendations for appointments 101; residential mortgage lending standards 118; scrutiny of banks 103; state anti-predatory lending laws 117; state consumer laws 116; state laws 113; states mimicking procedures of 68; supervision of banks 83–4; tenure and removal 93–5; Treasury Department 91–2, 98–9

Office of Thrift Supervision (OTS) (1989-2011) 4, 114; abolishing 143; Chicago Central Regional Office 142; community reinvestment 138; director 133; electronic and Internet banking 138; failure 129; federal savings associations and state-chartered thrifts 132; fees and assessments 133; financial crisis 129; Financial Institutions Regulatory Reform and Enforcement Act (FIRREA (1989)) 132–3; inability to carry out mission of 143–4; Net Portfolio Value (NPV) 135–6; new millennium 140–2; Prompt Corrective Action 141; Reports of Examination 134; structure 133–4; subprime and high loan-to-value lending 139; violations of thrifts 136

Ohio General Banking Act (1845) 12

Ohio State Journal 35

Olcott, Thomas W. 36–7

Ontario Mine 58–9

OTS Matchmaker program 136–7

Panic of 1857 33

Panic of 1907 68

154 *Index*

paper currency: banks of redemption 8; bond-secured 14; issuances 9; mini-bonds in form of 10; pre-Civil War issues 8; uniform i, 1
Patman, Wright 96, 97
The Pennsylvania Company for Banking and Trusts Company 44–5
Philadelphia Clearing House 76
Philadelphia Ledger 34
Philadelphia National Bank 76, 80, 82
Philadelphia North American 37
Philadelphia Press 39–40
Philler, George 43
politics and bank supervision 99–102
post-Civil War period 4
postmaster general 93
Post Office 94
pre-Civil War banks 2, 8–9
predatory mortgage lending 116–22; inferred 110; inhibiting state regulation of subprime lenders 121–2; laws and regulations prohibiting 116; National Bank Act (NBA) effect 112–13; Office of the Comptroller of the Currency (OCC) 113–16, 118; preemption 109–22; prior to 2004 regulation 114; subprime mortgage lending 118–21
president 94–5
private companies printing national currency 21
professional bank examiner 3

Qualified Thrift Lender (QTL) 135

Reagan, Ronald 130
real estate 59
receiverships 59
The Regulation and Reform of the American Banking System (White) 67
Regulation Q 130
Reich, John 141
reserve city banks 75
Resolution Trust Corporation (RTC) 133
Riegle-Neal Interstate Banking and Branching Efficiency Act (1994) 104, 113

Robertson, A. Willis 97
Roosevelt, Franklin D. 88–9, 99–101
Rue, Levi L. 82
Russell, W.S. 40
Ryan, Timothy 133

Salinger, Pierre 96
savings and loan holding companies (SLHCs) owning thrifts 140
savings and loan industry 83, 130, 132
Savings Association Insurance Fund (SAIF) 132
Saxon, James J. 96–7, 102
Second Bank of the United States 8
Secretary of the Treasury 35
Securities and Exchange Commission (SEC) 97
Seidman, Ellen 138
Senate 94–5
Senate Banking Committee 97
seven-thirties banknotes 34
shareholders and national bank 71
Sherman, John 11–12, 35, 70, 91
slow assets 58–9
Smith, James E. 45
sound money advocates 9
Spaulding, Eldridge G. 11–12
Spinner, Francis E. 10
Stanford, James T. 60
state banking law 12, 112–14
state banknotes 21
State Bank of Indiana 13
State Bank of Ohio 33
state-chartered banks 2–3, 33–4; competition from national banks 114; continued issuance of currency 111; public lack of confidence in notes issued by 33
state-chartered thrifts 131
state laws: conflicting with federal law 110; national banks 116; preempted into concise test 115
state-regulated financial companies and subprime mortgage lending 119
state regulators and subprime loans 121
states: anti-predatory lending laws 116–22; bank charters 68–9, 91; bank-issued notes 111–12; free banking acts 2–3, 8, 68–9; national

banks 111, 112, 113; Office of the Controller of Currency (OCC) procedures 68; professional bank examiner 3; subprime lenders 121–2; usury rates 69
Steamboard Inspection Service 93
Stiller, Deborah 4
stockholders and double liability 55
stock saving associations 133
subprime lenders 121–2
subprime loans 116, 122; Countrywide Financial Corporation 119; national banks 121; regulation of 120–1; state-regulated shadow financial institutions 119–20; state regulators 121
subprime mortgage lending 116–21
Summers, Lawrence 139
Sununu, John 104
Supremacy Clause 109, 110
Supreme Court: national banks 112–13; standard for preemption 115

Tennessee Savings and Loan League 130
Tenure of Office Act (1820) 94
Thompson, Fred 130
thrifts: acquisitions of 132–3; adjustable-rate mortgages 130; assets 130–1; bailouts 143; business model 130; changes (late 1970s and 1980s) 129–30; charters 131, 132; cleaning up troubled 136; competition 130; Congress 133; cost of doing business 137; deindustrialization sections of United States 130; disintermediation 129; Dodd-Frank Act (2010) 142–3; examiners and supervisors 134; failure 131, 133; financial resources 132; geographic concentrations of 134; high interest rates 130; holding companies 132; housing bubble 140–1; industry climate 136–7; industry evolution 138–9; IndyMac 141; interest rate 130, 135; interstate and intrastate branches 131; investment services 139–40; junk bonds 131; loans and assets 130; losses (1981-1982) 131; market value of portfolio 135–6; mergers and acquisitions 139; mortgages 130, 141; new millennium 140–2; new regulatory framework 132; oversight 132–4; pairing capital-deficient institutions with prospective purchaser 136–7; passbook accounts 130; profitable (1991) 136; Qualified Thrift Lender (QTL) 135; regulatory burden 137–8; reporting requirements 138; safety and soundness of 136; savings and loan holding companies (SLHCs) 132, 140; service corporations 131; state-chartered 131; state legislation 131; subprime and high loan-to-value lending 139; supervision of 135; Washington Mutual (WaMu) 141–2
treasury bonds 14
Treasury Department 97, 136; banknote companies 23–4; bond issue (1861) 34; bonds 11, 98; Comptroller of the Currency 36; customs taxes 9; Federal Reserve notes and gold notes 16; financing Civil War 21, 110–11; fixed terms 94; government printing office 21; injecting capital in banking system 141; legal tender notes 8; national currency 14, 92; National Currency Act (NCA) 1; obligating bankers to buy federal debt 7; Office of the Comptroller of the Currency (OCC) 3, 98–9, 110; Office of Thrift Supervision (OTS) 132; subprime lending 119–20
Trenholm, William 75
Troubled Assets Relief Program (TARP) 141
Tyler, George F. 40

unit banks 2
United States: 150th anniversary of Civil War 1; federal authority 21; financial system development i;

national policy 1–2; recessions 72; severe panic 72; state-chartered banks 33; uniform currency 33
United States Notes 21
U.S. Constitution, Supremacy Clause 109

Wachovia Corporation 45–6
Wainwright, Nicholas 80
Wall, M. Danny 133
Wall Street Journal 45
Wanamaker, John 80
War of the Copper Kings 59
Washington Mutual (WaMu) 141–2
Watters v. Wachovia Bank, N.A. 112
Weeks, Alonzo P. 81, 82
Welch, H.M. 38
Wells Fargo Bank 32, 45
Whitney, W.C. 80
Widener, P.A.B. 80
Williams, John E. 27
Williamson v. Mazda Motor of America 113
Wilson, Eugene T. 51–5, 57–8, 58–61
Wright, James A. 40